"A timely and indispensable work, not only [...] [...] [...] [...], [...] [...] [...] [...] ministers and caregivers who struggle to help people overwhelmed by traumatic events. *Crisis Counseling* is that rare book that combines theory with personal experience and application. Floyd understands the nature of crises and trauma, and he also speaks as one who has firsthand knowledge of counseling people in traumatic situations. His book has numerous examples and case studies from contemporary and biblical sources that inform and illustrate the multifaceted ministry of crisis counseling. Written from the perspective of a mature biblical counselor and scholar, *Crisis Counseling* is required reading for people who seek a clear and cogent introduction to the field and want guidance and biblical direction for effective ministry in times of crisis."

—Dr. Ian Jones
Professor of Psychology and Counseling,
Southwestern Baptist Theological Seminary
Ft. Worth, TX

"As a pastor, I'm often in situations in which this book has proven helpful. I heartily recommend it."

—Gregg Matte
Pastor, Houston's First Baptist Church
Houston, TX

"Scott Floyd has done the kingdom a great service by bringing together the wisdom of the counseling profession and the eternal truths of God's Word. . . . He draws upon years of personal counseling, wide reading in the field, and a deep understanding of Scripture. . . . This book is broad in its scope and comprehensive in its treatment."

—Dr. Al Meredith
Senior Pastor, Wedgwood Baptist Church
Ft. Worth, TX

"Those in the helping professions know the importance of ministry to those experiencing grief, crisis, loss, and trauma. Scott Floyd provides the playbook on how to effectively minister to those who have experienced traumatic events in their life and how to minister to caregivers. This book is a must-read for all ministers, lay counselors, and counseling professionals. It is a book I'll keep in my library and share with others."

—Dr. Daryl Eldridge
President, Rockbridge Seminary
Springfield, MO

CRISIS COUNSELING

A GUIDE FOR PASTORS AND PROFESSIONALS

SCOTT FLOYD

Kregel
Academic & Professional

Crisis Counseling: A Guide for Pastors and Professionals

© 2008 by Scott Floyd

Published by Kregel Publications, a division of Kregel, Inc., P.O. Box 2607, Grand Rapids, MI 49501.

ISBN 978-0-8254-2588-2

Printed in the United States of America

08 09 10 11 12 / 5 4 3 2 1

To Molly, Arie, Micah, Jilli, and Macy

ISAIAH 41:10

CONTENTS

ILLUSTRATIONS

ACKNOWLEDGMENTS

Writing a book is never a solo endeavor, but rather the culmination of patient support from others, their unselfish encouragement and wise guidance—contributions that most often go unnoticed by readers. As I labored toward completing this book, I was acutely aware of those contributions.

I appreciate my parents, who sacrificed for my education and who took a deep interest in this writing project, sharing from their years of wisdom. I'm thankful for my children, who've been patient with my times away from home, sharing their father with those in need. I'm most grateful for my wife, Molly, who's spent her married life hearing me think out loud, and serving as a sounding board for my ideas and theories, including the material for the book. Her encouragement and support have always been a source of courage and inspiration.

I'm also grateful for the help and backing of many of my colleagues. Ian Jones has long served as my friend and advisor, but especially so in this book. I also appreciate the input of Elias Moitinho, Mike McGuire, Dana Wicker, David Green, Bart McDonald, and Shannon Wolf for their perspectives on ministry and crisis counseling. I especially value Donna Moncrief's input based on her expertise in working with children and adolescents. I'm thankful also to Southwestern Baptist Theological Seminary for their allowing me time to work on this project, and to my dean, Bob Welch, for his support and assistance.

I'd be remiss if I failed to express my deepest gratitude to my counseling clients who, over the years, have bravely disclosed stories of the most difficult events, sharing the dark nights of their souls. Their courage has consistently given me courage, has driven me to learn more, and has fostered my desire to train others for effective crisis ministry. Special thanks go to all who allowed me to share their stories with you, the reader.

Most of all, I'm thankful to God for His grace and loving-kindness. In

2 Samuel 7:18, David says, "Who am I, O LORD God, and what is my house, that You have brought me this far?" (HCSB). When I look back at the things God has allowed me to do, I share David's sense of awe and amazement. I'm thankful that God would allow a wooden vessel like me to minister in His name to those who are hurting, confused, struggling, and in pain.

Introduction

Everything seemed typical on this particular Sunday morning. It was July 1995, and I was driving my wife and four children to our place of worship, Travis Avenue Baptist Church, located in Ft. Worth, Texas. As usual, we would attend Sunday school, followed by morning worship. This Sunday, however, was anything but typical. While helping our children out of our van, we heard the staccato report of multiple gunshots. They seemed to come from just beyond the church parking lot, about a hundred yards away. I recall thinking, *It's too early in the morning for gang activity. That would be more likely to happen on a Friday or Saturday night.* As the gunshots continued to echo across the parking lot, my wife and I made eye contact and hurried our children toward the church's education building.

As we entered the building, we could tell that something serious was unfolding behind us. Rescue vehicles were arriving from all directions, and the police helicopter was churning in low, tight circles over the north end of the parking lot. Like us, our fellow church members were scurrying for the safety of the building.

As the morning wore on, we heard that there had been a shooting in the apartment complex just to the north of the church's property. The initial report indicated that several individuals may have been injured, along with possible fatalities. Some friends told stories of arriving at church, but then ducking behind their vehicles as bullets whizzed overhead. Throughout the morning, and even as we left after the morning worship service, the shooting scene was a beehive of activity.

During the day, I heard rumors about the shooting, but not until I watched the evening news did I realize the impact of the morning's events. According to the newscaster, a man had gone on a rampage, shooting several individuals. He killed three children and wounded their mother. As apartment residents heard the shots, several Good Samaritans responded, two of whom were injured by shots from the gunman. The first police officer on the scene was also wounded. I didn't hear the newscaster mention the name of the shooter, but when his picture flashed on the TV screen, I thought, *He looks familiar.* The next morning I would find out why.

A month prior to the shooting near my church, I had attended a conference on trauma counseling. It was led by a friend of mine who worked with victims and rescuers following the Oklahoma City bombing. I had grown up with a father who was a paramedic, and both my brother and I worked with him on his ambulance crew as we transitioned from high school to college. During that time, I was regularly exposed to people in the midst of crises; I witnessed trauma events in their rawest form. This early exposure was invaluable in my later work as a licensed counselor, providing priceless preparation for the counseling work I would later do with hurting individuals and families. My clients often have experienced a personal crisis or trauma. So, too, the trauma counseling training I'd received a month before the shooting proved very beneficial. I was introduced to specific models for providing care following a large-scale disaster. Little did I know that within a few weeks I would use every bit of that training as I attempted to minister to my own church family.

On Monday morning following the shooting, I called the church offices. Dr. Pat Clendinning, the church's counselor, had just retired the previous week, and he and his wife were out of town. I knew the church might need some assistance as they dealt with this neighborhood incident. As I spoke to the receptionist, I began to realize the scope of this event. She informed me that the gunman was a member of the church security/maintenance staff, and he lived in the apartment complex where the shooting took place. Further, the two older children killed in the shooting had recently attended Vacation Bible School at our church and had spent the week prior to the shooting in our church's Day Camp, a ministry to underprivileged neighborhood children. I asked one of the church's ministers if there was anything I could do to help. He said that any assistance would be beneficial.

I recall thinking, *Where do we start?* The task seemed overwhelming. The gunman's fellow maintenance and security staff members were hurting, asking again and again if they had missed something that could have prevented their fellow worker from committing such an outrageous act. Our children's workers were stunned and numb. The shooter, as a security guard, had often escorted those workers to their cars following child-care duty. The Day Camp staff who had worked with the slain children were crushed. One related that the week before the shooting, he'd carried the boy on his back when they visited the zoo. Parents in our church worried about what to tell their children and about how much to discuss or withhold. Residents of the apartment complex were horrified. How could this happen near their homes?

The ramifications of the shooting were immense. I was acutely aware that neither my eleven years of counselor training nor my years of counseling practice had prepared me for an event with such an extensive impact. In the midst of feeling overwhelmed, I recalled the conference I attended just weeks before. In God's providence, those who had ministered to the victims of the Oklahoma City bombing had equipped me with the tools I needed to get started. I offered a silent prayer, asking for God's help, rolled up my sleeves, and went to work.

As a professor of counseling at Southwestern Baptist Theological Seminary, I had access to many gifted counseling students. Selecting one of the brightest, I took him with me; for the next week we worked with various groups and individuals from the church and community who had been touched by this horrible event, ministering to them during this time of crisis and loss.

A New Problem?

The last few years in American society have been marked by a number of notable violent events. In February 1993, the first World Trade Center bombings in New York City took place. Islamic extremists planted a car bomb in an underground parking garage, killing six people and injuring hundreds. In addition to the actual horror of the bombing, this terrorist attack on American soil was a foreshadowing of events to come.

The 1995 bombing of the Murrah Federal Building in Oklahoma City brought large-scale violence to the heartland of the United States. Timothy McVeigh, a Gulf War veteran, parked a Ryder truck packed with explosives on the street in front of the building. The blast killed 168 individuals, including nineteen children who were in a day care housed in the building. Hundreds of others were wounded, and surrounding buildings sustained extensive damage. Individuals watching the news were forced to wrestle not only with the location of the event, Middle America, but with questions of why a person would do something so destructive, displaying callous disregard of human life.

In 1997, a student shot and killed two classmates, wounding seven others in Pearl, Mississippi. This event was followed by other noted school shootings: West Paducah, Kentucky; Jonesboro, Arkansas; Springfield, Oregon. Then the most deadly school shooting so far exploded across our television screens: Columbine High School in Littleton, Colorado. The nation watched in horror as rescuers tried to help students flee the school. Inside, Dylan Klebold and Eric Harris had killed thirteen students and a teacher, and wounded twenty-three others before turning their guns on themselves. Large-scale trauma had happened not only in the heartland, it was now in our schools.

September 15, 1999, was marked by another mass shooting, this time in a church setting. A gunman entered Wedgwood Baptist Church in Ft. Worth, Texas, and made his way to the worship center. There, hundreds of teenagers had gathered for a concert and celebration service. Before taking his own life, Larry Ashbrook killed seven adults and teenagers and terrorized hundreds of others. Mayhem and terror had spread from our heartland into our schools, and now even into our churches.

In 2001, terrorists hijacked four airplanes, crashing them into the two World Trade Center buildings in New York City, and into the Pentagon in Washington, D.C. Thanks to the heroic responses of passengers on United Airlines flight 93, a fourth plane crashed into a field in Pennsylvania, preventing it from being used as a bomb on an additional strategic target. Much of the nation watched as the twin towers collapsed. Loss of life from the airplanes, the Pentagon, the towers, and rescue personnel totaled almost three thousand, far surpassing the death toll of any premeditated, violent human event in the United States.

In October 2002, residents of the Washington, D.C., area were targeted. Ten individuals were killed and three others injured by snipers, who seemingly picked human targets at random. For three weeks, John Allen Muhammad and Lee Malvo terrorized residents of Washington, D.C., southern Maryland, and northern Virginia. People were afraid to leave their houses to shop for groceries, buy gas, go to school, or drive to work.

In August and September 2004, Florida residents were left reeling as Hurricanes Charley, Frances, Ivan, and Jeanne ravaged the state. In addition to the numerous fatalities caused by the storms, many Floridians were left homeless and others went weeks without electricity. Even water and gasoline became precious commodities.

With all their devastation, the hurricanes in Florida were only a foretaste of the hurricane season of 2005. Anxious New Orleans residents watched as Hurricane Katrina moved through the Gulf of Mexico, strengthening into a category five storm—one of the most powerful ever recorded. Many Louisiana residents—veterans of many hurricane seasons or those lacking the resources to flee—attempted to ride out the storm. On Monday, August 29, the eye of the hurricane made landfall in the early morning. Around 11:00 A.M. the levees that separated Lake Pontchartrain from New Orleans gave way in several places, flooding the city. A horrified nation watched as individuals and families were rescued from rooftops and from makeshift floatation devices. The devastation to the Louisiana and Mississippi coastlines was immense.

Less than a month after Katrina decimated the Louisiana and Mississippi coastal regions, Hurricane Rita was forming in the Gulf of Mexico. It appeared to be headed toward Houston, Texas. In the wake of Hurricane Katrina, mandatory evacuations were announced. On this occasion, the nation watched as South Texas residents attempted to flee, but became stuck for hours in snarled traffic caused by the mass evacuation. The storm turned eastward and caused less damage than feared, but in a horrible twist of irony, a bus carrying nursing home residents away from the hurricane burst into flames just south of Dallas, killing twenty-three elderly individuals.

While many other deadly events have occurred in the past couple of decades, these are some of the more notable. The number and extent of such occurrences does lead to questions: Why have we seen so many large-scale crises in the last several years? Are we in a new chapter of society, one in which devastating events follow one another, becoming commonplace, a staple of our evening TV diet? Are we dealing with a new problem?

An Old Problem?

Catastrophic events are not unique to our time. Even in Jesus' day, people experienced devastation that sounds similar to that of present day. Luke, author of the third gospel, records a brief interaction between Jesus and some of His followers (Luke 13:1–5). They discuss a political murder for which Pilate was responsible—a group of worshippers killed while they were in the process of making their sacrifices. In the same conversation, Jesus mentions eighteen individuals killed in Siloam when a tower fell on them.

Here are two tragic events—one, the murder of individuals involved in a religious ceremony, and the other a terrible accident with multiple victims. Jesus' listeners seem familiar with the second event; perhaps people in the surrounding countryside had been talking, as we do today, about what had happened and why. As His followers question Jesus, He uses these events to point them to God and to His larger purposes. This passage is somewhat obscure, not one frequently used in sermons, but it demonstrates that devastating events are not unique to modern day.

Indeed, humans have always had to contend with natural disasters—earthquakes, volcanoes, fires, floods, famines, and hurricanes. Humans have also been responsible for some of their own disasters, including building collapses, plane crashes, and ship sinkings. Throughout the centuries, people have engaged in wars and other aggressive acts, producing countless loss of lives. Diseases, such as bubonic plague, influenza, tuberculosis, and small pox, have killed millions.

Crises and traumatic events have been a part of human experience since the creation. Each age has, indeed, had its own set of difficulties, dangers, and challenges to daily life.

A New Look at an Old Problem

While tragedy and crises are not unique to the late twentieth and early twenty-first centuries, some components of modern day tragedies are distinctive to our day. Certain aspects of how trauma is viewed, communicated, and experienced have become characteristic of our daily lives.

First, we live in an information age, a time of immediate, graphic, and detailed news about tragedies that occur any place in the world. In the 1940s, individuals went to the movies and saw newsreels about events of World War II. For many, this was their first glimpse at some of the enormous calamities taking place. Today, we get twenty-four-hour coverage of every possible crisis. Images of certain events, such as the collapse of the World Trade Center towers, are replayed endlessly on all-news channels. In the Iraq war, journalists have been imbedded in combat units, providing scenes of the soldiers' day-to-day activities, as well as live coverage of combat. Because of technological advances, we are exposed, over and over again, to crisis images, and inundated with information about tragic events.

Another seeming difference in modern society is the character of human violence—often extreme, rapid, and cruel. In more than one case, individuals, including adolescents, have gained access to automatic weapons, producing multiple fatalities or injuries. Various countries consistently threaten to develop nuclear weapons or other weapons of mass destruction. Suicide bombers kill or maim dozens of innocent bystanders, their means and methods seeming to have reached unprecedented levels of sophistication.

Yet another modern phenomenon is the capability of individuals to access information instructing them in how to carry out violent acts. The Internet provides details about weapons and bomb-making, as well as forums that share ideas about how to create and carry out destructive acts. Many movies and video games, as well as some popular music, glorify violence, reward those who commit violent acts, and fail to present any kind of consequence for destructive and evil exploits.

Some aspects of modernity seem, then, to promote, display, and even profit from violence and destruction. While tragedy is not a new thing, it's a very present thing. And whether or not the problems of such events are old or new, the unfortunate truth is that most individuals will, at some point in life, undergo some kind of tragic, crisis event. Those who work in ministry must be prepared to offer help when such incidents take place.

Ministering to Those in Crisis

While trauma and crises are not unique to modern times, our consciousness has risen in regard to their effect on humans. Many of the recent large-scale trauma events have, in fact, resulted in a more sophisticated understanding of how to work with those in crisis and how to assist individuals who have experienced a major trauma. Within the last decade, a growing number of professionals have focused on how best to help survivors in the aftermath of trauma. Terms like Crisis Intervention, Trauma Counseling, Disaster Psychology, Disaster Management, and Critical Incidents Stress Management have all appeared in the human relations and counseling literature. These terms represent attempts to arrive at the best methods of providing care for individuals, families, and communities who have undergone some type of traumatic event.

It is essential, too, for those in ministry to understand the nature of crises and trauma as well as to have specific knowledge about how to help people under such circumstances. It's inevitable that individuals involved in ministry will encounter persons in the midst of crises. Some ministers may, in fact, feel that they're simply moving from one crisis to the next.

Not all ministers, though, are trained to help people in the midst of difficult circumstances. Some ministers intuitively sense how to provide help and are effective in doing so, but other well-meaning ministers may inadvertently cause harm. Knowing how to provide crisis care is essential, then, to any type of effective ministry.

THE VALUE OF PROVIDING CRISIS CARE

Why is it vital to gain knowledge and develop skills that are a part of providing effective crisis care? There are many reasons why this is especially important for leaders in the body of Christ. Caring for those in need is a reflection of God's character, it imitates Christ's work, and it carries out specific scriptural injunctions. Caring for those in crisis is, in other words, an essential function of the body of Christ.

Providing care to others reflects God's character because God cares about those who are hurting. Isaiah 25:8 states, "And the LORD God will wipe tears away from all faces." God provides for those who are struggling to provide for themselves. The Old Testament is replete with passages indicating God's concern for the poor, widows, and orphans. The Bible contains story after story of God intervening in the lives of those who are suffering, confused, or in pain. Heaven itself is described as a place where God provides comfort: "He will wipe every tear from their eyes. There will be no more death or mourning or crying or pain" (Rev. 21:4 NIV). God is a caring God and He demonstrates this facet of His character both directly and through other individuals. When we provide care to those in need, we are both reflecting and expressing God's character.

Helping struggling individuals imitates Christ. In Luke 4:18–19, Jesus states His purpose in coming to live among us: "The Spirit of the Lord is on me, because he has anointed me to preach the good news to the poor. He has sent me to proclaim freedom for the prisoners and recovery of sight for the blind, to release the oppressed, to proclaim the year of the Lord's favor" (NIV). Crisis ministry not only reflects the spirit of Jesus' ministry, but it's an active way of freeing prisoners, restoring sight to the blind, and releasing the oppressed.

Knowing how to help in difficult circumstances is part of carrying out Paul's injunction in Galatians 6:2 to "bear one another's burdens." Paul understood the value of fellow believers' helping shoulder the load when life's cares become heavy. Paul notes that when those in the family of faith help one another, they are actually fulfilling the law of Christ.

Crisis ministry allows believers to have contact with those we might not otherwise encounter or have an effect upon. When things are going well, many nonbelievers go about their lives, often vigorously avoiding anything remotely religious. Crisis events open doors for believers to reach out to nonbelievers— to provide real and meaningful help in the midst of struggles and to represent God's care. In trying circumstances, clearly demonstrated care is extremely valuable and actively reveals God's concern for His creation.

Caring for hurting individuals in difficult times provides opportunities to point individuals to life's ultimate solutions. Tangibly demonstrating concern for others directs them to God's care. Reaching out to those who are hurting reduces their feelings of isolation and creates opportunities for the hurting person to seek answers to their questions. Crisis circumstances provide an occasion to introduce a person to Jesus Christ, the ultimate source of help in times of trouble.

OVERVIEW OF THE BOOK

It is essential to provide care in times of crisis. It's essential, too, that we know how to provide that care. This book is designed to help individuals understand the nature of crises, and to convey practical steps for ministering to those who struggle. It's written for counselors who deal with crises and trauma, for ministers who regularly encounter those in adverse circumstances, and for anyone in the body of Christ who feels a desire to help others who are experiencing crises.

To that end, this book weaves together Scripture, solid theology, principles of ministerial soul care, and research from the crisis counseling field. These are herein combined with my own personal experience from providing crisis intervention and counseling. Throughout the book, I include actual cases I've encountered through counseling and through supervising counselors. In these real-life stories, names have been changed and identifying information altered to protect the privacy of those involved. Other individuals have given me permission to tell parts of their stories. As individuals recover from traumatic events, they are often motivated to help others who struggle, using their own stories to minister to and to encourage others.

To accomplish the tasks of the book, we will first examine some key terms in the field: crisis, trauma, loss, and grief. Chapters 1–4 will help the reader develop a clear understanding of these terms, their scriptural bases, the processes they represent, and how and when they occur.

The book next turns to a model of how these terms function in relationship to each other. Chapter 5 sets forth a crisis ministry model, providing the reader with a map for following an individual through the experience of crisis, trauma, loss, or grief. Once the helper knows how these processes interrelate, he or she must know how to provide help. Chapters 6 and 7 focus on intervention points, or the practical components of when and how to provide help.

Chapter 8 is addressed to the minister. What aspects of crisis intervention are specific to ministry and what does the minister need to know to be most helpful to those in crisis? Chapter 9 deals with crisis and trauma intervention from the standpoint of the counselor and the formal counseling relationship. What does the counselor need to know in order to most effectively provide crisis or trauma counseling? Also, how can the counselor make use of spiritual resources in order to aid clients?

Chapters 10 and 11 discuss trauma related to children and adolescents. Crisis ministry during these developmental stages requires specialized knowledge, and can be quite different from working with adults. Chapter 12 considers large-scale disasters that happen in a church or community setting. How should the church respond? Can the church be ready to mobilize in the event of a larger disaster?

Last, chapter 13 turns our attention to caring for the caregiver. Crisis ministry is extremely stressful, and caring for caregivers assists helpers to stay vital and effective as they minister to others.

A White Blood Cell in the Body of Christ

Having functioned as a counselor in both community and church settings for almost a quarter of a century, I've run across those who do not see the value of this type of ministry. I've been asked, on more than one occasion, even by friends whom I respect, "What did people do before there were counselors?" This question always seems to imply that crisis counseling is a more recent creation and of questionable validity. A closely related question, which often goes unspoken but can be detected in some people's attitudes, is "Shouldn't people just 'tough it out' when they have hard times?" Occasionally, individuals tell me they don't need any outside assistance, that they're capable of making it through difficulties on their own.

It's true that not everyone who undergoes a crisis or trauma will need crisis ministry. Some individuals are strong enough to make it on their own.

Others make use of family, friends, and other resources to keep moving ahead in a healthy manner. Many other individuals, however, are desperate for help, but don't know how to ask for it or where to find it. These individuals live in incredible pain, but show up at church week after week, forcing a smile and uttering standard religious phrases. In private, though, they feel devastated, isolated, and paralyzed by their struggles. These are the people to whom crisis ministry is aimed.

At one point in my spiritual pilgrimage, I began to wonder about my place in the body of Christ. I was well aware of Paul's assertion in 1 Corinthians 12:12–30 that we are all part of the body of Christ, that we all have a function as a part of the body. What was my part in the Christian community?

As I looked at my spiritual gifts, what I enjoyed doing, and even at my career path, I realized that I was a white blood cell in the body of Christ. In the human body, certain foreign invaders create illness and disease. White blood cells were created by God as the body's means of attacking these invaders, which have the potential of doing much harm. In the body of Christ, individuals are often attacked by crises or traumatic experiences. For some individuals, such crises threaten to rob them of peace, destroy human relationships, and may even hinder their relationship with God. Those who provide crisis ministry function in much the same manner as white blood cells.

This book is written for all who, in the body of Christ, seek to help hurting individuals, couples, and families living in the wake of a crisis, loss, or trauma. It's designed to provide practical information and support for the never-ending battle of helping those who experience difficult times. In Galatians 6:10, Paul exhorts believers, saying, "Therefore, as we have opportunity, let us do good to all people, especially to those who belong to the family of believers" (NIV). The task of crisis ministry is to do good in ministering to believers and nonbelievers alike, battling those aspects of crisis and trauma that are devastating to so many.

CHAPTER 1

CRISIS

A CRISIS STORY

BRENDA WAS THE EPITOME OF someone in the midst of an agonizing personal crisis. Two weeks prior to her wedding, her husband-to-be was diagnosed with Amyotrophic Lateral Sclerosis (ALS), or Lou Gehrig's Syndrome, an extremely debilitating neurological disorder that causes progressive deterioration in a person's ability to function. Eventually, ALS patients lose their capacity to walk and talk and to carry out even the most basic aspects of everyday life. At the time I met with Brenda, most individuals died within five years of the disease's onset.

Brenda began counseling with me about six years after her husband contracted the disease. Although his mind was still alert, he was confined to a wheelchair, and she had to assist him with all of life's rudimentary tasks. He had outlived the doctors' expectations, but was only a shell of the athletic man she had married. Brenda's husband could not use his arms or legs and was having difficulty eating and swallowing. He spent each day in a specially designed wheelchair, utilizing a computer to communicate.

In counseling, Brenda discussed the daily struggles she faced. In addition to feeding, bathing, and helping her husband dress, she had to maintain a full-time job, transport her husband to all of his numerous doctors' visits, and deal with medical bills and insurance companies. Brenda never wavered in her love for her husband, but even simple tasks like mealtimes or an outing to the movies were now difficult and stressful. Each month, Brenda had to make a five-hour trip across the state, where her husband met with his physician specialist. Each month, as the couple returned from the specialist's office, they would discuss the husband's further physical deterioration, the bleak prognosis for his disease, and whether developing medications or treatment options would be available before he died.

Although Brenda was a remarkably strong woman in both her faith and her general approach to life, she was constantly exhausted and periodically frustrated and discouraged. Having no relatives in the vicinity, she alone bore the brunt of caring for her husband. We spent several months of counseling, discussing numerous crises she encountered each day and strategizing ways to cope.

All individuals face crises in life. Some are smaller and more temporary. Others may be extensive, like those encountered by Brenda. Some individuals cope effectively when they confront difficult circumstances. Some even thrive in the face of crises, seeking leisure activities or careers in which they function surrounded by crisis situations. While not all individuals in crisis need outside assistance from a counselor or minister, other individuals may greatly benefit from that kind of caring help.

DEFINITIONS

The word *crisis* is used in a variety of ways in everyday conversation. Some people use the term when speaking of a phase in human development—a teen is experiencing an identity crisis or an adult is undergoing a midlife crisis. Others might apply *crisis* to economic or political events, such as an energy crisis or a crisis in the Middle East. Still others might use the word to describe a spiritual struggle, such as a crisis in faith. Some individuals even use *crisis* to indicate small, everyday frustrations, such as losing one's car keys or running out of flour when cooking.

Just as general society uses an array of different meanings for *crisis*, so experts in the field of crisis counseling have a range of definitions for *crisis*. Most often, *crisis* connotes a negative or problematic state, event, or series of events, or an unstable time period with an uncertain outcome. *Crisis* can also refer to a turning point in human functioning. One researcher breaks the concept of crisis into components and considers each component as necessary in order to produce what could be called a *crisis*. Each of these attempts to define *crisis* bears further consideration.

Crisis as Problematic State

Some attempts to define *crises* highlight the negative or problematic nature of difficult events. Everly and Mitchell define *crisis* as, "a state of acute distress wherein one's usual coping mechanisms have failed in the face of a perceived challenge or threat and there results some degree of functional impairment."[1] Wright notes the potential adverse nature of crises, although he believes the effects may not be permanent: "A crisis usually involves a temporary loss of coping abilities, and the assumption is that the emotional dysfunction is reversible. If a person effectively copes with the threat, he then returns to prior levels of functioning."[2] Thus, one effort at defining crisis emphasizes the inherent difficulties and problems associated.

Crisis as Turning Point

Other attempts to define *crises* go beyond negative connotations. *Crisis* can also mean a critical time period or a turning point at which things may go one direction or the other. Thomas Oden observes that the word *crisis* is derived from the Greek word *krinein*, meaning "to decide," and adds, "Generally a crisis is a turning point or crossroad in the development of something, a crucial time, a decisive point."[3]

James and Gilliland, experts in the field of crisis intervention, also view a crisis as a turning point, defining it as "a perception or experiencing of an event or situation as an intolerable difficulty that exceeds the person's current resources and coping mechanisms."[4] They note that a crisis carries with it both danger and opportunity. Danger is present in many crises because of the inherent struggles that result. In extreme cases, crises may produce physical illness or could even lead to suicide attempts or other types of self-harm. On the other hand, a crisis may also produce opportunity. An individual who faces pressure situations or a difficult circumstance may experience positive outcomes such as personal growth or new ways of viewing circumstances and events. These difficulties even allow individuals to realize strengths they were unaware they possessed. During the Great Depression, some individuals were crushed by the weight of the economic hardships that engulfed the nation. Other individuals, however, faced the challenges, made it through that dark decade in American

---

1. Everly and Mitchell, *Critical Incident Stress Management*, 2–3.
2. Wright, "Crisis Intervention and Emergency Practice," 1:600.
3. Oden, *Crisis Ministries*, 4:3.
4. James and Gilliland, *Crisis Intervention Strategies*, 3.

history, and emerged strengthened by their ordeals. Thus, a crisis, while diffi-cult, is a turning point at which a person can actually grow as a result of tough times.

Trilogy Definition of Crisis

Kanel offers a clear and concise definition for *crisis,* which she refers to as a trilogy definition. She says, "The three parts of a crisis are these: (1) a pre-cipitating event; (2) a perception of the event that causes subjective distress; and (3) the failure of a person's usual coping methods, which causes a person experiencing the precipitating event to function at a lower level than before the event."[5] For a crisis to transpire, there must be an event that starts the sequence. Next, the person must actually perceive the event to be problematic. Last, a person's regular methods of dealing with problematic situations are not effec-tive. When this occurs, it places the person in a type of disequilibrium, with a resulting disruption of effective functioning. Kanel believes that understand-ing the elements of a crisis may give the helping individual an idea of where to intervene when working with a person in crisis.

TYPES OF CRISES

Of the many types of crises, James and Gilliland identify several, including developmental, situational, and existential crises.[6] Individuals may experience these as well as interpersonal and spiritual crises.

Developmental Crises

A human experiences many critical phases of development. These include birth, learning to walk, entering school, becoming a teenager (and traveling through the teenage years), leaving home, dating and getting married, having children, reaching midlife, and retiring. While many of these phases are natu-ral and expected, each can produce crises or turning points at which individu-als may have difficulty coping.

Situational Crises

Different from developmental crises, situational crises tend to be sudden and unexpected. These include physical crises, during which a person struggles

---

5. Kanel, *A Guide to Crisis Intervention*, 1.
6. James and Gilliland, *Crisis Intervention Strategies*, 5.

with health-related issues and concerns; economic crisis, during which an individual faces financial difficulties; any other event over which a person has no control and that challenges the person's ability to cope.

Existential Crises

Crises that impact a person's beliefs about the world tend to hit at an existential level. According to James and Gilliland, "An existential crisis includes the inner conflicts and anxieties that accompany important human issues of purpose, responsibility, independence, freedom, and commitment."[7]

Interpersonal Crises

Numerous crises occur between individuals or groups of individuals. These most often happen in close relationships and can be an outgrowth of unresolved conflict or of difficulty communicating effectively. Interpersonal crises can lead to either positive or negative outcomes, including relationship growth, relationship strain, or relationship termination.

Spiritual Crises

Individuals may experience spiritual crises when they wrestle with issues of faith, with some significant aspect of religious life, or with questions about spiritual matters. A spiritual crisis has the potential to lead a person into a deeper, more intimate relationship with God, or may result in a person's turning away from God. In some instances, a crisis may precipitate a decision to follow Christ, as was the case for Saul of Tarsus (Acts 9:1–19) and for the Philippian jailer (Acts 16:29–30).

THE BIBLE AND CRISIS

The specific word *crisis* does not appear in Scripture, but the Bible contains many accounts of crises. Such include unstable time periods or turning points in the lives of biblical figures. We do find in Scripture terms that parallel crisis—*trial, tribulation, test, persecution,* and *affliction.*

These terms seem to be common components of what all humans experience in life, even believers who are attempting to follow Christ. In 1 Peter 4:12, for example, Peter tells believers to "not be surprised at the painful trial you are

---

7. Ibid.

suffering, as though something strange were happening to you" (NIV). James encourages followers to, "Consider it all joy, my brethren, when you encounter various trials" (James 1:2). Just prior to the crucifixion, Jesus informs His disciples, "In the world you have tribulation, but take courage; I have overcome the world" (John 16:33). In the Old Testament, Genesis 22:2, God tests Abraham by asking him to sacrifice his son, Isaac. God, in Deuteronomy 8:2, tells the children of Israel that He led them into the wilderness to humble them and to test them. This testing involved allowing them to be hungry (Deut 8:3, 16), thirsty (Deut. 8:15), and in physical danger (Deut. 8:15). Paul informs the Thessalonians that "when we were with you, we kept telling you in advance that we were going to suffer affliction; and so it came to pass, as you know" (1 Thess. 3:4). Individuals in Scripture were no strangers to crises.

Other terms, too, used in Scripture are similar to crisis, including *suffering, hardship, adversity,* and *pain.* In Romans 5:3, Paul says, "We also rejoice in our sufferings, because we know that suffering produces perseverance" (NIV). Jesus also experienced suffering, telling His followers, "the Son of Man must suffer many things" (Mark 8:31). Peter states, "To this you were called, because Christ suffered for you, leaving you an example, that you should follow in his steps" (1 Peter 2:21 NIV). Paul writes to Timothy, encouraging him in the faith and exhorting him to "endure hardship with us like a good soldier of Christ Jesus" (2 Tim. 2:3 NIV). Proverbs 17:17 states that a brother is born for adversity, leaving little doubt that humans will experience unfavorable circumstances. Job references the "unrelenting pain" he is encountering (Job 6:10 NIV), as does Jeremiah, who wonders, "Why is my pain unending and my wound grievous and incurable?" (Jer. 15:18 NIV).

While the Bible does not use the term *crisis,* passages such as those above paint a partial but compelling picture of just how extensive human struggle is. Whether suffering, tests, affliction, or pain, these human experiences are discussed in the Bible, with numerous specific examples.

BIBLICAL EXAMPLES OF CRISIS

From Genesis to Revelation, we see examples of children of God as they face crises. Sometimes these events result from disobedience to God; on other occasions, individuals who are truly following God end up in difficult circumstances. A few examples follow.

Adam and Eve

Genesis 3 gives the account of Adam and Eve's disobedience to God, their resulting shame, and their attempt to hide from God. Because they choose to rebel against God, this couple faces the first crisis in Scripture—that is, being exiled from the Garden of Eden, their beautiful home and the place where they walked with God in the cool of the day.

Jacob

Throughout his life, Jacob endured a number of crises. After deceiving Esau and obtaining the birthright and blessing from his father, Isaac, Jacob is forced to flee from his enraged brother, who pledges to kill him (Gen. 27:41). Although Jacob locates relatives in Haran, he faces a rather unusual crisis: he awakens after his wedding celebration, having spent the night not with the woman he thought he was marrying, but with her sister (Gen. 29:25). Jacob faces yet another crisis when he returns to Canaan many years after leaving, fearing that Esau is still angry and wanting to kill him (Gen. 33).

Moses and His Family

Moses' family was subject to a very difficult crisis. His mother gives birth to him after the pharaoh decrees that all male Hebrew children are to be killed (Exod. 1:16). In his adult life, Moses must deal with a serious crisis after he kills an Egyptian who is mistreating a Hebrew slave (Exod. 2:11–14). Moses experiences yet another turning point when God calls him to return to Egypt as His spokesman and as the one chosen to lead the Israelites out of their Egyptian slavery (Exod. 3).

The Nation of Israel

The Israelites undergo a number of extreme difficulties as they escape from Egypt, year after year being forced to wander in the wilderness. Crises include being chased toward the sea by the Egyptian army, being hungry and thirsty, navigating around dangerous desert creatures like snakes and scorpions (see Deut. 8:15), and dealing with threats from hostile surrounding nations. Even the prospect of entering Canaan produces a crisis—disagreement between the spies who were sent to scout the land (Num. 13).[8]

---

8. Note how the various spies differed in their perceptions and interpretations of this particular crisis. Caleb and Joshua saw the wonderful opportunities of the land, whereas the other ten spies could see only the problems and dangers.

David

Like many other Old Testament figures, David faced numerous crises, beginning in his youth. Still a boy, David confronts the warrior Goliath, while older, more experienced soldiers are paralyzed with fear (1 Sam. 17). Later, after being anointed as the king of Israel, David must flee for his life, living several months behind rocks and in caves in the southern part of Israel. David is in crisis when he impregnates Bathsheba, and also as the child, born from this relationship, lies ill (2 Sam. 11–12). David also experienced various political and military crises throughout his time as king. Many of David's psalms were recorded in the midst of personal and political crises and are wonderful examples of his desire to seek God in difficult circumstances.[9]

Esther

Esther had to deal with a number of extremely critical situations. Her people are to be killed, according to the decree of King Xerxes, her husband, who has been tricked by the evil Haman (Esther 3:8–11). Esther finds herself in a predicament when Mordecai, her cousin and adopted father, urges her to speak to the king on behalf of the Israelites. Esther knows that when she approaches the king without his permission, she risks being put to death (Esther 4:15–16).

Daniel

As a young man, Daniel is taken from Israel and placed in servitude in a foreign land, a crisis of immense proportions. Immediately upon arriving in the new country, Daniel is given a new name and required to eat food inconsistent with Jewish dietary restrictions (Dan. 1:1–16). Daniel experiences another serious crisis later in his life when he is ordered to bow down and worship an earthly king. Despite his faithfulness to God, he is thrown into a lions' den because of his refusal to worship anyone other than the true God (Dan. 6).

Jeremiah

Jeremiah seemed to move from one crisis situation to another. He is placed in stocks (Jer. 20:1–2), thrown into a pit (38:6–13), imprisoned (37:15), and kidnapped and dragged to Egypt (43:7). The religious leaders of his day even pronounce him under a death sentence (26:11). In the face of many trials, Jeremiah continues to proclaim God's message to the people of Judah.

---

9. Psalms 34; 51; 52; 54; 56; 57; and 59 are all written by David during periods of personal and national crises.

The above are but a few notable Old Testament examples of individuals who faced various crises. Following are a few from the New Testament.

Joseph

Joseph is engaged to Mary and is likely within months of the wedding when he discovers she is pregnant (Matt. 1:18). Confronted with this crisis, Joseph must decide what to do. As a righteous man, he knows the law calls for Mary to be stoned to death (Deut. 22:23–24). An angel tells him that Mary will be the mother of the Messiah, but before receiving that revelation, Joseph surely spent many sleepless nights wrestling with the issues of Mary's pregnancy, their pending marriage, and how to uphold the law while still caring about Mary.

The Disciples

Walking around the countryside with Jesus, the disciples experience numerous crises, some of their own making and some that result from following Christ. One clear crisis occurs as the disciples are in the boat with Jesus and a storm arises on the sea (Luke 8:22–25). Interestingly, in the midst of this test of the disciples' faith, Jesus is calmly sleeping in the boat. The disciples are also in crisis around the time of the crucifixion of Jesus, both following His arrest and after the actual crucifixion. When Jesus is arrested, Peter attempts to stay close to Him, but is accused of being one of Jesus' disciples (Luke 22:54–62). After the crucifixion, we see the disciples locked in a room, fearing for their lives (John 20:19). Following Jesus' ascension, Peter and John face a crisis when they are arrested and forbidden to preach about Jesus (Acts 4). Their situation becomes even more critical as the persecution of believers intensifies. First, Stephen is stoned (Acts 7:54–60), then James and Peter are arrested and jailed (Acts 12:1–19). James is executed and Peter escapes with the help of an angel.

The Ill or Diseased

Perhaps some of the clearest examples of people in crisis are the numerous individuals in Scripture who seek out Jesus, hoping to be healed from illness or physical infirmities. It's easy to imagine the pain and suffering these individuals and their families experienced. For some, the suffering took place over a period of years. In the Gospels, Jesus constantly encounters people who are desperate for healing. Jesus heals the deaf and mute (Mark 7:32–37), paralytics (Luke 5:18–26), lepers (Luke 17:11–19; Matt. 8:2–4), the blind (Mark 8:22–26; Mark 10:46–52), a crippled woman (Luke 13:10–13), a woman with prolonged, uncontrolled bleeding (Mark 5:24–34), and Peter's mother-in-law, ill with a fever (Luke 4:38–39). These are but a few stories of those who seek Jesus in the midst of health-related crises.

On more than one occasion, crowds flocked to Jesus, bringing all their loved ones in need of healing. Luke identifies one such occurrence after Jesus heals Peter's mother-in-law: "While the sun was setting, all those who had any who were sick with various diseases brought them to Him; and laying His hands on each one of them, He was healing them" (Luke 4:40). Mark notes another such instance as Jesus, traveling by boat, lands at Gennesaret: "When they got out of the boat, immediately the people recognized Him, and ran about that whole country and began to carry here and there on their pallets those who were sick, to the place they heard He was" (Mark 6:54–55). The stories of those who seek Jesus for healing demonstrate the almost palpable desperation of people battling the ongoing crises of personal or family illness.

Paul

Even while still Saul of Tarsus, this great apostle faces numerous crises. These include watching Stephen as he was stoned to death (Acts 7:58; 8:1), and being confronted by Jesus on his way to Damascus (Acts 9:1–19). After becoming a follower of Christ, Paul has many crisis experiences. He recounts one of these in 2 Corinthians 1:8–9: "We do not want you to be uninformed, brothers, about the hardships we suffered in the province of Asia. We were under great pressure, far beyond our ability to endure, so that we despaired even of life. Indeed, in our hearts we felt the sentence of death" (NIV). Paul does not give specifics about the trouble he faced in Asia, but at one point it was so severe, he concluded that he would not survive.

John

John, the beloved disciple, encountered many crises, but perhaps none so serious as being exiled on the Island of Patmos, where he awaited his death. When John authors the book of Revelation, he has been banished, most likely to a Roman penal colony on Patmos, and is surely in the midst of crisis. It is interesting, too, that Scripture begins and ends with crisis situations, both involving exile: Adam and Eve are exiled from Eden, and John pens Revelation in the midst of political and religious exile.

FACTORS DETERMINING THE IMPACT OF CRISES

A great deal of variation occurs in how severe an impact a crisis makes. Some variation depends upon certain dimensions of the crisis event itself—the nature of the onset, the severity of the event, the length or duration of the crisis and related events, and losses produced by the crisis event. The impact of a crisis is also influenced by the person going through the crisis—the person's coping skills, perception of the event, support the person receives from others, and the number of additional stressors experienced. These factors interact to determine whether the outcome of a crisis event is positive or negative (see fig. 1.1).

Figure 1.1. Factors Determining the Impact of Crises

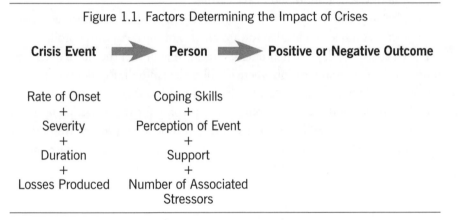

The Crisis Event

Certain events produce clear and recognizable crises. Being fired from a job, receiving information that a loved one needs immediate surgery, having a child born with a serious birth defect, discovering that your spouse is having an affair and wants to divorce, having your car totaled by an uninsured driver—all these are crisis events. The impact, too, of these various crises is unmistakable: the event produces an unstable circumstance with an uncertain outcome, with the person in crisis facing various turning points. While some crises are created by specific events, the causes of others may be more subtle. A person may believe, for instance, that he or she is in a crisis, but has a difficult time pinpointing an actual precipitating event. This lack of clarity may be related to the role played by one's perceptions or beliefs in deciphering difficult circumstances.

Rate of Onset

Rate of onset affects the impact of crisis. Some crises are gradual in onset, while others occur suddenly. A phone call from the state police informing a couple that their teenage daughter has been in an accident is a type of sudden crisis. The daughter may be a careful driver and not prone to taking risks. The parents may never have expected to receive a phone call of this nature and are forced to face this stunning turn of events. Other crises occur more gradually. A family may live in an area that's been deteriorating over time and has a rising crime rate that increases danger to family members. These changes in the neighborhood may be part of a gradual crisis that the family is facing in regard to staying in the neighborhood or relocating.

Similar to gradual versus sudden onset are crises that are expected versus unexpected. A hurricane headed toward an area of the coast often produces an expected crisis. For days, meteorologists track the course of the storm and often pinpoint the time and location where it will make landfall. Residents of coastal regions usually have time to decide whether or not to evacuate and are able to board up their windows, buy supplies, and prepare for the worst. Conversely, tornadoes can strike with minimal warning. People living in certain parts of the country know that, even if tornado sirens sound, there is little time to react, and a crisis produced by a tornado is most often quite unexpected.

Severity

Some crises are mild, while others are more powerful; some may even seem quite extreme. A person overdrawn at the bank encounters a mild crisis, but this experience pales in comparison to, say, a certain farmer. His land has been in the family for generations, but now he watches his drought-parched fields and realizes he'll lose his crops, his livestock, or, worse yet, his entire farm.

When crises are mild, individuals generally cope effectively, perhaps not even registering the event or events as a type of crisis. When crises are extreme, people can be devastated in terms of daily functioning, relationship health, and even spiritual awareness and growth.

Duration

Some crises are quite brief, ending in a few seconds. A mother whose two-year-old has wandered off in a department store is likely to experience an immediate crisis. If she finds the child right away, the crisis will be brief in nature.

symptoms - state
points - moments of opportunity
            to in crisis

CRISIS

As any parent in a like situation can attest, some crises begin unexpectedly, become intense, but also end suddenly.

Other crises are more protracted, lasting months or even years. For individuals whose homes are damaged or destroyed in a natural disaster like a flood, hurricane, or tornado, the crisis is immediate in terms of personal and family safety. The crisis is also protracted, however, relating to where the family will live and how they will function. If a crisis of this nature is combined with not having insurance, losing one's job, or having to relocate the family, the struggle can be severe and ongoing. A further example involves individuals who have supported relatives or loved ones facing terminal illness. This type of crisis generally lasts months or years. Relatives who provide care to those having Alzheimer's, cancer, or any degenerative illness know well the complexity of coping day to day, week to week.

James and Gilliland believe that most crises tend to be shorter in duration; a crisis will emerge, and then will be resolved. Some crises, however, are chronic and prolonged and the individuals undergoing the crisis suffer ongoing symptoms. James and Gilliland refer to the collection of symptoms produced by an ongoing crisis as a transcrisis state.[10] An individual experiencing a transcrisis state may feel a great deal of stress and anxiety and may be less effective in work productivity, personal relationships, and in general functioning.

When a crisis is prolonged and produces a transcrisis state, the individual will also experience a number of transcrisis points.[11] Transcrisis points are key moments within a larger crisis when an individual can grow, come to grips with the problem, or make adjustments to what is taking place within the larger crisis. These transcrisis points might be compared to hurdles that a runner must clear to complete a race. When a person—either the one going through the crisis or a caregiver—notices a transcrisis point, it becomes an opportunity for the crisis victim to progress in his or her overall effort to cope. Recognizing and navigating transcrisis points becomes, then, a key component in dealing with ongoing crises.

Losses Produced

Some crises result in minor losses; others result in significant losses. Those losses can be material, emotional, or spiritual. In the case of our farmer mentioned above, or the victims of Hurricane Katrina, the material losses are

---

10. James and Gilliland, *Crisis Intervention Strategies,* 5–6.
11. Ibid., 7.

devastating. If someone fails to repay the twenty dollars he or she owes you, that material loss is, for most people, nominal. That same twenty dollars, however, can result in the loss of relationship. The person might now be embarrassed to face you. You might feel betrayed that a friend would fail to repay such a small loan. In extreme cases, if the debtor were a Christian and the lender a non-Christian, the lender might harbor a spiritual loss: "If so and so is a Christian and doesn't repay a small loan, then Christianity isn't for me!" The more significant or extensive the loss or losses a person experiences, the more negative the overall impact is likely to be.

These dimensions of crises—onset, severity, duration, and losses produced—shape the trajectory of the overall crisis. Some crises have a sudden onset, are very intense, and end abruptly. Other crises may be slow in developing, but become increasingly powerful as time progresses. In the story of Brenda at the start of the chapter, her crisis had a gradual onset, but became increasingly intense. Because her husband outlasted the life expectancy for ALS, Brenda's crisis was ongoing, with little relief. She appeared to be in a transcrisis state, and she was struggling emotionally, physically, and spiritually. She also experienced a number of transcrisis points in the midst of the larger crisis. On one occasion her insurance company refused to pay for part of her husband's care. On another occasion, a home health-care nurse was causing numerous problems, leading Brenda to fire the nurse and to have to look for a replacement. Counselors and ministers who work with individuals in the midst of crises can understand the nature of the crisis most accurately if they pay attention to the various dimensions of the crisis event.

The Person in Crisis

The extent of the impact produced by a crisis depends, too, on factors related to the individual undergoing the crisis. These factors include the person's coping skills, perception of the event, support received from others, and additional stressors of the person experiencing the crisis event.

Coping Skills

How does the person respond when a crisis occurs? Individuals who possess adequate *coping skills* prior to a crisis are more likely to make adjustments necessary for effectively facing the crisis. Some individuals tolerate greater pressure and even function well under an enormous amount of stress. Other individuals lose their bearings if life events become even slightly stressful. What seems a severe crisis to one person may be circumstances more easily navigated by another individual. Thus, the outcome or impact of a crisis is affected by a person's ability to cope with crisis situations.

Perception or Interpretation of Events

Related to a person's coping skills is that person's *perception or interpretation of* events. Some circumstances indisputably constitute a crisis, as mentioned above. In some instances, however, a person may perceive him- or herself to be in crisis, when, in actuality, the person is not. Or, a person may perceive a crisis to be larger than it really is. If a man believes he'll be fired in the next round of layoffs, or misinterprets work-related information, or perceives certain circumstances as threatening, he may face the situation as a crisis. This man may feel anxious, discouraged, and frustrated. He may ponder other job possibilities and think of relocating to another city or state. The reality may be that the man's job was never in danger; his was not one of the jobs to be eliminated. If an individual believes something to be true, whether it is or is not, the person may conclude that he or she faces a crisis. Thus, some crises are actual events, while others are perceived. Even when a person perceives a crisis that does not actually exist, that person's emotional response will tend to be the same as if the crisis were real. Further, two individuals can confront a similar situation in markedly different ways. One person may view a situation as a challenge, whereas another person may view the situation as threatening, problematic, or even devastating. The first individual may vigorously face the challenge, not even interpreting the situation negatively, while the second person may become discouraged, ineffective, or even paralyzed.

Perception and interpretation, then, play a significant role in how a person recognizes and responds to various situations. According to Kanel, understanding how a person perceives a situation is central in offering help to that person: "The perception of the event is by far the most crucial part to identify, for it is the part that can be most easily and quickly altered by the counselor."[12]

Support System

Having a strong *support system* is also important in coping. A single, childless person with no relatives who live nearby is in a more precarious position than a person with a solid marriage, well-adjusted children, and extended family

---

12. Kanel, *A Guide to Crisis Intervention*, 2.

living close by. That same single person with a network of close friends and/or a church community is less at risk than the person who lives a life of virtual isolation.

Number of Stressors

Last, if a person faces a *number of stressors* apart from the crisis, effective coping is likely to be diminished. The person whose mother has just died but whose life is otherwise reasonably under control is less at risk than the person whose mother died and who is also three months behind on rent, has a rocky romantic relationship, and needs a new transmission.

The Crisis Impact or Outcome

Again, the outcome of a crisis, whether positive or negative, is a function of the nature of the crisis itself combined with the person's ability to make appropriate and healthy adjustments during and following the crisis. An individual who does not handle crises well is in danger of becoming what Kanel refers to as a crisis-prone person.[13] When individuals fail to cope effectively with a crisis event, the result is an ongoing disequilibrium and a vulnerability to future stressors or crisis events. When the individual faces more stressors, they again fail to cope, leaving them even more at-risk. Most ministers and counselors know individuals who fit the description of a crisis-prone person. They seem to go from one situation to the next, never coping effectively, and often requiring a great deal of help and support. Failure to cope effectively can send a person into a downward spiral, where the likelihood of future coping is diminished.

CONCLUSION: CRISES FROM A CHRISTIAN PERSPECTIVE

Crisis events can be challenging, disorienting, and, in some instances, devastating. When experiencing a crisis, a person is often tempted to see it as a negative event, thereby feeling discouraged and frustrated. The Christian caregiver must be careful, however, when working with those in trying circumstances to avoid viewing crises from a purely human perspective. In concluding this chapter, I offer a few observations on crises from a Christian perspective.

---

13. Ibid., 5–6.

1. *Being a Christian doesn't exempt us from all crises.* In some situations, God may protect someone in such a manner that he or she avoids a crisis. On other occasions, God will guide a person through a time of crisis. All individuals, however, will experience crises, exemplified by the number and types of crises identified in Scripture. Some crisis experiences seem necessary in order to conform an individual into the image of Christ. Even the godliest individuals experience multiple crises over the course of a lifetime.

2. *A crisis to us isn't a crisis to God.* God does not panic, nor does He wring His hands, wondering what He should do next. God does not lose sleep, or fret, or pace the floor. What we as humans view as a crisis is not a crisis from God's vantage point. God is in control; He knows where we are and the exact nature of our circumstances. God cares about us, even in the midst of what we interpret as a crisis.

3. *God comforts and promises to be present.* I'm amazed at how many times God encourages His children to "Fear not," often adding the assurance, "I am with you." Many of the most godly biblical figures received reassurance of God's care and presence when they faced crises: Abraham (Gen. 15:1), Jacob (Gen. 26:24), Moses (Num. 21:34), Joshua (Josh. 8:1), Gideon (Judg. 6:23), Solomon (1 Chron. 28:20), Jeremiah (Lam. 3:27), Daniel (Dan. 10:12), Zechariah (Luke 1:13), Joseph (Matt. 1:20), Mary (Luke 1:30), Peter (Luke 5:10), Paul (Acts 27:24), and John (Rev. 1:17). God cares for His children, provides words of comfort, and promises to be present in difficult circumstances.

4. *A crisis will not last forever.* One of my favorite phrases in the Bible is "And it came to pass . . ." Our timing is not the same as God's timing. God knows what we need and when we need it. Even difficult circumstances will eventually change or God will provide us strength to face and cope with the crisis.

5. *Hope is resident in crises.* Paul understood that crises do not have to end in hopelessness and despair. In Romans 5:3–5, Paul acknowledges that believers will have struggles, but difficult times do not have to dictate negative outcomes: "But we also exult in our tribulations, knowing that tribulation brings about perseverance; and perseverance, proven character; and proven character, hope; and hope does not disappoint, because the love of God has been poured out within our hearts through the Holy Spirit who was given to us." Difficult circumstances have the

ability to produced perseverance, character, and hope. It is, in fact, this hope that helps us look ahead, to face the crises that are so much a part of life in this world.

CHAPTER 2

TRAUMA

A TRAUMA STORY

LEONARD WAS A THIRTY-FIVE-YEAR-OLD, single adult who came to counseling in the aftermath of a harrowing experience. One warm May evening when returning home from work, he pulled into the driveway of his house. As he prepared to open the car door, a figure appeared at his car window. There, Leonard saw two young men, one of whom was pointing a gun at him and demanding he get out of the car. To Leonard's dismay, no neighbors were in sight. The gunmen took his keys and wallet and forced Leonard into the trunk of the car, beginning an ordeal that would last for the next several hours.

The gunmen drove to an ATM machine and, using one of Leonard's cards, withdrew cash. They drove around the city where Leonard lived, stopping occasionally to purchase alcohol. Even though it was after sunset, it was a hot evening, and even hotter in the trunk of the car. Leonard struggled to breathe, a task made more difficult by his asthma. At least twice the gunmen stopped behind abandoned buildings, took Leonard out of the car, and put the gun to his head, telling him they were going to shoot him. They seemed to see this as some kind of game. Leonard was convinced he would die that night. At about 5 A.M., after several hours of driving around town, the men stopped in a deserted area, opened the trunk of the car, took Leonard's shoes from him, and threw him out beside the road. After they drove off, Leonard walked several blocks to a convenience store, called a friend to come get him, then called the police.

Leonard came for counseling because he knew the extreme nature of his ordeal was hindering his work and relationships. A social worker by profession, he was aware of the impact of events such as the one he experienced. He noted, however, that knowing about trauma does not prepare a person to experience it. He talked of being anxious in general, but especially when driving at night. He had difficulty returning to his house and had temporarily been living with other young men from his church singles group. He experienced trouble concentrating at work and did not want to spend time with friends. Leonard was angry at the perpetrators, but he was also angry at himself. Because he had been in the military, he continually wondered why he couldn't have done more to protect himself. He felt guilty and embarrassed, consistently second-guessing how he had ended up in that predicament.

Leonard knew he'd experienced a traumatic event, but he was surprised at how it affected him and about his reactions to it. He came to counseling at the urging of his fellow social workers and wanted to know the best way to lessen the impact of his night of terror.

DEFINITIONS

According to Webster's dictionary, the most basic meaning of *trauma* is "wound."[1] Trauma may involve physical wounds; accordingly, hospitals have trauma centers, or emergency rooms. Trauma can also be emotional, striking at the core of a person's identity and sense of self. According to Lenore Terr, trauma occurs "when a sudden, unexpected, overwhelmingly intense emotional blow or series of blows assaults a person from the outside. Traumatic events are external, but they quickly become incorporated into the mind."[2] Therefore, trauma is an event outside of what is normally expected in the life of an individual, and that breaks past normal coping and defense mechanisms, causing strong emotional pain.

Trauma, then, contains several elements. First, trauma results from a specific event or set of events. Whereas a crisis may be somewhat vague and can involve a person's perception, trauma is very specific and is connected to a particular event. Second, trauma is not a part of general human functioning. Having a teenager obtain a driver's permit may produce struggles in some families, but no matter how hard this process might be for a family, it is not a traumatic event; it is an expected part of human functioning. In the same vein, having

---

1. *Merriam-Webster's Collegiate Dictionary*, 11th ed., s.v. "trauma."
2. Terr, *Too Scared to Cry*, 8.

a child begin school, become a teenager, leave for college, or get married may be stressful, but these are part of typical human experience and not trauma events. Third, a traumatic event tends to overwhelm normal coping mechanisms. God made humans to be resilient, and, generally, individuals show an amazing ability to cope with many difficult and trying life situations. Certain events, though, are so powerful they overwhelm a person's regular means of coping. Last, any traumatic experience tends to produce a set of symptoms in the person encountering the trauma. Symptoms can be cognitive, emotional, behavioral, spiritual, or relational. This chapter discusses these symptoms in greater detail at a later point.

TYPES OF TRAUMA

Type 1 Trauma

According to Lenore Terr, humans experience two general categories of trauma.[3] Type 1 trauma is also known as single-event trauma, or single-blow trauma in a person who experiences a sudden, unexpected event. Examples include accidents such as major car wrecks; experiencing natural disasters such as tornadoes or hurricanes; being victim of some criminal activity such as a robbery or assault; or sudden death of a family member, whether through an accident or self-inflicted. Type 1 trauma can result even if the specific trauma event happens to another person such as a family member or close friend. This type of trauma is usually referred to as secondary or vicarious trauma and will be discussed in more detail in chapter 13.

Type 2 Trauma

The second category, type 2 trauma, is also known as multiple-blow trauma. Type 2 trauma generally occurs in a couple of ways. First, a person experiences repeated instances of trauma. An example is a soldier who sees active duty during which, over time, he or she is exposed to several extreme events such as personal injury or the deaths of other soldiers. Another example is a child growing up in a gang-infested inner-city setting. This young person might witness, or even experience, events such as having friends killed or injured. Still another example is a child who is sexually molested on multiple occasions over a period of time. Sexual abuse always has a traumatic element, and if it happens

---

3. Terr, *Unchained Memories*, 11.

more than once, the individual will tend to experience many of the symptoms of type 2 trauma.

While type 2 trauma can result from repeated exposure to the same event, it also can be the outcome for a person who undergoes a series of different traumatic events. On occasion I see in counseling an individual who, in a short period of time, has been faced with several extreme, traumatic circumstances. Pamela, for instance, came to see me for counseling when her husband announced he was leaving her and their small child to marry another woman. As we talked about this, she also shared that, within the past eighteen months, her father suffered a heart attack and died suddenly, her brother died in her arms following an extended illness, and a family celebration turned tragic when her house caught on fire, resulting in injuries to both Pamela and her child. Each event was different, but because they happened in close chronology to each other, the effect was that of type 2 trauma.

THE BIBLE AND TRAUMA

The Greek word τραῦμα, or trauma, appears in various forms in the New Testament, twice in the book of Luke and once in the book of Acts.[4] As in modern usage, the word means *wound* and is used as both a noun and a verb.

On two occasions, Jesus used τραῦμα in parables He told to His followers. Τραῦμα first appears in the New Testament in the story of the Good Samaritan, recorded in Luke 10. A man is attacked by robbers, stripped naked, and left beside the road bleeding and wounded. Two highly religious individuals pass by this man without helping. When the Samaritan finds him, his reaction is recorded in Luke 10:33–34: "But a Samaritan, as he traveled, came where the man was; and when he saw him, he took pity on him. He went to him and bandaged his wounds [τραύματα], pouring on oil and wine. Then he put the man on his own donkey, took him to an inn and took care of him" (NIV).

Jesus used this parable to communicate what it means to love one's neighbor. The Samaritan finds an enemy, injured and lying beside the road. He has compassion on him and treats the man's trauma, or wounds. Bock notes the first aid provided by the Samaritan: "As he engages in the process of bandaging the wounds, he anoints the cuts with oil and wine. Oil soothed the wounds,

---

4. Trenchard, *Student's Complete Vocabulary Guide*, 112.

while wine disinfected it."[5] He then provides for the man's ongoing care. It's interesting that the Samaritan in the story helped the hurting stranger at the cost of time, money, and effort.

Jesus' second use of τραῦμα is also recorded by Luke in the parable of the tenants, found in Luke 20:9–19. A rich man purchases a vineyard and leases it to caretakers. At harvesttime, the owner sends a servant to collect some of the harvest from the tenants. Instead of responding appropriately, the tenants beat the servant and send him away. The owner sends a second servant, who is also beaten and "treated shamefully" (Luke 20:11 NIV). The owner sends yet another servant, with the account recorded in Luke 20:12: "He sent still a third, and they wounded [τραυματίσαντες] him and threw him out" (NIV). The attacks of the vineyard tenants became increasingly violent, from beating the first servant to killing the owner's son when he was sent.

The final New Testament appearance of the word τραῦμα occurs in Acts 19, when Paul is in Ephesus. Here, sons of Sceva, the Jewish high priest, are attempting to cast out demons using the names of Paul and Jesus. Acts 19:15–16 states, "And the evil spirit answered and said to them, 'I recognize Jesus, and I know about Paul, but who are you?' And the man, in whom was the evil spirit, leaped on them and subdued all of them and overpowered them, so that they fled out of that house naked and wounded [τετραυματωμένους]."

The Septuagint, or the Greek translation of the Old Testament, uses τραῦμα in Isaiah 53, describing Jesus as the suffering servant. Isaiah 53:5 says, "But he was wounded [ἐτραυματίσθη] for our transgressions, he was bruised for our iniquities; upon him was the chastisement that made us whole, and with his stripes we are healed" (RSV). What an amazing thought that Jesus was traumatized for us, taking our place and receiving what we deserved! When Hebrews 4:14–16 talks about Jesus as our Great High Priest, we know that He understands what it is to be wounded and traumatized. Those who have experienced trauma can approach Him with confidence that He comprehends suffering and pain.

In addition to the word *trauma* appearing in Scripture, the Bible gives specific examples of situations that are traumatizing to those involved. Three of these are the stories of the Egyptians following the tenth plague, Job and his struggles, and the crucifixion.

---

5. Bock, *Baker Exegetical Commentary on the New Testament*, 1033.

Pharaoh and the Egyptians

The book of Exodus gives an example of a traumatic event that occurred on a national scale. Moses has been talking to the pharaoh, requesting that the Israelites be freed from Egyptian slavery and allowed to return to Canaan. Pharaoh will not acquiesce, and although God sends a series of plagues on the Egyptians, the pharaoh refuses to relent. In Exodus 11:1, God tells Moses, "One more plague I will bring on Pharaoh and on Egypt; after that he will let you go from here. When he lets you go, he will surely drive you out from here completely." God then gives Moses instructions for the Passover and how to prepare the Israelite children to leave Egypt.

That night, about midnight, God passes through the midst of the people. For the Israelites who have followed the instructions of Moses, sacrificing a lamb and placing the blood on the doorposts of their houses, God passes over them, leaving them safe. Conversely, for the Egyptian families, the firstborn male in each is killed.

Exodus 12:30 notes, "Pharaoh arose in the night, he and all his servants and all the Egyptians, and there was a great cry in Egypt, for there was no home where there was not someone dead."

This was trauma on a national scale, having an impact on thousands of individuals. The most common modern example of trauma experienced on that scale might be natural disasters such as floods, hurricanes, or earthquakes. The resulting devastation often shocks entire nations, with individuals losing loved ones, homes, and in some instances, all life possessions. The tenth plague of Exodus was just such a large-scale event, having an impact on every family in Egypt.

One can imagine what it must have been like for the Egyptians to awaken the morning after the Passover. While the earlier nine plagues were certainly stressful and would have produced crises for those involved, they were nothing compared to the final plague. The Egyptians went to bed that evening, not expecting an extensive tragedy upon awakening. What happened is an example of an event that was not a normal part of human functioning and that burst past normal coping mechanisms. The "great cry" in Egypt surely was an outcome of this extensive trauma.

One final note about this particular example of trauma—Exodus 12:35–36 tells of the Israelite children plundering the Egyptians, taking objects of gold and silver and articles of clothing from them. The Israelites did not, however, steal these items. On their way out of the country, they simply asked the Egyptians for these treasures, and the Egyptians handed them over. This strange turn of events makes sense, though, in light of how trauma affects individuals. Immediately following a traumatic event, it is common for rescue personnel to find the victim stunned and in a state of shock, often still in the midst of danger. Rescuers can often take the person by the hand, speak simply and clearly to him or her, and lead the person out of harm's way. It's as if the victim's regular coping mechanisms have shut down. It is common for one undergoing a traumatic event not to be thinking clearly.

This appears to be the case for the Egyptians, who handed over prized possessions to their slaves, who were walking off the job and leaving the country. The Egyptians eventually came out of their state of shock, as noted in Exodus 14:5. They ask themselves, "What have we done?" They then make haste to pursue the Hebrew children, trying to reclaim their slaves and their possessions. For the Egyptians, the loss of firstborn children was a traumatic event occurring on a national scale. The outcry and shock that followed were clear examples of the impact of trauma.

Job

A second example of trauma appears in the book of Job. Job is a man of great character, who "was blameless, upright, fearing God and turning away from evil" (Job 1:1). Satan takes note of Job and, in essence, makes a wager with God: if Job were to experience hardship, he would cease to worship God. Satan is allowed by God to put Job to a test. In quick succession, Job sustains incredible losses. First, Job loses his livestock, including oxen, donkeys, sheep, and camels (1:13–17). Many of his servants are killed as raiders from neighboring countries take his animals. Following these disasters, Job is informed that his seven sons and three daughters have all been killed when a great wind struck the house they occupied, causing the walls to collapse (1:18–19). As if this is not enough, Satan inflicts Job with painful boils that cover his entire body (2:7). Job's losses are intense and severe.

Job experienced, in today's terms, type 2 trauma as he faced a rapid series of extremely difficult, traumatic events. Any one of the specific losses Job encountered would challenge the average person. He lost his possessions, his children, and his physical health. Job had no way of knowing of the meeting that took place between God and Satan; he only knew what had just happened to his family, his health, and his belongings. The remainder of the book of Job discusses his struggle to understand what has happened and why it has occurred.

The book of Job, then, presents a clear picture of a person in the wake of a series of traumatic circumstances.

The Crucifixion

Perhaps the clearest example of trauma recorded in Scripture is what takes place for the followers of Jesus in the period between His arrest and His resurrection. The Gospels provide us with a great deal of information about how the disciples and other followers of Jesus responded to the events surrounding Jesus' crucifixion.

Because the Passover is a festive time for the Israelites, it is assuredly with anticipation that the disciples spend the days prior to the celebration. They had traveled with Jesus around the countryside for three years, leaving family and occupation to follow the Messiah. Earlier in the Passover week, the disciples witnessed the crowds worshipping Jesus, laying palm branches in the road, crying "Hosanna" as He entered Jerusalem, riding on the back of a colt. Although Jesus had told the disciples He would be killed in Jerusalem (see Matt. 16:21–23), they did not comprehend what He was saying.

The disciples had no idea of the events to come as they prepared to celebrate the Passover. Sharing the meal with each other and with Jesus, they surely marvel at seeing Him convey a message about leadership by washing their feet. They hear Jesus talk about peace, about the Holy Spirit, and about the vine and branches. They also hear Him announce that one person around the table will betray Him. Even in all this, the disciples have no idea of what is to come later in the evening.

As the disciples spend time with Jesus in the Garden of Gethsemane, struggling to keep alert while Jesus prays, a crowd approaches the group. At some point, the disciples realize that something is wrong. We can easily imagine their state of confusion. Do they immediately understand what is happening, that Jesus is being arrested? What is Judas doing with the group? Why are there soldiers, the chief priest, officers of the temple, and elders in the group? Why is Judas kissing Jesus?

At some point, at least one of the disciples recognizes danger. Seeing Jesus being arrested, Peter pulls his sword and strikes the slave of the high priest, cutting off the slave's right ear. Again, the disciples must have experienced tremendous confusion as Jesus healed the servant, then was led away by the group.

If a traumatic situation is ongoing, it is common for individuals to undergo confusion and not know what to do. Thus, some of the disciples flee the danger. Peter, at least, follows at some distance and observes the events from the courtyard of the high priest's house. As a man of action, Peter may be trying to help Jesus.

If Thursday evening was confusing, Friday had to compound the struggle for the disciples. They surely witnessed parts of the legal proceedings and heard rumors and stories about Jesus' arrest. Maybe they saw Pilate wash his hands of the matter. Perhaps they heard the crowds call for the release of Barabbas, a notorious criminal. They may have observed the Roman soldiers, in mock worship, putting a robe and crown of thorns on Jesus. Some saw Simon being recruited to carry the cross to Golgotha.

What ran through the disciples' minds on Friday? Did they doubt what they were experiencing? Were they numb? Were they confused? Did they talk with each other or did they retreat from the crowds? Maybe they thought about how quickly things had gone from good—celebrating Passover with Jesus—to bad—the soldiers arresting Jesus—to horrific, as their Lord was nailed to the cross. We do know that John, Mary the mother of Jesus, and other women followers saw the entire crucifixion (John 19:25–26). How difficult was it to stand nearby and watch the prolonged and agonizing death of this One they loved so much?

Prior to the resurrection of Christ, the crucifixion could not but impact the disciples as a clear, large-scale trauma. We see in their behavior many of the characteristics of traumalike symptoms. The disciples scatter, not knowing what to do. Some attempt to care for Jesus after the crucifixion. Joseph of Arimathea and Nicodemus take His body for burial. Some of the women help in the burial process. Other followers flee and hide away, fearing for their lives.

Even though Jesus had told them about this very day, the followers seem stunned, even paralyzed. Perhaps one of the best examples of a trauma response can be seen in Mary Magdalene. She comes to the tomb Sunday morning (John 20:1–18). Not only has her Lord been killed, but as she comes to tend to the body, it appears that Jesus has been stolen out of the tomb. Mary's struggle gives the impression that the stress of the preceding days has become too much to bear. Although Jesus talks to her, she doesn't even recognize Him. Only when Jesus speaks her name does she come out of the trauma-induced fog in which she seems to be functioning.

The trauma of Jesus' death seems so great that not everyone believes the resurrection stories related by the women and disciples. Jesus appears to a group of followers who are barricaded in a room. Thomas will not believe the stories for another week, and does so only after Jesus allows him to touch the nail prints in His hands (John 20:26–29).

The crucifixion is an unambiguous example of a trauma event. Something unexpected and outside the realm of regular human experience—having a loved one suddenly and viciously killed—bursts into the functioning of the followers of Jesus. The event is so extreme that normal coping mechanisms do not seem to work. The nature of the crucifixion also gives a picture of the individual variability regarding how the followers responded to the pressure of the situation. Some help while others hide. Some act, but others are frozen, paralyzed. Some mourn; others are too stunned to grieve. Some experience a great deal of fear. All of them are confused. All of them feel the impact of the events. Trauma is certainly not a respecter of persons.[6]

Scripture provides clear examples, then, of individuals and groups of people coping with traumatic events. The accounts of the Egyptians following the tenth plague, the sufferings of Job, and the crucifixion allow us to see the impact of traumatic events on those involved.

EFFECTS OF TRAUMA

Those who have worked with trauma victims in the immediate aftermath of a traumatic event are well aware of how an extreme ordeal may affect a person. The impact of traumatic events is felt by survivors in all their functions—cognitive, behavioral, emotional, spiritual, and relational. And while individual responses vary greatly, the symptoms of trauma are clear and noticeable. Immediately following a traumatic event, a person's body and mind appear to function in a manner that serves to protect him or her, buffering the person from the full brunt of the trauma event. Following are some common symptoms of trauma.

Cognitive Symptoms

Trauma often impacts how a person processes information. This includes how the person thinks or what the person believes about the world. The impact on cognitive functioning can range from mild to severe.

---

6. See Jones's excellent description of the impact of the crucifixion on the disciples in *Counsel of Heaven on Earth*, 80–83.

Difficulty Concentrating

It is common for victims of trauma to have trouble concentrating. They lose focus and are easily distracted, making it challenging to return to work or school following a traumatic event. Tasks once performed automatically may now be much more arduous to complete. A very capable person may, for instance, find him- or herself having trouble making out and following a grocery list. A person may experience difficulty in doing simple math calculations, as when counting out correct change or trying to compute a restaurant tip. It may be harder for the person to participate in everyday conversations, especially when required to listen for any length of time. Students often find it difficult to focus on lectures and homework assignments.

Flashbacks

In the aftermath of most trauma experiences, survivors repeatedly replay the event in their minds. Some do this willfully, trying to make sense out of what happened. Others see the event repeated in their minds whether they want to or not. For some individuals, it's like watching a movie. They see the entire ordeal in great detail. For others, components of the trauma event appear more as individual snapshots. Often, these flashbacks are unwanted and intrusive, producing great frustration in the victim. Small reminders can serve as cues to produce flashbacks, although the flashbacks may occur with no cue. Some individuals experience the flashbacks when they attempt to relax. Others have flashbacks when they're attempting to concentrate or complete a task. At best, flashbacks are irritating; at worst, they're debilitating, and trauma survivors may feel as if they're reexperiencing the event, often multiple times a day.

Reacting to Similar Circumstances

Persons surviving traumatic events often react negatively to other people or events that remind them of their trauma experiences. A person may have trouble returning to the location of the trauma. A survivor of an automobile accident may have difficulty driving or riding in a car. If the trauma involved some kind of attack or physical assault, it's not unusual for the survivor to believe he or she sees the perpetrator in a crowd of people. The survivor may even react to others wearing the same color or style of clothing as the perpetrator.

Guilt

In virtually all trauma events, survivors feel and express guilt over various components of the experience. A survivor may express guilt over not saying "good-bye" to a loved one who was killed suddenly. Guilt can be exacerbated if a person had a fight or disagreement with the deceased loved one the last time they were together. In large-scale trauma events, victims experience a phenomenon known as survivor guilt. Those surviving may feel guilty for living when others died, wondering whether they, too, should have died. Often, survivors mentally run through the events over and over, thinking about what would have happened if they'd left sooner or had done something differently prior to the event. Survivor guilt, however, is rarely a belief or emotion founded in fact—most often, the survivor could not have changed the circumstances or prevented the event. Frequently, individuals feel the guilt so strongly, that reasoning with them does little good in alleviating the guilt feelings.

Futurelessness

In extreme trauma cases, individuals sometimes express a futurelessness, or an inability to see themselves as part of the future. This sense of having no future is not unusual to hear from a child or teen who has experienced type 2 trauma. This young person may say something like, "I think I'll die when I'm eighteen" or "I just can't see myself living past my twenty-first birthday." In milder forms, a person may have difficulty making plans, both short-term and long-term. In more severe forms, futurelessness contributes to suicidal thoughts or behavior.

Altered Worldview or Belief System

Trauma challenges a person's assumptions about the world, how one believes the world works. As an individual travels through life, he or she comes to conclusions about the nature of the world, or how the world works. The individual's beliefs, or worldview, allows the person to make decisions, interact with others, and to function day to day. Following a traumatic event, it is common for trauma survivors to struggle with these beliefs. For trauma survivors, it's as if the structure, the framework that helped them make sense out of the world, is suddenly gone. To them, it often feels like the rules for life have changed. A person who lived a reasonably trouble-free life may suddenly believe the world is unsafe. A fairly trusting person may become very guarded and suspicious. Survivors may question the motives of others, even of formerly trusted friends and loved ones. Survivors may also struggle with their faith and with their understanding of God. Traumatic events challenge, then, how individuals view themselves, the world, and God.

Emotional Symptoms

In addition to the cognitive effects, trauma survivors often experience a range of emotional symptoms. These can be confusing and frustrating, and may drain energy from the victim, who is already emotionally depleted.

Numbness

Perhaps the most common emotional symptom following trauma is a general sense of numbness. This tends to be more pronounced the more severe the event. Victims feel like they're functioning in slow motion. I often ask trauma survivors, "Do you feel like you're living underwater?" Most will agree, acknowledging this numbness. Survivors frequently feel sluggish in both their thinking and in their reactions to what occurs around them.

Anger

Even individuals who are rather placid by nature may feel anger following a traumatic experience. The anger can range from mild—the person feels irritable at everything and everybody—to extreme, with the survivor experiencing a sense of rage about what has taken place. This rage can be specific, directed at certain individuals or entities, or it may be more diffuse and general. Often, individuals feel angry, but then might feel guilty because they're experiencing anger. This seems especially common among Christians, many of whom falsely believe that all anger is sin, or that anger is not appropriate for Christians to experience.

Sadness

Most individuals experience some amount of sadness following trauma, especially if the trauma involves some clear loss—losing a loved one, for instance, or some specific possession. In more extreme circumstances, the sadness may lead to, or be part of, depression, a more ongoing sense of hopelessness and helplessness. While not all depression is negative—and may at times actually serve a useful purpose—depression for some individuals involves thoughts of self-harm, suicide, or revenge. Counselors who work with trauma survivors must be alert to the possibility that those persons are having thoughts and feelings about harming themselves.

Hypervigilence

Survivors of trauma may find themselves being overly alert, and even overly cautious. A survivor of a shooting may have difficulty being in an enclosed space such as a small room or any room where an exit is not readily accessible. If a survivor goes to see a movie, it's not unusual for him or her to locate the exits and plan an escape, should it be necessary. Trauma survivors may also notice that they are easily startled. Loud or sudden noises may send their hearts racing, producing feelings of wanting to run. Some individuals have difficulty relaxing and constantly feel alert or on guard.

 ## Behavioral Symptoms

Symptoms impact not only how a trauma survivor thinks and feels, they also affect how that person behaves or functions in daily activities.

Sleep Disturbance

Following a traumatic event, some individuals have difficulty sleeping. This is especially problematic since lack of sleep tends to reduce productive functioning and leads to exhaustion. Sleep disturbance can involve a person's having difficulty falling asleep; other individuals may fall asleep, only to awaken a short time later. After awakening, the person may find it impossible to fall asleep again. Some individuals experience nightmares. Like flashbacks, these nightmares can be extremely vivid. Dreams may involve a type of replay of the trauma event, or components of the event, sometimes with bizarre twists. Conversely, sleep disturbances may involve sleeping much more than normal. Some survivors have difficulty getting up and may also take long naps. Some individuals sleep excessively, but report not feeling rested, even after several hours of sleep. Lack of feeling rested tends to fuel other symptoms such as depression and reduced concentration.

Eating Disturbance

As with disrupted sleep habits, some trauma survivors experience changes in eating habits. Some eat more than they did prior to the trauma event, while others have difficulty eating. Some experience stomach discomfort and do not feel hungry. Others may feel hungry, but do not have energy to prepare meals. When a person doesn't obtain adequate nutrition following a traumatic event, he or she may struggle with decreased energy, fatigue, or other related symptoms.

Trouble with Routine Tasks

Often, in the aftermath of trauma, individuals have trouble completing routine tasks. A person may find him- or herself struggling to do housework, general maintenance, everyday errands, and common chores. Survivors may fail to pay bills on time or keep necessary household records. Students often have difficulty with schoolwork, homework, and school-related projects. In one counseling session, a college student and trauma survivor told me, "Usually in my schoolwork, I have been able to 'step on the gas' when I need to get an assignment done. Now, I step on the gas and nothing happens. I find myself sitting and staring into space a lot."

Overcautious/Taking Risks

Some survivors become overly cautious. They may avoid risks at all costs. A man who survives an automobile accident may experience frustration as he checks, double-checks, and triple-checks his car before a short trip. During the trip, he may travel at reduced speeds and may avoid even the slightest risk. Even though this behavior is not characteristic of his previous functioning, he might feel helpless as he repeatedly behaves in such a manner to avoid another accident. While some survivors become excessively cautious, other survivors might suddenly take unnecessary risks. One counseling client who survived a robbery told me that the night following the robbery she walked outside alone, in a bad neighborhood, looking for her missing cat. She thought, "I almost died yesterday; what's the worst that could happen to me now?" This unnecessary risk taking may be evidence of self-harm thinking, or it may represent a belief that nothing really matters, a sense of helplessness in a dangerous world.

✳ Spiritual Symptoms ✳

In addition to cognitive, emotional, and behavioral symptoms, trauma also produces spiritual symptoms, impacting a person's spiritual beliefs or functioning.

Questions About God's Existence

Trauma commonly results in concerns about whether or not there is a God. Both Christians and non-Christians may find themselves struggling with the most basic questions about God. Following a traumatic experience, nonbelievers often struggle with issues of mortality in a way they did not prior to the event. Believers, even committed Christians, may find themselves questioning whether God really exists. Extreme circumstances can produce doubt, even in the strongest believers. Matthew 11:1–19 relates the story of John the Baptist who, from prison, sends his followers to ask Jesus if He really is the Messiah. In prison, and just prior to being killed, John seems to struggle with doubt and appears to be asking a question not uncommon when life is confusing: "Have I done all this for nothing?"

Questions About God's Character

Some individuals may not wrestle with questions about God's existence, but trauma commonly produces questions about God's nature or character. Following a traumatic event, survivors will ask such questions as, "Is God really good?" "Does God care about what I'm going through?" "Is God taking care of me?" "Why do bad things happen?" "Did God cause this to happen?" All of these questions have to do with God's character, what God is like.

Trauma often leads a person to reexamine his or her conclusions about God's nature. The Psalms present many examples. In Psalm 10:1, the writer asks, "Why, O LORD, do you stand far off? Why do you hide yourself in times of trouble?" (NIV). Asaph poses a series of questions: "Will the Lord reject forever? Will he never show his favor again? Has his unfailing love vanished forever? Has his promise failed for all time? Has God forgotten to be merciful? Has he in anger withheld his compassion?" (Psalm 77:7–9 NIV). Even David, a man after God's own heart, struggles with questions about God. In Psalm 13:1 he asks, "How long, O LORD? Will you forget me forever? How long will you hide your face from me?" (NIV). These questions seem even more extreme in Psalm 22:1, where David cries, "My God, my God, why have you forsaken me? Why are you so far from saving me, so far from the words of my groaning?" (NIV). In each of these instances, the psalmists struggle with God's nature, and with what God is like, especially during difficult circumstances.

Anger at God

As discussed, trauma produces a range of emotions, one of which may be anger. While anger can be expressed at many different targets, individuals often feel anger toward God. This anger may be expressed openly. Some trauma survivors are very clear that they're angry at God, blame God for what happened, and some even attempt to walk away from God. For others, the anger at God produces guilt, or can be turned toward self or others. Some individuals seem to be angry at God, but deny that the trauma has produced the anger.

Some may believe it's dangerous or sinful to be angry at God. Some individuals feel anger toward God, but it's expressed in a form of attempting to hide or distance oneself from God. These individuals avoid thinking about God and may take pains to stay away from situations where they will be confronted with spiritual matters.

Difficulty with Religious Practices or Expressions

Following trauma, a person may discover that he or she is having difficulty with common religious practices such as prayer, Bible reading, or attendance of religious services or activities. Even a devoted believer may notice a lack of desire for religious matters. Often, this lack of desire for familiar religious expressions produces guilt, compounding matters. Some individuals may not experience a lack of desire for religious expressions, but may note frustration or impatience with religious expressions that seem shallow or simplistic. Some believers find themselves feeling alienated from their religious traditions or from their regular places of worship. Many individuals wrestle with such matters but may keep attending religious services out of habit or out of fear of what will happen if they stop. This particular expression of trauma can be confusing and frustrating. The very source of comfort and support in days past now seems unsafe as one struggles with various spiritual symptoms.

Relational Symptoms

Not all symptoms take place within an individual; some are expressed in relationships. If the trauma is severe, even close relationships might be affected. In extreme circumstances, a traumatic event can result in a relationship breakup such as divorce.

Relationship Withdrawal

It's not unusual for survivors to pull away from significant relationships, even withdrawing from those who, in the past, have been their most stable sources of comfort. In most circumstances, this withdrawal is temporary, and gentle support of loved ones results in a return to the relationship. Survivors often feel overwhelmed by their own emotions and struggle to make sense of the event. It's an added strain when the survivor believes that he or she must be the emotional caretaker of others following the traumatic event. After a large-scale trauma, some survivors have difficulty talking to loved ones about what took place or how the survivor feels about the event. The survivor may feel more comfortable talking with other survivors and may believe that those who weren't directly involved cannot understand what took place.

Difficulty Being Alone

Some survivors do the opposite of withdrawing from relationships; they appear to be compelled toward others. A survivor may have difficulty being alone or away from others whom they feel close to. A parent may find it extremely trying to be separated from children. One adult survivor told of her experience following a traumatic event that occurred when she was an older teen. She found herself driven toward her boyfriend, believing he was the only one who could understand and comfort her. Some trauma survivors report increased anxiousness if they're not around loved ones following an extreme event.

Relationship Strain

When an individual experiences an extreme event, he or she may notice relationship struggles in the aftermath. In their book written for survivors, *Life After Trauma*, Rosenbloom and Williams note how relationships are affected following trauma: "But traumatic experiences can challenge and change some or all of our existing relationships. Even when you have supportive friends, family, a partner, or work environment, you may nevertheless feel isolated after trauma. Previously supportive people in your life may not know how to help you. Old friends and family may not be able to understand what you are going through and this can greatly increase your sense of loss."[7]

Even with loved ones, the survivor may be irritable or argumentative. Survivors often experience the greatest relationship struggles as they interact with those closest to them. Relationship struggles can occur in other arenas, as well, such as school or work. The relationship strain is especially likely if both individuals in the relationship experienced the same trauma event.

Symptoms: Concluding Comments

Following a traumatic event, all individuals experience some symptoms, whether cognitive, emotional, behavioral, spiritual, or relational. The specific symptoms depend on the type of trauma, the extent of the trauma, and the personality of the person encountering the ordeal. No two individuals experience the same symptoms to the same degree, but all individuals do experience symptoms.

---

7. Rosenbloom and Williams, *Life After Trauma*, 23.

Symptoms of trauma are not a sign of weakness. Some survivors might think, "If I were stronger, I wouldn't be feeling this way, functioning like this." This belief may actually exacerbate what the individual is undergoing, as the survivor then adds guilt to the other emotions he or she is experiencing. It is common for people to feel crazy for having symptoms following trauma. Clients often tell me they feel like they're losing their minds because of how the event is affecting them.

In some instances, symptoms may be delayed, even occurring some time following a traumatic event. After a particular traumatic event in my city, I received phone calls from clients three to six months following the actual event. They all said basically the same thing: "I thought I was doing okay. I wasn't really struggling with anything. Suddenly, a couple of weeks ago, I started _____." The individual might have begun having nightmares, feeling panicky, or struggling with depression. The more severe the trauma event, the greater chance that some symptoms will be delayed. Most often, the delay will be a matter of weeks or months. If the trauma is extreme, or if a person experiences type 2 trauma, symptoms can appear months or even years after the event.

Post-Traumatic Stress Disorder

In some circumstances, a person who experiences trauma will develop Post-Traumatic Stress Disorder, or PTSD. Post-Traumatic Stress Disorder is an anxiety disorder that develops in response to extreme psychological and emotional distress caused by a specific traumatic event.[8] According to physician Michael Lyles, "PTSD is a big deal because it's not just an emotional issue. People who develop PTSD get sick a great deal. They often have health problems and overutilize health services. They frequently become functionally impaired. They can't do their work as a spouse or parent, and they can't do their job well."[9]

To be diagnosed with PTSD, a trauma survivor must meet certain criteria.[10] First, the person must be exposed to a specific traumatic event. Second, the person consistently reexperiences the event, either through flashbacks, dreams, or ongoing memories of the incident. Third, the individual shows a general numbing of responsiveness and tends to avoid any situation or stimulus that reminds him or her of the trauma event. Next, the individual displays a

---

8. Sue, Sue, and Sue, *Understanding Abnormal Behavior*, 156.
9. Lyles, "Trauma and PTSD," 48.
10. Holmes, *Abnormal Psychology*, 167–68.

heightened state of arousal or hypervigilance. And last, these types of symptoms must occur for more than thirty days. If symptoms appear following trauma, but last between two and thirty days, the person can be diagnosed with Acute Stress Disorder.[11]

Not all individuals who experience trauma develop PTSD. According to Lyles, around 50 percent of individuals will undergo a traumatic experience at some point in their lives, but only about 20 percent of these will develop symptoms consistent with PTSD.[12] Researchers and counselors have long been curious about why two individuals can go through the same traumatic experience, but each will be affected differently. One may develop ongoing symptoms, whereas the other seems to experience a lesser blow.

Several factors play a role in whether or not a person develops PTSD. A person's general level of functioning prior to a trauma impacts how the person experiences the event. An individual who is prone to anxiousness and who is emotionally vulnerable prior to encountering a traumatic event will be more likely to develop PTSD. The severity or magnitude of the trauma also plays a crucial part in the development of PTSD. A person is likely to develop symptoms when the trauma is extreme, and certain types of traumatic experiences will negatively impact the vast majority of those experiencing the event. Thus, any trauma event that threatens a person with injury or with death is much more likely to result in PTSD.[13]

An individual's perception of what took place also plays a role in the development of PTSD. How a person interprets a traumatic experience—what the person concludes about God, about self, and about the nature of the world—greatly influences how he or she will cope in the days to come. If an individual is prepared for traumatic experiences, the likelihood is reduced that the person will be affected. Thus, medical, military, and law enforcement personnel may not be as easily traumatized by certain circumstances as would an individual with no training, preparation, or knowledge of specific trauma events. A key factor that mitigates how a person responds to trauma is the individual's level of social support before, during, and following a traumatic occurrence. A person who has close, supportive relationships has a better likelihood of coping effectively.

---

11. Sue, Sue, and Sue, *Understanding Abnormal Behavior*, 157.
12. Lyles, "Trauma and PTSD," 49.
13. Barlow and Durand, *Abnormal Psychology*, 156.

PTSD is a phenomenon that experts in the field have begun to understand only in the last few decades, and as a result of how individuals respond to extreme trauma situations. Those who work in ministering to individuals following traumatic events would do well to keep abreast of ongoing developments in the understanding of this particular disorder.

CONCLUSION

Occasionally I catch a televised news channel where a reporter interviews a survivor, a young man perhaps, following a notable traumatic event or large-scale disaster. I watch the survivor's eyes and listen to his voice as he answers questions. I note that the survivor looks glassy-eyed and in shock. The young man gives answers, but they often sound flat and robotic. It's highly likely that he is at the beginning point of a journey with an uncertain outcome.

A person may go through this journey well, recover, and move ahead with life. Conversely, the person may struggle to overcome various trauma-induced symptoms and may live with many days of frustration, confusion, and strained relationships. Some individuals will develop PTSD and may struggle for years to overcome the effects of the trauma event. Others may deny, ignore, or even repress the symptoms, only to have these very symptoms emerge at a later date, often with a vengeance.

When I see a survivor after trauma, either on television or in my counseling office, I offer a silent prayer. I pray that God will be very present with the person and will bring him or her through the difficult days that lie ahead.

CHAPTER 3

LOSS

A little girl faces the death of a favorite grandparent. A little boy buries a beloved hamster. A teenaged girl's best friend moves to another state. A young man experiences the breakup of a serious dating relationship. A middle-aged woman deals with a threatened layoff at work while attending to the declining health of her parents. A senior male retires and must adjust to life apart from the career that he valued so dearly.

Over the course of a lifetime, we'll all suffer losses, of both meaningful people and objects. Some losses are, of course, less important, passing with little notice. Other losses are enormous, a blow to our functioning, producing a great deal of pain and sadness. Some losses require little adjustment. Others demand time and attention as we struggle to live without the lost object or person.

While many losses require adjustment, not all losses are negative. A child's losing her first baby tooth, for example, usually calls for a small family celebration. For an overweight man with high blood pressure, losing weight is a triumph. When a man or woman breaks up from a bad relationship, the loss is generally positive. In counseling, I occasionally encounter a situation where a loss unexpectedly turns out to be a good thing. One couple I saw in marriage counseling was dealing with several areas of conflict, especially over family finances. Despite my best efforts, the couple was not progressing. They came to their session one week and announced that the husband had been fired from his job. I remember thinking, "Oh no, this will really strain the relationship." I expected the job loss to make the marriage even more fragile. Over the next few weeks, though, I was surprised to learn that the husband's layoff had a positive effect on the relationship and thus on counseling. The husband's company gave him a nice severance package, including two or three months of extra salary. The couple paid off their debts, which reduced the financial strain, and the husband began training in a new job field, one he'd desired to enter. In this instance, the loss turned out to have many positive aspects.

Loss

Ministry involves working with individuals who have suffered losses. Often, the loss is easily recognizable, and it's clear that it contributes to a person's struggle. On other occasions, the loss is subtle, with the person who experienced the loss not cognizant of its ultimate effect. An individual may not recognize the connection between the loss and how it expresses itself in the person's functioning.

A key component of crisis ministry is understanding the nature of loss and knowing how to minister accordingly. Consider the following story: What losses did this young woman sustain?

A STORY OF LOSSES

I MET JANELLE AND HER HUSBAND at a marriage conference. They were a young couple, deeply committed to their relationships with Christ. Janelle, an intelligent and mature young woman, phoned me one day, asking if she could speak with me about some problems in her family of origin. As we met, she told me the story of the previous several months, a time of pain and confusion.

Janelle had received a phone call from her father, a noted minister who lived in an east coast state where she was born and had lived until leaving for college. Her father said, "I just need to tell you before you hear it from someone else: I've been having an affair. The church just discovered it and I've been fired. Your mom and I are not doing well right now. I don't know if our marriage will make it."

Janelle was stunned at the phone call. Several hundred miles away from her parents, she was caught completely off guard. She spoke to me of growing up in a deeply devout family in which service to God and love for family were central to all of life. She spoke of the respect her father had in the community and denomination, but how this admiration had been shattered by the disclosure of his unfaithfulness with a married woman from his congregation.

As she conveyed the story, Janelle was obviously in pain. Even though the initial phone call from her father came about twelve months earlier, she discussed it as if she'd received it only the previous evening. She spoke of feeling depressed, tired, and lonely. She attempted to talk about her family difficulties with Christian friends, but they encouraged her to "cheer up" and to just "get over it."

In the months following the phone call, her parents continued to experience difficulty. Their marriage was fragile, and sometimes Janelle would spend several nights a week on the phone with one or the other of her parents, encouraging them to not abandon their marriage. She related that her parents had moved out of their home, the only home Janelle had known in her growing up years. Her parents were now living in a small apartment and struggling financially. Her father was attempting to sell real estate, but not having much success. Her mother wrestled with thoughts of suicide. Janelle traveled to see them once following the disclosure of her father's affair, but felt the hurt of not being comfortable attending the church where she grew up. As she walked around town, she sensed the stares of those who knew of her father's misdeeds. She felt out of place, even in her hometown.

Not only was Janelle dealing with depression, but she spoke of spiritual struggles, as well. Her father had been the most committed Christian she knew. How had he thrown it all away? She also began to question her understanding of God. How could she have served Him so diligently, only to have this happen? She talked of the past several months—she had stopped praying and reading her Bible. She found it painful to attend church. Janelle admitted that her world seemed upside down.

As Janelle and I discussed what had transpired in her family, one of our counseling activities was to focus on the losses she experienced over the previous months. She agreed to make a list of the losses she could identify. The obvious ones were the loss of trust in her father and the potential loss of her parents' marriage. She had also lost her family home and the comfort of returning to her family's church or walking down the streets in her hometown. She felt alienated from church members who had been part of her life from birth. She noted her loss of sleep and depleted energy reserves, which accompanied trying to help her parents.

I encouraged Janelle to consider other losses that may have occurred, ones that might be less obvious. Janelle talked of losing a clear sense of who God is or what He is like. She noticed that she was confused about her relationship with both her earthly father and her heavenly Father. She noted the loss of a sense of identity. She had been the daughter of a prominent and respected minister; everyone in town knew her family. The town no longer seemed safe. She talked of the losses in her family role. As an only child, she always felt secure in her family. Now, the security was gone. Not only was the family unit in peril, but she had reversed roles with her parents. She, in many respects, had become the parent. Janelle spent time with each parent, attempting to provide encouragement in the midst of their pain. She advised them in basic decision-making and coping strategies. Instead of her parents being a source of support in her first year of marriage, she became her parents' support in their marriage crisis.

Janelle noted that she'd had many losses in the past year. She was somewhat surprised at the number, and some she hadn't recognized. Identifying the losses was a helpful part of her overall process of coping with the difficult things that occurred in her family. My giving her support as she made sense of the hurt and sadness helped her renew her relationship with Christ and allowed her to make good decisions about relating to her parents, about taking care of her own marriage, and about intentionally progressing through her own time of struggle.

DEFINITION AND ELEMENTS OF LOSS

Literature on crisis, trauma, and grief often acknowledges the importance of loss. H. Norman Wright, pioneer Christian counselor and author of books on crisis and trauma, states, "At the heart of trauma and crisis is loss. In order to understand and appreciate fully the significance of crisis and trauma, we need to understand the multitude and complexity of loss."[1]

While many writers in the crisis counseling field note the importance of loss, they rarely define the term and seldom delve into the characteristics of loss. This absence of focused attention on loss suggests an insufficient understanding of the nature of loss, how it impacts individuals, and perhaps most importantly, how we help individuals cope with their losses.

Ultimately, loss is the separation from or removal of something meaningful to an individual. Something is taken away from a person in such a manner that, generally, the person is not able to retrieve it. A loss is composed of several elements, as identified below.

Focus of the Loss

Loss generally has a focus. Perhaps the most notable is the loss of a person. This happens most obviously through death, but it may occur in other ways,

---

1. Wright, *New Guide to Crisis and Trauma Counseling*, 60.

as well. Loss of a person may happen when a friend moves away, when a child leaves for college, or when an aging relative ceases to recognize loved ones. The focus of a loss can also be an object. A person might lose his or her home in a fire, an automobile in an accident, or a pet that runs away.

In some instances, the focus of a loss is obvious, as when the loss is a person or object. The focus of some losses however, is more subtle, like the loss of freedom, the loss of a dream, or the loss of hope. When the focus of the loss is subtle, it becomes more difficult to identify. A person may have a feeling or sensation that something is wrong, but may be unable to recognize or pinpoint the source of the feelings of loss. Thus, the loss is more felt than understood.

Value of the Loss

Most often, there is a value associated with losses. The more we value some-thing, the more noticeable the impact of the loss. The more meaningful the person or object, the greater the sense of loss. In some instances, we might choose to lose something in order to gain something of more value to us. A person, for instance, might sacrifice sleep to gain time to work on a project. Another individual might spend his or her own money to go on a short-term mission trip to an impoverished country. The gains (time, helping others) are of more value than the losses (sleep, financial resources). Ultimately, though, the more valuable an object or person, the greater the impact of the loss.

Means of the Loss

Most losses that have an impact on a person are involuntary; something is taken away or removed from an individual. Involuntary losses produce feel-ings of helplessness, frustration, hurt, and even anger. In some circumstances, however, losses are voluntary. Giving a child up for adoption is an example of a loss a person might sustain, although that person fully chooses to do so. Other voluntary or intentional losses include turning down a promotion, allowing a child to attend college in a distant city, or choosing to leave a job or a church family. While voluntary losses may not affect a person to the same extent as an involuntary loss, voluntary losses still have an impact. Although a young woman who gives a baby up for adoption may believe doing so is in the child's best interest, the birth mother is still likely to feel the impact of the loss even though she chose to relinquish the child to another family.

Permanence of the Loss

Most losses are permanent. Death, destruction of property by a natural disaster, and some types of declining health are examples of permanent, irreversible losses. For individuals, the permanent nature of many losses is the most difficult part of initial coping. Following a permanent loss, many individuals spend great amounts of time or energy trying to restore the lost person or object. A person may even beg God to return a deceased loved one, perhaps even attempting to strike a bargain with God. Permanent losses, especially those that are involuntary, are generally painful and difficult.

While many losses are permanent, other losses can be retrieved, restored, or revived. In counseling, I occasionally see couples who divorce, then remarry each other. Some dating couples may break up then reunite. At times, a loss may seem permanent, but, ultimately, it was not. A lost object might be returned, a lost child found, and a lost dream might become infused with hope. Some individuals might try to replace a loss. Dating soon after the death of a spouse or having a baby soon after the death of a child is, for some individuals, an attempt to ease the pain associated with the loss. Efforts to replace permanent losses, however, often compound the struggles to adjust to that loss.

THE BIBLE AND LOSS

The subject of loss is woven into Scripture in a number of different ways. Many of the Bible's writers and many biblical figures directly discuss various aspects of loss. The Bible also contains many unvarnished stories and examples of individuals who experience loss. In some instances, loss is presented as good or necessary. In other instances, loss is obviously negative and problematic. In the final analysis, however, the Bible offers yet a third frame of reference to God's children for understanding and making sense of loss.

Loss as Good or Necessary

While it's common to think of loss as negative, some losses, according to Scripture, are necessary, even desirable. As Jesus made His entry into Jerusalem just prior to His crucifixion, He made a statement about loss that foreshadows His own death on the cross: "Truly, truly, I say to you, unless a grain of wheat falls into the earth and dies, it remains alone; but if it dies, it bears much fruit. He who loves his life loses it, and he who hates his life in this world will keep it to life eternal" (John 12:24–25). For a seed to produce fruit, it is necessary for it to die, and the person who makes the preservation and promotion of his or her own life a priority will end up losing it.

On many other occasions Jesus indicated that not all losses are negative, and He called attention to the importance of losing one's life, or not putting one's self at the center of the universe. In Matthew 10:39, Jesus states, "Whoever finds his life will lose it, and whoever loses his life for my sake will find it" (NIV). Variations of this particular saying of Jesus appear in each of the Gospels and occur more than once in two of the gospels (Matt. 10:38–39; 16:24–25; Mark 8:34–35; Luke 9:23–25; 14:26–27; 17:33; John 12:25). According to Foster, "No other saying of Jesus is given such emphasis."[2] Jesus repeatedly emphasized the necessity of losing one's life in order to gain eternal life, stressing that some losses are necessary, even desirable.

Loss as Negative or Problematic

Many losses presented in Scripture are highlighted as negative or problematic. Hebrews 12:3 and 2 Corinthians 4:1 both refer to losing heart. John warns his readers to consolidate gains they have made in the Christian life, stating, "Watch yourselves, that you do not lose what we have accomplished, but that you may receive a full reward" (2 John 8). Part of Jesus' mission has to do with lost things. In Luke 19:10, Jesus states, "For the Son of Man came to seek and to save what was lost" (NIV). Humankind's lostness is so problematic that Jesus came to rescue us from this state.

Another passage that clearly considers the subject of problematic losses is Jesus' story in Luke 15:3–32, in which He tells followers about a lost sheep, a lost coin, and a lost son. In this parable, Jesus speaks of individuals who lose meaningful objects or loved ones and how the shepherd, the woman, and the father are affected by the losses. In each of these stories, an individual actively searches for the object of the loss. Jesus uses this story to demonstrate God's care for us and His active pursuit of us in our lost state.

Losses Experienced by Biblical Figures

The Bible also gives many examples of losses through the lives of biblical figures. In the Old Testament, Lot loses his wife, who turns around to look as Sodom is destroyed (Gen. 19:26). Esau loses his birthright (Gen. 25:31–32) and his father's blessing (Gen. 27:30–41). Ruth and Naomi lose husbands, and

---

2. Foster, *Zondervan NIV Study Bible*, 1589.

Naomi also loses both her sons (Ruth 1:3–5). Hosea loses his wife, who leaves him and his children and returns to a life of prostitution (Hosea 3:1).

Joseph faces many losses in his early years. His mother dies when Joseph is still young (Gen. 35:18), and when he is only a teenager, his brothers sell him into slavery (Gen. 37:18–36). He loses his family, his country, and his freedom as he is made a slave in Egypt. In his new land, he faces loss of reputation when he is accused of sexual involvement with Potiphar's wife (Gen. 39:7–18). His losses are exacerbated when he is thrown into jail, again losing freedom, status, position, identity, and safety.

Throughout the Bible, many females are identified as facing the difficulty of childlessness. Those in the Old Testament who struggled with infertility include Sarah, Rebekah, Rachel, Hannah, and in the New Testament, Elizabeth. Besides the obvious loss of not being able to have children, these women also faced societal losses, as people presumed that the inability to conceive was evidence of God's disfavor.

Perhaps one of the more difficult losses to experience is the loss of a child. Adam and Eve not only lost a child, but had to live with the knowledge that one son killed the other. Another account of losing a child is presented in 2 Kings 4:8–37, the story of the Shunammite woman and Elisha. Elisha tells the woman, who is unable to have children, that by the next year, she will have a son. The Shunammite woman does give birth to a son, but a few years later, the child suddenly dies. We see the Shunammite woman wrestle with this tremendous loss as she seeks help from Elisha, who raises the child from the dead. A similar story occurs in Luke 8:41–56 as Jairus, a ruler in the synagogue, approaches Jesus following the death of his daughter. As did Elisha, Jesus heals the child. Even though these two children are ultimately healed, all their parents suffer difficult, albeit temporary, losses.

In Scripture, many individuals deal with loss of health. This is seen most clearly in the Gospels, where people continuously flocked to Jesus for healing. Reading those accounts gives a picture of the incredible range of losses these individuals must have experienced. Lepers faced not only loss of physical health, but loss of social status and loss of ability to interact in a normal manner. Blind individuals couldn't experience the joy of seeing colors. Lame individuals couldn't walk or run. Deaf individuals did not hear the sounds of God's creation. Some in Scripture had been coping with loss of physical health for many years. We get a glimpse into the struggles of these individuals when we see the sheer joy they express as they regain health resulting from Jesus' healing touch.

A Different Frame of Reference Regarding Losses

Most often, when a person experiences a loss, the result is negative or problematic. For the follower of Christ, however, there is a paradoxical nature to many kinds of losses. One was identified earlier: only by losing one's life does a person actually gain life. The apostle Paul also seems to understand losses from a different frame of reference. One clear example appears in his letter to the Philippians: "But whatever was to my profit I now consider loss for the sake of Christ. What is more, I consider everything a loss compared to the surpassing greatness of knowing Christ Jesus my Lord, for whose sake I have lost all things" (Phil. 3:7–8 NIV). Paul was able to see all his accomplishments as losses compared to what he gained in his relationship to Christ.

Paul again demonstrates his perception of loss from a different frame of reference in his discussing whether it is better for him to continue living or to die and be with the Lord. In Philippians 1:21 he says, "For to me, to live is Christ and to die is gain" (NIV). Paul did not despair even of the possibility of losing his life, as he viewed living and dying from the perspective of what he would gain. Paul's perspective regarding loss is even more remarkable since his statements to the Philippian believers were written from prison, where he undoubtedly experienced many losses (see Phil. 1:13–14).

In Scripture, the issue of loss is, then, multifaceted. Some loss is negative, producing pain and struggle. Other loss is good, even necessary. Some loss, though, can and should be viewed from a different frame of reference, which may mitigate many of the negative or problematic aspects of the loss.

CHARACTERISTICS OF LOSS

As with crisis and trauma, losses are quite complex. Loss can be experienced physically, emotionally, or cognitively. Two individuals may undergo the same event, but experience losses differently. Following are various characteristics of loss that have an impact on how a person experiences and adjusts to loss.

Gradual or Sudden

Some losses occur suddenly. A three-year-old, playing in the front yard, runs behind his father's vehicle as he backs out of the driveway. What had been a pleasant family evening turns tragic. Conversely, loss may take place over an extended time period. A person diagnosed with a terminal illness may gradually notice a general deterioration in functioning. The person may first detect a decrease in energy. Later, tasks once performed with ease must be done by others. This person might eventually be confined to a wheelchair, then to bed. Declining health can take place over a period of weeks, months, or years, and associated losses occur gradually.

Big or Small

Losses may range from inconsequential to enormous. Whether a loss is big or small, however, cannot be easily determined by an outside observer. What seems insignificant to one person may be of great concern to another. Parents might not feel distraught over the death of their child's pet gerbil, but to the child this may be the saddest day of his or her first six years of life.

Cumulative Effect

One loss by itself may not have all that great an impact on an individual. If, however, the individual has experienced other losses in recent days, the most current loss is often magnified. A person who is normally very functional may struggle if he or she faces a series of losses in rapid succession.

Conscious or Unconscious

Some losses are very apparent. In certain instances there is no doubt about what has been lost or about how the loss is affecting the person. Other losses, however, occur outside a person's conscious awareness. As a counselor, I've noticed that it's not unusual for an individual to experience a loss, but to be unaware of the loss and of how he or she is affected by it. People tend to be more aware of concrete losses (e.g., death of a loved one or loss of a job). They are less aware of the more abstract types of losses (e.g., loss of identity, loss of a sense of security). While individuals might not initially be cognizant of some losses, they tend to quickly recognize them if prompted by a counselor. If individuals are unaware of the losses affecting them, they are often relieved to pinpoint the loss as it helps them understand why they are struggling, feeling sad, or feeling angry.

Reminder of Other Losses

At times, losses become more complex when a person is reminded of other losses experienced in the past. An adult who goes through a divorce may be reminded of experiencing his or her own parents' divorce. A coworker dying of cancer may be a reminder of a person's own relative who died of cancer. Losses associated with extreme events are commonly reminders of all the other losses a person has experienced. In some instances, a current loss causes past losses to be brought to the forefront of a person's awareness. One of the first classes I taught at the college level was Lifespan Development. Near the end of the semester, we were covering the unit on older adulthood, specifically dealing with death and dying. I asked the class to tell me words we use for death in American society. As the class began what I'd envisioned to be a rather safe and factual discussion, I became aware that a number of students were tearing up and wiping their eyes and noses with tissues. One individual put her head on the desk. Another got up and left the class. It was obvious that, as we were discussing terms for death, class members were recalling the deaths of loved ones. That afternoon, I called the student who left the class during our discussion, and, like the others, she had been overcome with thoughts of her grandmother, who had died within the previous year. In this instance, a mere discussion of terms for death produced for many of the students memories of other losses.

TYPES OF LOSSES

Not all losses are similar. Even following a specific loss event, such as the death of a loved one, the surviving individual will experience an array of other types of losses. Some large crises or trauma events produce several types of losses, whereby an individual must simultaneously deal with a range of different loss experiences. Some losses are obvious, but others are much more subtle and require the caregiver to pay attention to what may be occurring for the person suffering the loss.

Real, or Objective, Losses

Some losses are tangible and concrete, creating no confusion about whether a loss has occurred. The clearest example of an objective, concrete loss is the death of a loved one. When a loved one dies, the impact is immediate and profound. Most societies have ceremonies, funerals, and memorial services to mark death. These ceremonies are designed to help recall the life of the deceased person and to aid in the transition to a new phase of life for those left behind.

While death is the most notable example of an objective loss, it is not the only one. Other objective losses include loss of a job, loss of home or property, or loss of health. All of these are clearly identifiable losses, experienced by the person undergoing them.

In May 1997, an F5 tornado struck the small town of Jerrell outside of Austin, Texas. As families assessed the damage, they discovered that twenty-seven individuals had been killed and several homes destroyed, with the Double Creek Estates housing addition wiped completely off the map. This powerful tornado took not only houses, automobiles, and livestock, it even pulled up about twelve inches of topsoil in certain places, marking the path of destruction. The residents of Jerrell, like others who experience a natural disaster, were left to cope with a number of real or objective losses, including deaths of friends and loved ones, loss of homes, damage to cars, property destruction, and loss of livestock and pets.

Abstract, or Subjective, Losses

Abstract or subjective losses are generally more difficult to identify. These losses are not always immediately apparent and can be quite subtle.

- A fifty-year-old businessman is notified that he's been "downsized" as his company restructures. He will experience a number of subjective losses. He might grapple with losses related to identity, especially if he has difficulty finding a new job. He may experience the death of a dream, of what he thought he could accomplish in his job or on his career path. He might also struggle with losses of purpose, drive, and ambition.
- An engaged female's fiancé breaks off the engagement. Along with the concrete loss of relationship are the more subjective losses of her role as an engaged person, loss of confidence, and loss of both the object of her love and the source of love directed toward her.
- A bank teller is robbed at gunpoint. The teller may not have personally lost money, but his subjective losses involve feelings of security and safety along with a sense of control. He might also experience a loss of freedom, as his movements might be restricted due to anxiousness produced by the attack.
- A couple's last child leaves for college. Although they are proud of the child, they also feel a sense of sadness at this change in life. The house is empty and quiet. They miss the laughter of teenagers watching movies or playing games upstairs. They miss going to their children's sporting events and music performances. They even miss providing food for hoards of hungry teenagers parading through the house. Even though

the couple is excited about their child beginning a new phase in life, the parents recognize losses associated with their changing parental roles.

While generally harder to identify than objective losses, subjective losses are often very powerful. It is common for a person to experience subjective losses more at an affective level—at the level of feelings or emotions—than at a cognitive level. Subjective losses may produce sadness, anxiousness, frustration, guilt, and a number of other responses that affect a person's immediate functioning as well as his or her long-term recovery from the losses.

Imagined Losses

Some kinds of losses may never actually occur. A person's ability to imagine certain losses can, though, be almost as powerful as an actual loss. A woman who's had previous miscarriages may be quite anxious when she becomes pregnant again. Even though the baby inside her uterus is doing fine, she may spend sleepless nights worrying that she'll lose the baby. A married woman whose first husband left her may imagine that her current spouse is making plans to leave. Those fleeing a powerful hurricane may imagine losses and destruction that they'll encounter when allowed to return to their neighborhood.

Even though the feared outcome in an imagined loss may never happen, the ability of humans to dwell on imagined losses can produce a sense of being overwhelmed. Some individuals are adept at immediately fearing the worst. A person's mind can automatically travel to images of the most extreme negative outcome that could possibly happen. Imagined losses produce many of the same symptoms as real losses, the most notable of these being strong feelings of anxiety and dread.

Threatened Losses

Like imagined losses, threatened losses may or may not actually occur, but the chance that the loss will occur can cause a person great discomfort. Wright states, "The most difficult losses of life often are the threatened losses. The possibility of their occurring is real, but you can do little about it. Your sense of control is destroyed."[3] One example of a threatened loss is that of an individual who is notified that his company will lay off five hundred employees at the end of the year. There is a real threat: people will lose jobs. A specific individual, however, may not know for certain if his or her job is to be eliminated. Another

3. Wright, *Recovering from the Losses of Life*, 18.

example of a threatened loss is that of the divorced female whose ex-spouse informs her that he's retained a lawyer and will be taking steps to gain custody of the children. The custodial parent now lives under the threat of having her children taken away. Threatened losses produce much of the same anxiousness as other kinds of losses, but these threats also create a very real sense of dread. The threatened loss may ultimately occur, becoming a concrete loss, or it may not take place, allowing the person to move on with life.

Ambiguous Losses

Some loss experiences are vague and unclear; an individual may not be completely sure whether or not a loss has taken place. In these instances, grieving is extremely difficult, and emotional support tends to be nonexistent. Boss identifies two types of ambiguous loss.[4] In the first, a person is physically absent from loved ones but still emotionally present with loved ones. An example of this type of ambiguous loss is when a family member is missing as a result of a natural disaster, in times of war, by kidnapping, or through running away. In these instances, the remaining family members have no closure and may not know whether the loved one is dead or alive. Grieving is extremely difficult in such circumstances. This first type of ambiguous loss also takes place when a child moves away from home, when a parent divorces and leaves the home, or when a person places a child for adoption. In all these instances, there is an emotional presence, but a physical absence, of a loved one.

A second type of ambiguous loss occurs when a person is physically present, but psychologically or emotionally absent. Examples include having family members who have Alzheimer's disease, a brain injury, severe drug or alcohol addiction, or extensive depression.[5] In these instances, the person tends to be a shell of his or her former self. Again, family members must care for the person, so grief and closure remain elusive.

THE IMPACT OF LOSS

Reactions to loss involve a great deal of individual variability. One person may react stoically while another becomes immobilized. How a specific individual reacts to loss depends on the personality of that individual, on the nature of the loss itself, the number and extent of other stressors present, recognition and

---

4. Boss, *Loss, Trauma, and Resilience*, 7–9.
5. Ibid., 8.

understanding of the loss, the amount of support present while the individual undergoes the loss, and even on family and cultural guidelines for reacting to loss. At one point in life, an individual may cope quite well with a significant loss, but on another occasion, the same person could struggle with a seemingly minor loss.

Losses impact an individual at an emotional level, at a cognitive level, and on a behavioral level. Again, though, a great deal of variation is seen within these levels.

At an emotional level, loss produces a range of responses, including sadness, frustration, and anxiousness. A person may feel guilty about the loss, and anger over the loss is not uncommon. The interplay between beliefs and emotions following a loss may get quite complex, as well. Following the death of a spouse, for example, the remaining spouse might feel anger at the spouse who died, followed by strong guilt feelings for the anger. Perhaps most significantly, loss often leads to grief, a topic that the next chapter considers.

Loss affects individuals at the cognitive level. A person experiencing loss often struggles to understand, to make sense out of the circumstances. Following the loss, the person may replay events over and over in his or her mind, sometimes second-guessing choices or decisions. A person may wonder whether he or she could have done anything different to change the outcome. A significant loss can cause a person to struggle with what he or she believes about the world and how it works, about the person's place in the world, and even about God, what God is like, and how He functions. Following a loss, a person may expend energy trying to make sense out of what has taken place.

Losses also influence a person's behavior, or what the person does following the loss. If the loss is large in magnitude, an individual may feel virtually paralyzed, not knowing what to do. Other individuals may not be paralyzed, but feel completely depleted of energy and vitality. Some individuals become hesitant following a loss. A young man receiving a "Dear John" letter from his girlfriend, for instance, may be slow to ask out another young lady. Still other individuals may become active in attempting to replace the loss. While this may not always be a bad thing, some people try to replace a loss with a behavior or habit that numbs the emotions produced by a loss. Drinking, drugs, sexual pursuits, spending money, overeating, and dangerous activities may all be attempts to provide diversions away from the sadness or hurt that results from losses.

In many instances, a person will not recognize the connection between the loss experienced, the resulting emotions, beliefs, and behaviors. In extreme circumstances, it is not unusual for a person to become suicidal following a significant loss. Emotions (sadness, anger), cognitions ("there is nothing to live for"), and behaviors can all interact to produce a dangerous situation in which a person may ponder harming him- or herself as a solution to the pain produced by the loss. Ministers and counselors must be aware that if a person's losses are extreme, self-harm thoughts are not unusual.

CONCLUSION

While a common human experience, loss is nevertheless difficult to endure. Some aspects of loss are recognizable, but other effects may be more felt than understood. We have rituals such as funerals for some objective losses, but we don't have anything similar for subjective, threatened, or ambiguous losses, making them more complicated to understand and navigate. While losses can be big or small, they tend to produce feelings and beliefs, and to affect behaviors of the one undergoing the losses.

One of the most common products of any significant loss is grief, or a person's attempt to adjust to the loss. The following chapter thus addresses grief and the grief process, considers the nature of grief, how it happens, and how individuals tend to journey through the heartache that follows many of the losses in life.

CHAPTER 4

GRIEF

A STORY OF GRIEF

BOB AND JAN APPROACHED ME FOR counseling following a very difficult year. Bob was minister of a small church, and Jan was the worship leader. They notified me in our first counseling session that they had chosen me because I was not a member of their denomination; they specifically wanted to see a counselor with an outside perspective. Bob and Jan lost their seven-year-old son, Ricky, to cancer eleven months before showing up in my office. Naturally, the couple's year had been difficult, and they were currently experiencing a great deal of strain in their marriage.

After being diagnosed with cancer, Ricky deteriorated rapidly. Their church and denominational leaders offered extensive support and encouraged the couple to have faith that Ricky would overcome the cancer. The couple's prayers appeared to have been answered when Ricky improved and the cancer went into remission. Their church members and denominational leaders rejoiced with them, noting God's victory.

A few months later, however, to the couple's dismay, their son relapsed. His deterioration was swift, and within a few weeks, their little boy was fighting for his life. Torn between watching their son struggle and wanting to believe he would be healed, the couple wrestled with issues of healing, faith, and God's will. Right before their son died, Bob leaned over the bed, kissed Ricky's forehead, and whispered that it was okay for him to stop battling. Within hours Ricky died.

Desiring solace, the couple sought out one of their mentors, a professor and denominational leader. Far from being comforting, this leader stated, "This was a battle and a soldier fell," implying that the couple had not demonstrated the right level of faith to keep their son alive. Bob and Jan were stunned. Not only did they experience waves of painful sadness, they now were filled with guilt.

As we talked about the past several months, Bob and Jan informed me that they'd continued in their ministry positions, but were just going through the motions. They were not sleeping well, and eating had been a chore. They said that they were barely communicating with each other; neither knew how to help the other, and neither had the emotional energy to provide support for the other. They wanted to know two things: "Why does it hurt so much?" and "When will this stop hurting?" Their questions led us to talk about grief, and specifically, its impact on each of them.

DEFINING GRIEF

Grief is not easy to define. It comes from a word that means heavy or grave.[1] In its mildest sense, it can mean an annoyance or an inconvenience as when Charlie Brown is bothered by Lucy and exclaims, "Oh good grief!" In its more serious sense, the word *grief* tends to be utilized in two different ways: (1) a collection of emotions, usually associated with loss; (2) a process or journey that follows a significant loss.

First, grief is a collection of feelings related to some notable distress. If a person is grieving, we know that he or she is experiencing a combination of different emotions. These may include sadness, hurt, fear, confusion, anger, and frustration, along with many other possible emotions.

Second, grief is also used to identify the progression or journey subsequent to some significant bereavement or loss. Following the death of his wife, Joy Davidman, C. S. Lewis chronicled his own experience with the process of grief:

> I thought I could describe a *state*; make a map of sorrow. Sorrow, however, turns out to be not a state but a process. It needs not a map but a history, and if I don't stop writing that history at some quite arbitrary point, there's no reason why I should ever stop. There is something new to be chronicled every day. Grief is like a long valley, a winding valley where any bend may reveal a totally new landscape. As I've

---

1. *Merriam-Webster's Collegiate Dictionary*, 11th ed., s.vv. "grief," "grieve."

already noted, not every bend does. Sometimes the surprise is the opposite one; you are presented with exactly the same sort of country you thought you had left behind miles ago. That is when you wonder whether the valley isn't a circular trench. But it isn't. There are partial recurrences, but the sequence doesn't repeat.[2]

We might talk about a person grieving or in the grief process, using this term interchangeably with the word *mourning*. Wofelt distinguishes between grief and mourning, seeing grief as, "the internal experiencing of thoughts and feelings following a death," and mourning as a person's "external shared social response to the loss."[3] H. Norman Wright also differentiates between grief and mourning, noting that mourning "is the process where grief is expressed. It's a natural, God-given process of recovery. It's his gift to us to help us get through the pain. Everyone has grief, but mourning is a choice."[4]

Whether referring to a specific set of emotions or the overall process, grief is inextricably intertwined with loss. The combination of strong feelings and the grieving process tend to follow loss. The more significant the loss, the more likely a person is to mourn the loss. Grief, then, is the process of separating away from some specific loss or losses as well as the collection of emotions associated with the loss.

Ultimately, grief seems to have some relationship with a person's ability to form connections in life. We do not tend to grieve over lost items that, or persons who, are not meaningful to us in some respect. When we form deep connections—a close relationship for instance—the loss of that relationship is not easy to navigate. Feelings of grief and the grief process seem to be God's way of helping us adjust to losses, allowing us to say good-bye and to begin life anew without the object of our grief.

THE BIBLE AND GRIEF

The various authors of the Bible treat grief as a normal part of the human experience. Grief may result from interpersonal relationships, such as the foolish son in Proverbs 10:1, who brings grief to his mother. Grief can occur on a much larger scale, as when Ezra grieves over the behavior of the nation of Israel

---

2. Lewis, *A Grief Observed*, 68–69.
3. Wolfelt, *A Child's View of Grief*, 22.
4. Wright, *Experiencing Grief*, 3–4.

(Ezra 9:5ff.). Lamentations is an entire book expressing the sorrow of Israel over the destruction of Jerusalem. Nearly one-third of the psalms are laments, a formal channel for expressions of grief, both for individuals and the entire community of Israel.[5] Responding to grief is a part of ministry, as can be seen when Paul encourages the Roman believers to mourn with those who mourn (Rom. 12:15). Grief, then, as presented in Scripture, is woven into the fabric of life and is a natural component of life.

Nor is grief in Scripture limited to humankind. In Genesis 6:6, God is grieved with the wickedness of the humans He created. Jesus is described as, "A man of sorrows and acquainted with grief" (Isa. 53:3). Isaiah 63:10 notes that the Israelites grieved the Holy Spirit of God. Similarly, Ephesians 4:30 is an injunction not to grieve the Holy Spirit. Perhaps the fact that humans are created in God's image includes having the ability to experience and express grief.

While grief may be a normal part of life, there appears to be a difference in how believers, as apposed to nonbelievers, are to understand and respond to grief. Jesus spoke about grief in the Sermon on the Mount, noting, paradoxically, that those who mourn are blessed and will receive comfort (Matt. 5:4). Stagg comments, "Probably the reference is to the comfort that is found now and in the final judgment by those who mourn now, whether over the hurts and hardships of life or over their sins and those of the world."[6]

Not only are those who mourn blessed but, for believers, there is a transitory nature to grief. In some of His final words to His disciples prior to the crucifixion, Jesus says, "Truly, truly, I say to you, that you will weep and lament, but the world will rejoice; you will grieve, but your grief will be turned into joy" (John 16:20). Jesus acknowledges the impact His death will have on His followers, but also notes the temporary nature of the associated grief. In verse 22 He adds, "Therefore you too have grief now; but I will see you again, and your heart will rejoice, and no one will take your joy away from you." Thus, grief, for the follower of Christ, does not appear to be a permanent condition.

For the believer, another crucial element of grief is hope. Even though believers may mourn a loss, they have the ability to understand the loss from a more complete perspective. In his letter to the Thessalonians, Paul states, "But we do not want you to be uninformed, brethren, about those who are asleep, so that you will not grieve as do the rest who have no hope" (1 Thess. 4:13). Paul

---

5. Anderson, *Book of Psalms, Volume 1*, 36–37.
6. Stagg, *Matthew and Mark*, 8:105.

acknowledges that believers who lose loved ones will grieve, but they have the hope of seeing their loved ones again, being united in heaven. Thus, grief for the believer is tempered by the knowledge of the bigger picture, of being united with Christ after death.

Grief, then, is a natural part of human functioning—a part of how God made humans to separate from what has been lost. The Bible, in fact, contains many specific examples of God's children in grief and mourning.

Abraham and Isaac

Both Abraham and Isaac were deeply affected by Sarah's death. Genesis 23:2 notes, "Sarah died in Kiriath-arba (that is, Hebron) in the land of Canaan; and Abraham went in to mourn for Sarah and to weep for her." Isaac's grief persists, even up until the time of his marriage to Rebekah. Genesis 24:67 states, "Then Isaac brought her into his mother Sarah's tent, and he took Rebekah, and she became his wife, and he loved her; thus Isaac was comforted after his mother's death." It seems that Isaac grieved his mother's death for around three years.[7]

Jacob

In Genesis 37, Joseph goes in search of his older brothers, who are taking care of the family's sheep. Jealous of Joseph, the brothers sell him to Ishmaelite traders, but tell their father, Jacob, that their brother has been killed by wild animals. Joseph's brightly colored coat, a gift from his father but now covered in blood, seems to confirm the brothers' story. Upon receiving the news, Jacob "tore his clothes, put on sackcloth and mourned for his son many days" (Gen. 37:34 NIV). Jacob is inconsolable. Verse 35 states, "All his sons and daughters came to comfort him, but he refused to be comforted. 'No,' he said, 'in mourning will I go down to the grave to my son.' So his father wept for him" (NIV).

Years later, Jacob still struggles with the loss of Joseph. Canaan is experiencing a severe drought and Jacob's sons travel to Egypt for grain. There they meet Joseph, who is in charge of Egypt's grain, although the brothers do not recognize him. Joseph tells the brothers that they must return with Benjamin. When the brothers inform Jacob, he initially denies their request, obviously

---

7. Isaac was born when Sarah was ninety years old. Sarah died at the age of one hundred twenty-seven (Gen. 23:1), making Isaac thirty-seven at her death. Isaac was forty when he married Rebekah (Gen. 25:20); thus it appears that Isaac's grief lasted at least three years.

still remembering the loss of Joseph: "My son will not go down there with you; his brother is dead and he is the only one left. If harm comes to him on the journey you are taking, you will bring my gray head down to the grave in sorrow" (Gen. 42:38 NIV). Jacob's grief over the loss of Joseph was still very present several years after Joseph's disappearance, and even later in life, Jacob's grief seems to drive decisions he makes about Benjamin.

Naomi

As discussed earlier, Naomi experienced a number of painful losses, including her husband and two sons. When Naomi and Ruth return to Bethlehem from Moab, the townspeople recognize her, saying, "Is this Naomi?" Naomi's response in Ruth 1:20–21 shows the depth of her pain. She replies, "Do not call me Naomi; Call me Mara, for the Almighty has dealt very bitterly with me. I went out full, but the LORD has brought me back empty. Why do you call me Naomi since the LORD has witnessed against me and the Almighty has afflicted me?" Naomi's statement made clear the hurt she felt in the midst of numerous painful and trying circumstances.

Hannah

Unable to have a child, Hannah grieves openly. Her husband, Elkanah, says, "Hannah, why do you weep and why do you not eat and why is your heart sad?" (1 Sam. 1:8). Hannah's grief over her childlessness is so strong that her husband notices her sad countenance and her lack of eating. Hannah's grief endures over a prolonged period of time; 1 Samuel 1:7 notes that she struggles with her inability to have children "year after year."

David

The greatest king of Israel, known as a man after God's own heart, experienced many instances of grief. When David is informed of the deaths of Saul and Jonathan, his reaction is prompt: "Then David took hold of his clothes and tore them, and so also did all the men who were with him. They mourned and wept and fasted until evening for Saul and his son Jonathan and for the people of the LORD and the house of Israel" (2 Sam. 1:11–12). David then composes a dirge, chants it, teaches it to those around him, and records the dirge in memory of Saul and Jonathan (2 Sam. 1:17–27). Perhaps writing the dirge facilitated the grieving process for David and helped him remember and grieve over the lives of his friend Jonathan, and Saul, his king.

Another instance of David's grieving occurs after his adultery with Bathsheba. The child she bears becomes extremely ill, and prior to the baby's death, David fasts and prays for the child. Second Samuel 12:17 says, "The elders of his household stood beside him in order to raise him up from the ground, but he was unwilling and would not eat food with them." When the child dies, those around him are afraid to inform David, and they are surprised when David gets up, cleans himself up, worships God, and eats. Perhaps David not only grieved the child, but grieved his own sin, as appears to be apparent in Psalm 51.

Yet another example of David's grief is apparent as he dealt with his sons Absalom and Amnon. When Absalom flees after killing his brother Amnon, 2 Samuel 13:37 notes that David, "mourned for his son every day." Later, David is notified that Absalom has been killed. His grief is unmistakable, as depicted in 2 Samuel 18:33: "The king was deeply moved and went up to the chamber over the gate and wept. And thus he said as he walked, 'O my son Absalom, my son, my son Absalom! Would I had died instead of you, O Absalom, my son, my son!'"

Mary and Martha

Mary and Martha experienced the death of their beloved brother, Lazarus. John 11 paints a picture of their grief following his death. Mary weeps when she talks to Jesus about the loss of her brother (v. 32). Both women express frustration with Jesus for not preventing Lazarus's death (vv. 21, 32), demonstrating the human tendency to question why a loss has to happen. Martha struggles to fit the death of her brother into her understanding of spiritual matters (vv. 21–27). All the while, the women are surrounded by friends and mourners: "and many Jews had come to Martha and Mary to comfort them in the loss of their brother" (v. 19 NIV). Although Jesus demonstrates His power in raising Lazarus from the dead, in this passage we see many elements of the earliest stages of the grief process, including tears, questions, frustration, and unmitigated sorrow expressed by these women, who obviously loved their brother.

SPECIAL BIBLICAL EXAMPLES OF GRIEF

The Bible presents many illustrations of grief, but three examples are especially noteworthy for how individuals respond to losses. Each of these instances gives insight into grief as a natural part of human functioning.

Joseph, Following the Death of Jacob

Genesis 50 relates the story of the days following the death of Jacob, Joseph's father. Jacob moves to Egypt during the drought in Canaan, being reunited with Joseph, his beloved son. Later, Jacob knows he is about to die and communicates his last wishes to Joseph and his other sons, including his desire to be buried in Canaan in the cave where Abraham and Sarah are buried. Even though Joseph knows his father is dying, he still expresses great sadness when the death takes place. Joseph weeps over his father (Gen. 50:1) and prepares him for the burial.

Following Jacob's death, Genesis 50 provides a clear picture of a series of grieving rituals undertaken by Joseph and those around him. Joseph commands the physicians to embalm his father, a process that takes forty days (Gen. 50:2–3). The Egyptians weep for Jacob for seventy days. These specific activities were part of a mourning period, a sanctioned time frame for grieving the death of a loved one.

Joseph requests and gets permission to return to Canaan for Jacob's burial. For this trip, Joseph takes with him a number of individuals, including all Pharaoh's servants, the elders of Pharaoh's household, the elders in charge of Egypt, and all of Joseph's brothers and their families (Gen. 50:7–8). The traveling entourage includes both chariots and horsemen. All of these individuals travel from Egypt to Canaan, taking Jacob's body to the cave in the field of Macphelah.

When the group arrives in Canaan, they stop at a certain spot called the threshing floor of Atad. Genesis 50:10 notes what happens next: "They lamented there with a very great and sorrowful lamentation; and he observed seven days mourning for his father."

Following forty days of embalming as part of seventy required days of mourning in Egypt, the group, led by Joseph, now lamented for seven more days. The act of mourning was so pronounced that those living in the area took notice, commenting, "This is a grievous mourning for the Egyptians" (Gen. 50:11). They even changed the name of the threshing floor to reflect the mourning of the Egyptians.

In this passage, we see the grief response of a great man like Joseph. Even knowing his father is about to die, he weeps and grieves for him. We also see a clear picture of a cultural influence on grieving. Joseph keeps his promise to his father regarding where Jacob wants to be buried. The Egyptians embalmed the bodies of those important to the culture and had a designated number of days for mourning. Grief following the death of a loved one was to be expected, and many cultural customs assisted a person or family in adjusting to the loss of a loved one.

An important aspect of this particular passage is our being able to see a process—a progression through the early mourning period. Joseph expresses initial grief, but makes preparations for the body. He then goes through several weeks of grieving. He travels to Canaan for the burial. He then grieves for another week. Joseph prepares and grieves, prepares and grieves. It's very likely that the ritualistic nature of having times of preparation and periods of intentional grieving greatly assisted Joseph, his brothers, their families, and even the Egyptians who had come to love Jacob, in beginning their adjustment to life without Jacob. This is perhaps the clearest biblical example of a structure to mourning a loved one.

Ezekiel, Following the Death of His Wife

Ezekiel was a prophet of God and was among those Israelites taken captive to Babylon in 597 B.C. In Babylon, God used him to speak to the Israelite exiles, calling for their return to the Lord. Perhaps more than any other prophet, Ezekiel was instructed by God to vividly depict God's message, often physically acting out the part of Israel or of God's judgment against His people. Ezekiel was directed to engage in some fairly bizarre activities, including making a small model of the city being attacked (Ezek. 4:1–3), shaving his head and beard and using his hair to demonstrate how God would deal with the nations (Ezek. 5:1–4), and packing his belongings twice a day and leaving the city, as if he were being taken into exile (Ezek. 12:1–16). All of these activities were visual in nature and were intended to communicate to the people a picture of their behavior and of God's judgment.

One of the most notable and striking examples of these symbolic activities occurs in Ezekiel 24:15–27. Here, God tells Ezekiel that his wife is going to die and that he is not to grieve for her. As is clear in the passage, Ezekiel obviously loves his wife; God says to Ezekiel, "I am about to take away from you the delight of your eyes" (24:16 NIV). He instructs the prophet not to mourn or weep (v. 16). Even though Ezekiel will groan silently, he is not to do so publicly (v. 17). The prophet is not to behave according to any of the normal customs following death. He is not to take off his turban, whereas customarily, mourners would remove their turbans and put dust on their heads. He is not to remove his sandals, cover his face, or eat a funeral meal, all common customs of the day.[8] These particular acts were appropriate for the death of a loved one, and the people would have expected Ezekiel to follow custom. As He did with Ezekiel's other symbolic expressions, God uses the aftermath of the death of Ezekiel's wife to vividly and graphically portray what He was doing, and to give the people a chance to recognize His work (vv. 24, 27).

In this passage, God does not tell Ezekiel to avoid grieving. He acknowledges that Ezekiel will groan silently (v. 17). Ezekiel is to avoid the outward signs of grieving in order to get the people's attention, to make them notice God's intervention in the nation of Israel. This symbolic portrayal apparently worked. In verse 19, the people come to Ezekiel and ask what his actions mean. God uses the absence of an expected, natural process—grieving the death of one's spouse—to get the attention of the wayward nation of Israel.

Jesus, Following the Death of John the Baptist

As Jesus walked around the countryside, He encountered individuals in every facet of life, including those who were grieving. Jesus demonstrates compassion toward those who mourn, recognizing their pain. When Mary and Martha are hurting following the death of their brother, Lazarus, Jesus comes to see them and raises Lazarus from the dead. Just prior to restoring their brother to life, John 11:35 notes that Jesus wept. It seems that, in part, Jesus is responding to the pain that His friends are experiencing.[9]

Jesus responded to others who were grieving, but did Jesus experience grief? Matthew records one such example in which Jesus expresses His lament over Jerusalem. Although chosen by God, the people of Israel had squandered countless opportunities. Jesus states, "Jerusalem, Jerusalem, who kills the prophets and stones those who are sent to her! How often I wanted to gather your children together, the way a hen gathers her chicks under her wings, and you were unwilling" (Matt. 23:37). Jesus seems to experience grief over His people's lack of understanding their role in God's plan.

Perhaps the best example of Jesus and grief occurs when He is informed of the death of His cousin, John the Baptist. Matthew 14 gives the account of Herod's executing John. John's disciples retrieve the body for burial and get word to Jesus of what has just occurred. Matthew 14:13 states, "Now when Jesus heard about John, He withdrew from there in a boat to a secluded place by Himself."

Upon receiving news of His cousin's death, Jesus left His disciples and the

---

8. Cooper, *Ezekiel*, 17:239.
9. Boice, *Gospel of John*, 3:244.

crowds and went to a place where He could be by Himself. It appears that Jesus was affected by the death of John. Although Jesus is fully divine, He is fully human, as well. In this instance, it seems that we get a glimpse of Jesus as He grieves the loss of His beloved cousin.

The Bible is replete with information about grief, and with examples of those in the midst of grief. Caregivers are most likely to help when they are armed with knowledge of what Scripture says about grief. Additionally, caregivers should have information about the nature of grief, about expressions of grief, and about the intensity and duration of grief. It is to these we now turn.

THE NATURE OF GRIEF

Grieving is part of being human. God designed us in such a manner that we are able to become attached to both people and objects, and depending on how important these are to us, we experience sadness and hurt when we lose them. Grief helps us separate from a lost person or object. If a loved one dies, for instance, grief allows us to adjust to life without the loved one. Ideally, humans will advance through the grief process to the point of being able to function without the object of the grief.

Grief, as mentioned, is not a simple, single entity that can be easily described. There is, in fact, great variability in the grief process. No universal, correct mode of grieving applies to all individuals in all circumstances. The way grief is experienced is related to the loss situation or the circumstances producing the grief process. The death of a casual acquaintance would not have as great an impact as would the death of a close relative. A sudden, tragic death of a young person affects the bereaved far differently than does the expected death of an older adult. The events surrounding the loss dictate at least some components of how an individual experiences grief.

EXPRESSIONS OF GRIEF

Following a loss, should a person be stoic and unemotional? Should a person wail and mourn? Are some behaviors associated with grief right or wrong, acceptable or unacceptable? Expressions of grief vary greatly. No two individuals grieve in precisely the same manner. Part of the caregiver's task is to support the hurting person according to the unique manner in which that person experiences and expresses grief.

General Expressions

How people express grief is influenced by their personalities, by families, and by their culture. An individual's personality influences whether he or she grieves internally or publicly, silently or vocally. Some individuals want to talk about their losses and are comforted with the support of friends. Others want to be left alone and work through the grief on their own. Some individuals have stoic personalities and are nonexpressive when they grieve, whereas others have no qualms about expressing a range of emotions.

Families influence and even regulate grief expressions, having both spoken and unspoken rules about grief. One family talks openly about a loss, listening to each other and checking on each other. Another family never mentions the death of a loved one. Some families may go so far as to forbid members from expressing grief in public. One family may move fairly quickly to part with the belongings of a deceased relative, attempting to get on with life. Another family may leave the deceased person's belongings untouched for years, building a type of monument or shrine to the deceased person. Families, then, are very powerful in influencing how and when grief is expressed, as well as in shaping how an individual interprets and experiences loss and grief. In ideal circumstances, supportive families give members permission to grieve, and they provide reinforcement for members as they do so. In less than ideal circumstances, families hinder or block the necessary grief processes of their members.

Culture impacts how grief is expressed, in that some cultures are quite stoic, and death is seen as a natural part of life, while other cultures are much more expressive, often with dramatic displays of grief. Still other cultures seem uncomfortable with the idea of death. In America, for instance, we battle the aging process, with people spending billions of dollars each year trying to ward off the effects of getting older. When a person dies, we often speak in hushed tones and use euphemisms like "passed on," "passed away," or "went to meet his maker." We may even prevent children from attending funerals of older relatives, not wanting to upset them. Often, culture influences families, which, as seen, exert a great deal of influence on individuals going through the grieving process.

Emotional Expressions

It is normal and appropriate for those encountering loss to experience and express a wide range of emotions as they grieve (see fig. 4.1).

When experiencing loss, individuals usually feel the emotions of sadness and hurt, but other emotions are generally present, as well. When a spouse dies, for instance, loneliness is common for the remaining partner. A surviving spouse often has thousands of daily reminders of the emptiness related to the absent spouse. Dreams of the deceased spouse can also leave one feeling lonely. Sometimes the remaining spouse may even feel abandoned.

Figure 4.1. Emotions Associated with Grief

Sadness	Hurt	Anguish
Fear	Loneliness	Helplessness
Longing	Lethargy	Guilt
Emptiness	Weariness	Confusion
Anger	Frustration	Irritation
Rage	Numbness	Discouragement
Relief	Isolation	Regret
Despair	Abandonment	Vulnerability

Often, this feeling of abandonment is accompanied by emotions such as frustration, or even anger. Feelings of anxiousness and guilt are also frequent visitors to the surviving spouse.

Many individuals feel numb following a significant loss, especially following the death of a close family member. Numerous counseling clients have conveyed to me that they feel nothing; numbness is the most salient sensation they are experiencing. Numbness subsequent to a loss is common, especially immediately following the loss. Later, the numbness tends to come and go, almost like the person is thawing out after having his or her emotions frozen.

As with other grief-related expressions, emotions vary from person to person and can be quite diverse over the course of the grieving process. Individuals may sense that they are coping effectively for a few months, but may be disconcerted when they feel suddenly and unexpectedly sad or angry. Emotions often ebb and flow through the months that follow a significant loss.

Behavioral Expressions

As with the other ways of expressing grief, behavioral expressions are quite varied. The most common expression of grief might be tears. While not everyone cries as a manifestation of grief, many do express feelings through tears. Tears mean different things to different individuals. Tears might represent sadness, fear, frustration, or hurt. Allowing people to cry, if they desire to do so, is certainly a part of helping them grieve.

Other individuals express grief quite differently. Some individuals find themselves easily irritated and may vent their emotions at those around. Even a fairly even-tempered person may be abrupt with others. Children, not able to understand emotions they experience, often express sadness through acting out, even through physical aggression. It's not uncommon for individuals to vent emotions at those closest to them.

Following the death of a loved one, some individuals engage in ritualistic behavior that may appear odd to others. They may talk to the deceased person or visit a gravesite and spend hours sitting near the deceased person's grave. They may keep mementos of the deceased person, buy the deceased person a birthday present, or leave a Christmas tree up for months after the holiday season. Unless a person is doing something dangerous, these expressions can be part of the necessary process of grieving and are generally temporary.

Cognitive Expressions

In addition to emotional and behavioral expressions, grief may also make itself known through a person's cognitive processes, through how the person thinks, perceives events, and interprets information. Sometimes following loss, a person will feel mentally sluggish and may have trouble thinking, concentrating, or recalling information. Grief may even affect how a person perceives events. The surviving individual may think he or she sees the deceased loved one in crowds of people, or even in the survivor's own house. It is also not unusual for a remaining spouse to think he or she hears a deceased partner's voice. Instances such as these may cause the surviving person to wonder if he or she is going crazy, but cognitive expressions of this nature are not unusual following the death of a loved one.

Again, how one experiences and expresses grief is unique to each person. Expressions of grief, whether emotional, behavioral, or cognitive, will vary over the life cycle of the grief process. Knowing that such expressions are typical allows the caregiver to provide comforting reassurance to the person in the midst of grief.

INTENSITY AND DURATION OF GRIEF

At the beginning of this chapter, I conveyed the story of Bob and Jan, whose son died of cancer. The couple wanted to know why the loss of their son hurt so much, and how long the pain would last. These questions are two of the most common questions grieving individuals ask during counseling. Those ministering to grieving individuals should know basic information about the intensity and duration of grief.

Intensity

According to Clinton and Ohlschlager, the intensity of grief is affected by three variables: the attachment to a person or possession, the way the loss came about, and whether the loss was sudden, premature, or violent.[10] Grief can vary in intensity from mild to extreme. Following a significant loss, an individual may face periods during which grief is particularly powerful. Generally, times of grief will come and go. A person may not feel strong emotions for a period of time, only to have them come rushing back, like an unwelcome visitor.

Often, when individuals describe the intensity of the grief, they may use metaphors to communicate what they're experiencing. Some individuals compare grief to ocean waves—some waves being smaller with less impact, others being extremely powerful. Other individuals express the feeling as being on a roller coaster. Just when they think they're doing better, they feel like they plummet down a steep decline, twist and turn, and then perhaps start slowly uphill again. Others report that grief-related emotions change quickly, like dropping off a cliff. Still another person might describe the intensity of grief in terms of breathing, that when things are particularly difficult, it feels as if someone is squeezing his or her chest, making it difficult to breathe. All of these word pictures are attempts to describe the intensity of the pain associated with the grieving process.

On occasion, a grieving person tells me they have no words to describe the pain they're experiencing. The grief is so intense that word pictures in terms of waves or roller coasters fail to capture the depth of the pain. A caregiver must be patient when a grieving individual struggles for words to describe the loss. The caregiver must never put words into the grieving person's mouth, as those words may trivialize what the person is experiencing.

---

10. Clinton and Ohlschlager, "Movements of Grief," 16.

Duration

Grief follows no timetable. Because individuals go through grief in such different ways, no technique has been developed to predict precisely how long it will last. Duration of grief following a loss is generally affected by how meaningful the lost person or object was, whether or not the individual feels permission to grieve, and support available to the individual in the aftermath of the loss.

Because the grief process ebbs and flows, individuals may feel confused about whether they're making progress as they attempt to cope with loss. This confusion is illustrated by C. S. Lewis: "Tonight all the hells of young grief have opened again; the mad words, the bitter resentment, the fluttering in the stomach, the nightmare unreality, the wallowed-in tears. For in grief nothing 'stays put.' One keeps on emerging from a phase, but it always recurs. Round and round. Everything repeats. Am I going in circles, or dare I hope I am on a spiral? But if a spiral, am I going up or down?"[11]

Over time, grieving individuals have hours, then days, then weeks when they feel better and when they feel more like they did prior to the loss. It is not uncommon for a person to mistakenly assume he or she is through with grieving, only to be caught off guard when the powerful emotions return. Counselors can help grieving individuals understand that emotional variability is part of the overall process, and a necessary component of working through the grief.

It's not easy for a grieving individual to determine when the journey is done, when the person has completed the grief process. Susan Zonnebelt-Smeenge and Robert Devries, authors of books on grief, are a married couple who both experienced the deaths of their first spouses. They believe that most individuals can make it to the other side of the grief journey. They state, "We define resolution as the bereaved no longer experiencing the pain associated with their loss, while still able to remember the pain and recollect at will all the cherished memories of the deceased loved one."[12]

As C. S. Lewis began to recover from the loss of his wife, he noted how subtle the recovery process can be:

Something quite unexpected has happened. It came this morning early. For various reasons, not in themselves at all mysterious, my heart was lighter than it had been for many weeks. For one thing, I suppose

---

11. Lewis, *A Grief Observed*, 66–67.
12. Zonnebelt-Smeenge and Devries, "Establishing Core Positive Constructs," 29.

I am recovering physically from a good deal of mere exhaustion. And I'd had a very tiring but very healthy twelve hours the day before, and a sounder night's sleep; and after ten days of low-hung gray skies and motionless warm dampness, the sun was shining and there was a light breeze. And suddenly at the very moment when, so far, I mourned H. least, I remembered her best. Indeed it was something (almost) better than memory; an instantaneous unanswerable impression. To say it was like a meeting would be going too far. Yet there was that in it which tempts one to use those words. It was as if the lifting of the sorrow removed a barrier.[13]

A FINAL NOTE ABOUT GRIEF

We live in a culture that values comfort and is not particularly tolerant of pain. Thus, we have many strategies for avoiding things that tend to produce pain. Strong emotions are usually part of the grieving process, and I often see people who wish to shortcut the process because of their pain. "Just tell me what I need to do to get through this," they say to me, "and I'll do it quickly." Because the grief process is anything but pleasant, individuals understandably desire to bypass it. When they ask me about a formula for more quickly getting through the pain, I tell them that I don't know any shortcut.

Oftentimes, individuals seek out their own shortcuts to avoid the pain of grieving. Many people consume alcohol to dull the pain. Some use drugs. Others may numb the pain through sexual behavior, either related to pornography or through direct encounters with other people. Still other individuals may throw themselves into work, hobbies, ministry, or other types of busyness that, they hope, will distract them from the hurt. All of these attempts, though, paradoxically slow the grieving process.

The grieving process may also be unfortunately hindered by well meaning friends, relatives, and even by religious entities. Following funerals, I often hear someone making the observation that Mrs. Smith "Is doing really well" or that Mr. Thompson "Is really strong." These comments usually mean that the one who has experienced the loss is not outwardly or overtly demonstrating emotions such as sadness or hurt. Absence of expressed grief does not necessarily mean the person is doing well. Following a funeral, the survivor is often either

---

13. Lewis, *A Grief Observed*, 51–52.

too numb to feel anything or is running on a type of automatic pilot, taking care of necessary details that surround the death of a loved one. It almost seems that, in modern American society, grief is something to be avoided, is negative if it does take place, and that the individual is doing well if he or she is not expressing grief.

Christian caregivers must understand the nature of grief and its role in how we function as humans. We must understand that God created us to exist in relationships with others. The part of us that gains joy in relationships can also be hurt through losses of these relationships. Grief is separating from loss. If we comprehend this as a necessary part of human functioning, we are better positioned to help those in the throes of grief. We can interpret what is taking place in hurting individuals and provide comfort and support in the midst of difficult times. When we do this, we are truly engaged in "mourning with those who mourn" and serving an incredibly important function in the body of Christ.

CHAPTER 5

A MODEL FOR HELPING

S o far, we've examined the nature of crisis, trauma, loss, and grief, what each of these entail, and their impact on humans. But how do these experiences interact with each other? How do they occur in relationship to one another when a person undergoes difficult circumstances? This chapter presents a model depicting the interplay of these human experiences (see fig. 5.1). The model provides helpers with an understanding of what humans experience surrounding crisis, loss, or trauma. The model's ultimate function is to present information for intervention. Caregivers can use the model as a basis for decision making when trying to provide effective help to a hurting person.

Figure 5.1. Crisis Ministry Model

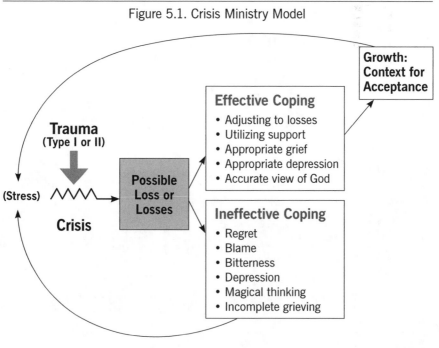

STRESS

The beginning point of the Crisis Ministry Model is understanding the role that stress may play in a crisis situation. Crises or traumatic experiences are undoubtedly accompanied by stress. Both crisis and trauma, in fact, produce stress. Stress, however, can occur by itself, long before a person encounters a crisis or trauma.

In general, stress results when one object pushes, pulls, or exerts force against another object. In physics, engineers design bridges and buildings to withstand stress. For humans, stress is not always problematic or a negative experience. Stress in moderate amounts may drive or motivate a person to be productive or to accomplish tasks. For many individuals, not having a sufficient amount of stress can produce boredom. Individuals may seek to add stress by riding roller coasters, climbing sheer rock cliffs, or running marathons. Stress in moderation makes life interesting.

When a person has too many stressors, or if the stressors last for too long, the effects can be problematic. Long-term stress leads to fatigue, burnout, and a host of medical concerns. Whereas moderate amounts of stress are part of human life, extreme stress negatively impacts humans in a number of ways.

If a person is under a good deal of stress, his or her coping resources tend to diminish and become depleted. This is especially unhelpful if the individual encounters a crisis or trauma event. A person who is already struggling with exhaustion, burnout, or depression will be less able to cope with tough life circumstances when they occur. Thus, stress paves the way for a crisis or trauma event to render a person less effective in overall attempts to cope.

CRISIS

Stress and crises are often interconnected, although not always. As discussed in chapter 1, a crisis can have either a sudden or gradual onset. A crisis may occur suddenly, even emerging when life is going well. A crisis having a sudden onset is less likely to be precipitated by stress. Crises that have gradual onsets are more likely to result from stressors. If a person faces too many stressors and becomes depleted, the outcome is likely to be some variation of crisis (see fig. 5.2).

Figure 5.2. The Relationship Between Stress and Crisis

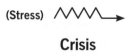

(Stress)

Crisis

Similarly, for a person who usually copes with crises, but who is exhausted from facing a number of life stressors, effectively coping with a crisis becomes much more tenuous.

TRAUMA

As identified in chapter 2, trauma is something that bursts into human functioning, often overwhelming normal coping mechanisms. Unlike crisis, trauma is not the result of stress, and functions independently from what else is taking place in a person's life. In other words, trauma is not a respecter of how stressful or stress free a person's life might be at any given time. A person may also experience a crisis without the presence of trauma. Crisis does not produce trauma. Conversely, trauma *always* produces or results in a crisis (see fig. 5.3). When people undergo traumatic events, they will, as a result, be in crisis. The more powerful and extensive the trauma, the greater the crisis will tend to be.

Figure 5.3. Trauma and Crisis

Trauma
(Type I or II)

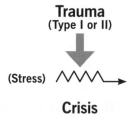

(Stress)

Crisis

LOSS

A crisis may or may not result in loss. Many crises do produce losses, as presented in fig. 5.4. A person facing a crisis in the workplace may actually lose a job, or a person in marital distress may have a spouse who leaves the marriage. Some crises produce multiple losses. A young woman in a car wreck may lose her car, suffer injuries, and deal with fear of driving. A brief crisis, however, may be resolved quickly, with little or no loss resulting. A medical test, for example, may cause concern for a person but may come back negative, resulting in a clean bill of health. What appeared to be a crisis was satisfactorily resolved.

Figure 5.4. Trauma, Crisis, and Loss

Trauma
(Type I or II)
(Stress)
Crisis
Possible Loss or Losses

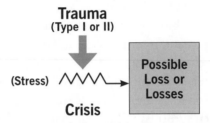

Whereas a crisis may not be traumatic and may not result in loss, a trauma event *always* leads to crisis and *always* ends in losses. These losses can be small or large, mild or extreme, real or imagined. One of the main struggles following a traumatic event is identifying, understanding, and making sense of the losses that result.

A Fork in the Road

Up to this point, the model is fairly straightforward. Specifically, individuals who encounter trauma will undergo an associated crisis and will experience loss or losses. At this juncture, however, there's a fork in the road (see fig. 5.5). Not all individuals progress through the aftermath of trauma or crisis in the same manner.

Figure 5.5. Two Pathways

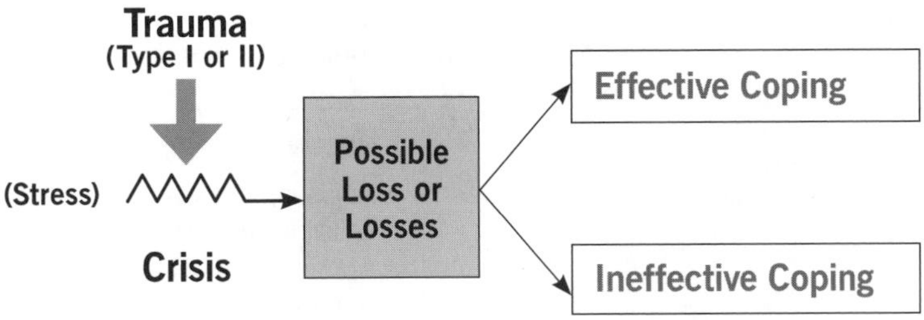

Trauma
(Type I or II)
(Stress)
Crisis
Possible Loss or Losses
Effective Coping
Ineffective Coping

Some individuals who experience trauma seem to make it through in fairly good shape. These individuals face some of the most extreme circumstances possible, but in the long run, they seem to cope effectively and develop a perspective on the trauma that becomes a helpful component of their general functioning.

Other individuals do not fare as well. On occasion, I see a person in counseling who experienced a traumatic event several years previously, but does not appear to have gotten over the event. This inability to recover from the trauma may be subtle or very apparent. In certain cases of extreme or extensive trauma, the person appears to be stuck in time and never progresses past the event. On more than one occasion a counseling client has told me about a trauma event, and by the emotion involved as they relate the story, I think the event has occurred recently. I'm then surprised to find out that the event took place many years before.

That some individuals overcome trauma and others do not begs the question: Why? Why do some people cope while others struggle? What takes place for individuals that may make it easier or more difficult to recover from a significant trauma and the subsequent losses? How can caregivers ultimately aid the process of recovery?

EFFECTIVE COPING

Individuals who do well in the aftermath of crisis, trauma, or loss seem to find ways to cope effectively (see fig. 5.6). Whether they do so intuitively, through reading and learning about coping, or through the use of available support, they seem to adjust. If they've faced a significant trauma or loss, effective coping generally involves going through the grieving process. These individuals are able to successfully separate from the losses they've experienced and are prepared to function productively in both the present and the future.

Figure 5.6. Coping Effectively

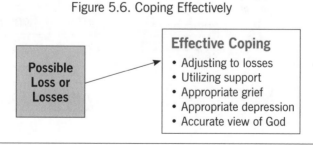

Those who experience crisis, trauma, and associated losses can make healthy adjustments and learn to cope effectively. Although recovery from losses is generally a difficult and even painful process, it's possible to adjust following tough events and to ultimately move ahead.

While recovery is possible, it's seldom easy. The more extreme the trauma or crisis and the more extensive the losses a person endures, the more difficult it is to smoothly transition through the grief process. Patience is key— both for the individuals who have experienced losses, and the caregivers attempting to provide comfort and help. Neither person should rush the process. Healing can come, but it usually takes time.

Effective coping following losses is comprised of a number of elements. These include adjusting to the loss or losses, utilizing available support, appropriate grief, appropriate depression, and having an accurate view of God and of His role in the crisis, trauma, or loss. Let me emphasize again—these elements of effective coping take place over time; rarely will a person experience these immediately after a significant loss.

Adjusting to the Loss or Losses

Part of effective coping is adjusting to losses that result from crisis or trauma. Adjusting involves several components. First, adjusting entails being able to make basic, day-to-day decisions in the aftermath of a loss. This can be difficult, especially initially. Second, adjusting involves the process of moving into new roles that may result from loss. A person losing a job has to adjust to being unemployed. When this person finds work, he or she will also have to make further adjustments to a new work environment, new coworkers, different responsibilities, and perhaps an unfamiliar work schedule. An individual who loses a spouse, whether through death or divorce, must become accustomed to single life, and perhaps even single parenthood. Effective coping involves being able to go through the journey of assuming and adjusting to new roles.

Effective coping means eventually making plans for the future. In the immediate aftermath of trauma and loss, most people do not focus on the future. Following severe trauma, a person is wise, in fact, to avoid making significant decisions about the future until things stabilize. At some point, though, consideration of the future is necessary and often beneficial. Plans regarding moving or staying in the same location, finding a new job, returning to school, beginning to date again, or having other children are all decisions that could be a part of the overall process of adjusting to a loss.

Utilizing Available Support

Another component of effective coping is making use of available support. When an individual encounters a personal struggle or tragedy, it's difficult to go though this trying time alone. In the aftermath of trauma or loss, it is common for a person to feel isolated and lonely. The person might believe that no one understands him or her, or the person may wonder if anyone really cares. While some individuals have no hesitation in seeking help from others, some find it difficult and even painful to ask others for help or to accept assistance when it's offered.

God designed us as humans to be in relationships, both with Him and with others. As discussed, the Bible is replete with passages that urge believers to help others, encourage others, mourn with those who are hurting, and bear each other's burdens. Support is essential when life is normal. It is crucial when life is difficult.

Support may take many forms. Often it's in the form of family members or friends who make themselves available following a tragedy or difficulty. Support may also come from church members or from others in the body of Christ. When the body of Christ functions as designed, it is available to offer aid and comfort when a person or family encounters trouble. In many instances, the support of family, friends, and fellow church members is sufficient to help a person navigate through trying times.

Another possible source of support is counseling. While not every individual needs counseling following tragedy, it can be beneficial to many. Counseling can provide a safe, supportive atmosphere in which a person is able to talk freely about what has taken place, develop strategies for coping, and make decisions about the present and the future. Counseling gives an individual a place to regularly talk about, and work on, the adjustment process. If a person seeks counseling following a trauma or loss, he or she should search for a counselor who has knowledge and experience related to crisis, trauma, and grief counseling. This is especially important if the trauma is extensive.

When seeking support from others, it's essential that the hurting person look for others who alleviate, rather than add to, the struggle. In my counseling, I often talk to trauma survivors about being selective when they accept support from others. Some individuals listen patiently, love unconditionally, and offer the kind of care that aids in the recovery process. Other individuals pry, scold, and make the survivor feel unnecessary guilt. Such individuals may encourage the person to "just get over it." They may offer platitudes that seem harmless, but are less than helpful. A client couple of mine had a baby who was born with a serious birth defect. Several church members, attempting to be encouraging, told the couple that God had given them this particular child because He knew they were strong enough to handle it. The couple found such statements to be of little help. Another client couple lost a child and were told by a friend that "God needed another angel in His heavenly choir." The couple told me they wondered why God had to choose their child. These types of comments are not only unhelpful to those who are grieving, but they seem more designed to comfort the speaker than the one hurting. Also among those who fail to offer safe, helpful support are individuals who have trouble with confidentiality, informing others of information the hurting person has confided.

When individuals seek support, I encourage them to be sensitive to, and keep their eyes open for, those whose support is helpful and comforting. Sometimes this will come from close friends, but not always. Not all friends know how to offer support following a crisis. Sometimes the best sources of support come from others who might not be expected to provide such support—a casual acquaintance who's been through similar circumstances, for instance. A sign of a person's actively progressing toward recovery is their looking for and accepting offers of support.

Appropriate Grief

When a person experiences losses, recovery involves grieving. You may recall that grieving is the process of separating from the losses one experiences. Going through the grief process in a healthy, constructive manner involves time and effort on the part of the grieving individual.

Time is a necessary ingredient to grieving effectively, because there's no shortcut to the grief process. In my counseling office, individuals often express a desire to hurry through the process. This is understandable, considering the pain involved. But even time, in itself, will not heal grief. Many individuals have lived months or years past a significant loss but have not even entered the earliest phases of the grief process. Time must be accompanied by investing effort in working through the grief.

The grieving person should also be free to feel a range of different emotions, as discussed in chapter 4. While emotions vary greatly among individuals, part of the grief process involves facing and experiencing such emotions. Some emotions may be quite transitory in nature, some more prominent than others. One way to block the grief process is to block the emotions or to deny them.

Recognizing emotions and acknowledging them is part of how a person makes sense of the impact of his or her loss. A hurting person needs a helper who will allow that person to talk about his or her emotions related to loss and grief. The sharing can be a powerful part of the journey through grief.

Rituals are also important in working through grief. Just as Joseph journeyed to bury Jacob, stopping to grieve along the way, rituals can facilitate adjustment to a loss. Rituals might include visiting a loved one's gravesite on certain days or at a certain time of the year, observing a morning or day whereon the loved one is remembered through talking or looking at photographs, taking a walk or a brief trip where one recalls good times with the deceased loved one. My oldest daughter, Arie, had friends in the sanctuary during the shooting at Wedgwood Baptist Church. One year following the shooting, on the anniversary of the tragic event, she and I got up before sunrise, bought flowers, drove to the memorial outside the church, and prayed for the church and for families who lost loved ones. This simple ritual was part of helping both of us make sense of a terrible event. Rituals, then, can be a powerful part of working through grief.

Appropriate Depression

At first glance, this element of effective coping may seem out of place. When I first mention depression as potentially beneficial to clients who are in the grief process, they often seem puzzled as to how depression may be a necessary part of coping with loss. Let me explain: When I'm counseling with individuals who've experienced a traumatic event, many tell me they're experiencing depression, or they describe having symptoms of depression. When they do so, I'll sometimes say, "It makes a lot of sense to me that you might be experiencing some depression-like symptoms. If a person had gone through what you've just described and told me they were doing great, *then* I'd be surprised. If you tell me, however, that you're struggling and that you may be depressed, it makes sense in light of what you've gone through." I relate to them that in some instances, depression is our body and mind's method of saying "time-out," in order to make sense of an extreme situation. I believe that God, in fact, made humans in such a manner that many individuals experience brief, temporary periods of depression, especially following trauma or some significant loss. I wonder, at times, if God might use brief depression as an opportunity for a person to look to Him and hear from Him.

I don't believe, however, that all depression is productive and beneficial. Later, I'll discuss a type of depression that is a more problematic aspect of grief.

Appropriate depression, however, is at times a part of the journey through grief, and a necessary component of separating from and adjusting to significant losses.

An Accurate View of God

Extreme events, such as trauma or large-scale losses, can affect a person on multiple levels, including where a person attempts to understand and make sense out of the world. Trauma often produces confusion, the person's being unsure how the world works. A world that was safe and orderly in the morning may be quite upside down by evening, seeming harsh, confusing, and disordered.

A person's understanding of God can also be affected by trauma or loss. A man who believes God is loving and caring may question that assumption when he hears that his only child has been killed in an accident. A woman who believes God is near and has a plan for her life may struggle with that belief after her home is destroyed by a tornado. Trauma, as discussed in chapter 2, can have an impact on both cognitive beliefs and an affective sense of who God is.

Part of effective coping involves developing or returning to a more accurate understanding of who God is and what He is like. This, alongside grieving, can be a process that occurs over time. In the immediate aftermath of trauma, a person may struggle with many questions about God. A caregiver can provide support and comfort about God's role following the tragic event, hoping that, as time goes by, the individual will gain reassurance of God's love and care. This assurance of God's nature will often be linked with the support of friends, church family, or of a caring counselor. Making sense out of one's relationship to God, though, is a key facet of the journey through grief.

All of these things—adjusting to the loss, use of support, appropriate grief and depression, and an accurate view of God—are part of the larger coping process. The person who works through these has a much higher likelihood of taking the productive fork in the road following trauma or loss. Again, this journey is not an easy one. Nor is progress smooth and easily made. Even the person who effectively navigates the larger grief process will have ups and downs. Some days he or she will feel better. On other days, the pain will feel fresh and raw. In many respects, the grief process is like a slow roller coaster, traveling up and down, up and down. On any given day, a person may not feel as well as he or she did the day before. Over time, however, if coping effectively, the person begins to feel better. He or she will experience periods when the pain is not as sharp, like he or she can breathe. The person notices feeling a little more like he or she used to, describing the feeling as "a little more like myself." The person will also have down days, but eventually these will become fewer and fewer. Generally, individuals will notice that they're doing better than they were a few months ago. When individuals start to notice that they're doing better, it's usually a confirmation that they're progressing well through the grieving process.

INEFFECTIVE COPING

At the fork in the road, not all those struggling with trauma and loss cope in a healthy, productive manner (see fig. 5.7). Some never seem to face the difficult circumstances, even denying that anything difficult happened. It's not unusual for a person who experienced sexual abuse as a child to downplay the extent and the significance of the trauma. This person might say, "What happened to me is so much less serious than what has happened to others." This denial of the severity of the event makes it difficult to grieve effectively. Other individuals may acknowledge they've experienced trauma, but still struggle to cope effectively.

Figure 5.7. Ineffective Coping

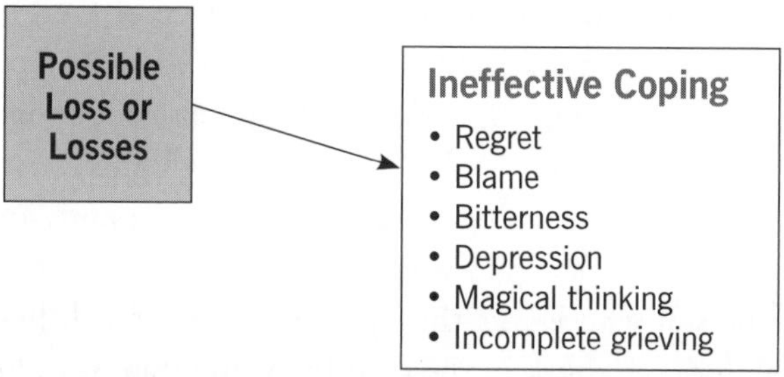

Possible Loss or Losses	Ineffective Coping
	• Regret
	• Blame
	• Bitterness
	• Depression
	• Magical thinking
	• Incomplete grieving

There are a number of markers of ineffective coping, which contribute to difficulty recovering from trauma or loss. These include regret, blame, bitterness, depression, magical thinking, and incomplete grieving. An individual struggling to cope following a trauma or loss may be affected primarily by only one, or by a combination of these.

Regret

Following crisis, trauma, or loss, a person may find him- or herself repeatedly reflecting on the events and questioning what he or she should have done differently. This second-guessing may be mild or powerful. As regret becomes stronger, it can lead to self-blame, resulting in a type of paralysis in the coping process.

Regret can take many forms. When individuals lose loved ones, they often regret not spending enough time with those loved ones, not saying "I love you" enough, or taking the relationship for granted, assuming the person will always be around. Sometimes, the last encounter between a person and a deceased loved one was not pleasant. If a couple had an argument the last time they were together, then one dies unexpectedly, this last conversation will likely be the source of regret.

Blame

As humans, we seem prone to blame. In Genesis 3, God asks Adam if he has eaten of the tree after God had instructed him not to. Adam manages to blame both Eve *and* God: "The woman you put here with me—she gave me some fruit from the tree, and I ate it" (Gen. 3:12 NIV). Eve also takes part in the blame game, pointing to the serpent as she attempts to deflect responsibility. This natural tendency, demonstrated so clearly by the first man and woman, is to avoid taking responsibility and to attach blame to others. With trauma, blame may not be so much about avoiding responsibility as about deflecting the pain associated with the traumatic event. If a person focuses attention on others, it may keep him or her from having to deal with the pain, sadness, or fear accompanying losses.

Following trauma or loss, the temptation to blame comes naturally. We blame the bosses who fire us, FEMA for not responding quickly enough, the legal system for paroling the individual who harmed a loved one, or the emergency room physician who treated a friend.

Blame can also be directed toward loved ones. It's not uncommon for a surviving spouse to even blame the deceased partner for dying. This happens in situations in which the loved one contributed to his or her own death, driving while drunk, for instance; but it can also happen when a traumatic event was not necessarily the loved one's fault: "If only she'd been driving more carefully" or "If he'd only watched his diet more closely."

Humans are also prone to blame God when bad things happen. It's not unusual for individuals to feel angry at God for their losses or to blame God for what has taken place. Following tremendous tragedy, Job's wife urges her husband to "Curse God and die!" (Job 2:9). The author of Psalm 44 seems to struggle with blaming God, stating in verse 12, "You sell Your people cheaply, and have not profited by their sale." Even God Himself, then, is not immune from humans' placing blame when difficult circumstances occur.

Following trauma or loss, some desire or tendency to blame is understandable and is not an unusual aspect of effective coping. Individuals who do not cope effectively, however, get stuck in blaming others; they can't seem to get past it and repetitively blame others. When an individual gets mired in blame, the grieving process slows or can be short-circuited entirely.

Bitterness

One of the clearest signs of ineffective coping is bitterness. Bitterness occurs when some of the emotions that are a part of the normal grieving process crystallize into resentment, anger, and even hatred. Bitterness can be like a corrosive acid, eating at the person who doesn't deal with those things that created the painful feelings.

Bitterness can be directed along a number of different pathways. It can be aimed at self, linked with regret and self-blame. It can be directed toward those who contributed to the trauma or loss. It can be directed toward the church or organized religion. It's often aimed at God. Bitterness can also be directed at loved ones, or even toward humankind, in general.

The writer of Hebrews comprehended the problems of bitterness. In Hebrews 12:15, he states, "See to it that no one comes short of the grace of God; that no root of bitterness springing up causes trouble, and by it many be defiled." The author of this passage understood the powerful and dangerous nature of bitterness. He describes it as causing trouble and having the ability to affect, even defile, many. Bitterness is a potentially dangerous outcome of trauma and loss. When bitterness becomes crystallized in a person's life, it will almost always result in hindered progress through grief or in a cessation of the entire process.

Depression

As discussed, depression at times can be productive, even a part of healthy grieving. Not all depression, however, is this type. For some individuals, being depressed is like being stuck knee-deep in mud. Everything becomes slower, more tedious, and more difficult. Simple tasks require a great deal of energy. Even getting up in the morning can be a chore.

The biggest difference between depression that is a part of healthy grieving and depression contributing to ineffective coping is that the latter is nonproductive. In effect, instead of progressing through grief, the person either feels stuck or feels like he or she is going in circles. Productive depression helps a person slow down enough to make sense of the trauma or loss. Nonproductive depression clouds a person's judgment and contributes to the sensation of struggle.

One of the difficulties in discussing depression as related to trauma is that the symptoms of both depression and trauma are often very similar. While a traumatized person may not become depressed, and a depressed person may not have been traumatized, both might, for instance, have difficulty sleeping, eating, and concentrating. Both might be irritable, have reduced energy, and might experience relationship problems. Because the symptoms of both are similar, it may be difficult for the person who's experienced trauma to determine when the aftermath of trauma has produced depression. This can be problematic for the caregiver to determine, as well.

Depression that is part of ineffective coping, though, can be marked by certain elements. For instance, the depressed individual tends to see the world through a dark lens. This person may quickly notice the negative in what occurs around him or her, but may have problems identifying the positive. The depressed person may even rewrite the past to fit the negative outlook he or she is experiencing. Depressed individuals are self-focused, having difficulty in thinking outside of him- or herself. The accompanying reduced energy makes it harder to meet anyone else's needs. The depressed person tends to focus on emotions, on how things feel. Emotions such as sadness, frustration, helplessness, and hopelessness most often drive their experience of the world and how they interpret events. All this negative perception and emotion make the depression cyclical: individuals become depressed, they can't accomplish what they used to accomplish, they feel anger toward self, they blame self and others, all of which leads to more feelings of discouragement and depression.

A person struggling with nonproductive depression bears a greater likelihood for thoughts of self-harm or suicide. Pain and hopelessness are powerful contributors to such thoughts. Counselors and ministers should be alert to those struggling with depression and should assess for suicidal thoughts and feelings in order to provide appropriate protection for the depressed individual.

Magical Thinking

Magical thinking occurs when a person makes connections between events that are not truly connected. Children, for instance, may avoid cracks in the sidewalk, saying, "Step on a crack, break your mother's back." In reality, there is, of course, no connection between a person avoiding cracks in the pavement and the spinal health of the person's mother. For an adult, believing that the rain started because you just washed your car is an example of magical thinking. Generally, adult magical thinking is much more sophisticated and subtle than that of children, but both make connections between things in the universe that have nothing to do with each other.

In the aftermath of trauma or loss, it's not unusual for an individual to struggle with magical thinking. A person may believe that he or she is responsible for an accident, when the person really had nothing to do with it. Sexual trauma survivors often believe some behavior or action on their parts caused the assault.

Magical thinking can also be evident in a person's understanding of God's role in a traumatic event. A man may believe that he lost his house to a fire because he wasn't having regular devotional times or because he failed to tithe the previous month. Even smaller events such as a flat tire can be attributed to the person's engaging in some behavior believed to be displeasing to God.

Magical thinking may be mild or extreme. When it becomes extreme, individuals draw faulty conclusions about their own role in a trauma event, and/or about God's character or functioning in the world. In extreme circumstances, the magical thinking often contributes to a person's becoming stuck in the grieving process. Regret, self-blame, and even bitterness can result.

Being intelligent, caring, and even being a committed Christian does not exempt one from having magical beliefs, as the following example illustrates:

JILL LOST HER FATHER TO A degenerative neurological disorder. As the oldest daughter, she was active in his daily care as he deteriorated, moving toward a painful death. In his last few months, he was often verbally abusive toward his family, and especially toward his daughters. I saw Jill in counseling a few years after his death. She was the wife of a minister but was struggling with her marriage. As we discussed her father's death, she did not express sadness or anger over her involvement with him near his death. Finding this somewhat curious, I questioned her about the time period immediately prior to her father's death and about this absence of sadness and anger. She finally confided that she believed if she expressed anger about her father, God would be displeased. She believed that God would punish her by taking away another person in her life about whom she cared. She thought that expressing feelings of grief would be a sign that she did not learn whatever lesson God wanted her to learn, and that God would teach her the lesson again by taking away another loved one. Therefore, in our discussions of her father's demise, any perceived negative feelings were off-limits for her. Through acknowledging her faulty belief system and in talking about what God is like, she was able to begin grieving the death of her father.

When practicing grief counseling, it's not uncommon to discover that a client is engaging in magical thinking. Because people do not tend to voice these thoughts, they generally go unchallenged. Some examples of magical thinking can be quite insidious, as was the case with a client of mine, a young adult named Jeanette.

JEANETTE HAD BEEN A SHORT-TERM missionary and was training for further ministry at the time we met together. Jeanette had been in the sanctuary of Wedgwood Baptist Church when a gunman entered and killed several people. Jeanette ducked down between pews as the gunman walked back and forth past her. Crouched there, she prayed that God would end the ordeal and would stop the horrible events unfolding around her. At the moment she finished her prayer, the gunman put the gun to his head and shot himself. In the days that followed, Jeanette concluded that her prayer had been responsible for killing the gunman. She further believed that if she'd been behaving in a Christlike manner, she would have been praying for the gunman's salvation instead of focusing on her own needs. Her guilt following the shooting, combined with the magical belief that she'd contributed to the gunman's death, resulted in her having a great deal of difficulty eating, sleeping, and performing at work.

When Jeanette and I first met for counseling, she was, by her own admission, "barely hanging in there." Not only did she believe that she played a part in the gunman's death, she worried that because of this "sin," God could take her life at any moment, just like He did the gunman's. She was jittery, confused, and exhausted. When Jeanette was able to verbalize her magical thoughts, we began the process of examining these against the reality of the situation and against what the Bible reveals about the nature of God.

Magical thinking is rooted in the belief that God is, at best, distant or displeased and, at worst, angry with us. We must behave in certain ways to gain good from Him or to ward off the bad things He might do as a result of His displeasure. If we get it wrong, God is punitive, waiting to get us.

When a person struggles with magical thinking, counseling involves pointing the individual to God's character as identified in Scripture, including His loving-kindness, mercy, and grace. It involves helping clients understand that God is like a perfect parent who cares about the pain that we experience. Helping struggling individuals to an accurate understanding of God can often jump-start them toward productive movement in the grief journey.

Incomplete Grieving

On occasion, an individual may begin the grieving process but have difficulty completing it. The person may seem to be adjusting to the loss he or she has experienced and even grieving in an appropriate and healthy manner. Along the way, however, the person becomes stuck, unable to continue.

A number of factors contribute to a person's inability to continue the grieving process. The pain associated with grief may seem too acute, causing a person to abandon the process. Fatigue, a natural outcome of the energy required for grief, may play a part in a person's having difficulty making progress. The busyness with other life demands short-circuits the grief process. Some individuals may lack support during the grief, isolated in their attempts to work through the grief of a significant loss. Other individuals may even face resistance from family members or friends who misunderstand the necessity of grief.

Further, if a person faces a loss while still bearing unresolved grief from the past, it's difficult for that person to appropriately and successfully navigate current or future losses. Some individuals may not complete the grief process because they lack knowledge or information about how to make it past a loss. A person may do his or her best to cope and adjust, but may lack a basic map for the grief journey. Some individuals may have received bad advice about grief. Well-meaning friends, loved ones, or even religious leaders who are devoid of a healthy understanding of grief might guide a person astray.

Any single factor or combination of these factors may contribute to a person coping ineffectively in the aftermath of loss. The result may be incomplete grief and a sense of being stuck in one's attempt to overcome a loss. Thus, it's not unusual for a person to begin, but not complete, the journey through grief. In many respects it's easier, in fact, to travel down the pathway of ineffective coping than to face losses and work through grief in a productive, healthy manner.

GROWTH THROUGH GRIEF: DEVELOPING A CONTEXT FOR ACCEPTANCE

When people are able to progress through the grief process, they eventually reach a point at which they begin to recover. Individuals may notice fewer painful moments or days, an increase in energy, a desire to return to abandoned activities or interests, or they may ponder new ventures. Individuals may observe that they feel more like they used to prior to the trauma or loss.

Along with these important markers of recovery, persons will also develop a context for making sense out of what has taken place in their lives. The context for acceptance is a central part of recovery, especially if individuals have experienced traumatic events or significant losses (see fig. 5.8). The context for acceptance is a clear indication that these persons are not only recovering, but may also be experiencing growth through their trials.

Figure 5.8. Context for Acceptance

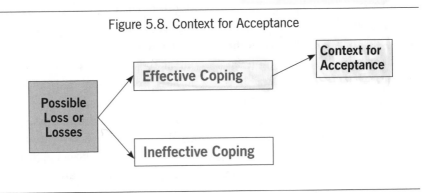

Developing a context for acceptance involves building a framework for making sense of what has happened or seeing how the trauma or loss fits into the greater scheme of life. You'll recall that one of the major components of a trauma or loss is a person's inability to decipher what has happened and the way that he or she reacting. "Why" questions are common. With trauma, especially, there is no framework for understanding what took place. The context for acceptance occurs when the person develops instead the framework for fitting the events into a bigger picture. While an individual may never have answers to all of the "Why" questions, the context for acceptance seems to serve the function of providing a sense of meaning and purpose. The context for acceptance usually emerges as an outcome of effectively grieving and adjusting to losses.

When people begin to develop the context for acceptance, they may say certain types of things:

- "This was the worst thing that has ever happened to me, but I'm beginning to see how God may be using this in my life."
- "The last several months have been really painful, but I think I'm a stronger person for it."
- "Because I know what it's like to go through _____, I think God may want to use me to work with others who are in similar circumstances."
- "I don't want anyone to go through what I've been through, but I realized the other day that if I hadn't gone through this, I would be headed down the wrong pathway in life. God used these horrible circumstances to help me understand a lot about myself and about who He is."

These statements provide clues to the caregiver that the person is well into the grief journey and generally is recovering from what took place. Statements such as these do not necessarily mean the grief journey has ended, but they're indicators that the person is on the route to recovery.

In some instances, an individual's context for acceptance is detected not through what the person says, but through the person's actions or decisions. For instance, a parent whose child is killed by a drunk driver might join Mothers Against Drunk Driving or may crusade for more stringent drunk driving laws. A survivor of sexual abuse may feel compelled to help others who've undergone similar struggles, or may even decide to become a counselor specializing in sexual trauma. An individual who knows the strain of losing a home to a natural disaster may become active in assisting others in like circumstances.

One's context for acceptance, then, often involves helping others. The apostle Paul is perhaps one of the best biblical examples of a person's developing a context for acceptance after difficult events. In 2 Corinthians 11:23–27, Paul lists the struggles he encountered in his service of Christ, including being jailed, beaten, stoned, and shipwrecked. Paul endured a number of traumatic events and his life was in danger on numerous occasions. Earlier in 2 Corinthians, though, Paul conveys an example of a context for making sense out of these events: "Blessed be the God and Father of our Lord Jesus Christ, the Father of mercies and God of all comfort, who comforts us in all our affliction so that we will be able to comfort those who are in any affliction with the comfort with which we ourselves are comforted by God" (2 Cor. 1:3–4). He could see these trials as part of his apostleship and he knew God's hand was on him during difficult circumstances. He saw what God was doing in him and through him, and he recognized the bigger picture of God's activity and of his own role in God's work.

Individuals who develop a clear context for acceptance generally notice how much they've grown, even through the difficult and dark times. This growth becomes a powerful part of the person's identity and life story, even overshadowing the effects of the traumatic event or of the losses incurred. People who have received comfort are thus often more than willing to help others who are hurting.

When individuals cope ineffectively following trauma—when they get stuck in the grief process—the trauma *event* tends to define who they are. When they cope effectively, develop a context for acceptance, and grow through the experience, the *growth* defines who they are. One of my favorite Bible characters is Joseph. Joseph encountered crises, losses, and assuredly grieved over being separated from his family and his country. And yet, when he had the opportunity to retaliate against his brothers who authored his struggles, he said to them, "Don't be afraid. Am I in the place of God? You intended to harm me, but God intended it for good to accomplish what is now being done, the saving of many lives" (Gen. 50:19–20 NIV).

Joseph had clearly developed a context for making sense out of the bad things that happened to him. He saw God's hand in bringing good out of evil, recognizing how God used the trials of his past to help many others, his brothers included. He responded not with bitterness, regret, or anger but with love and concern. What an incredible example of overcoming losses!

PROBLEMS ASSOCIATED WITH THE CONTEXT FOR ACCEPTANCE

While a context for acceptance is a marker of healthy progress, it may entail a couple of dangers or problems. One occurs within the person going through the trauma or loss; the other can be introduced by a caregiver.

Premature Adoption of a Context for Acceptance

The first problem happens when individuals prematurely adopt a context for acceptance, often immediately following a trauma or significant loss. The individuals may downplay the significance of the trauma or the impact of the loss. They may not admit to experiencing common emotions such as sadness or fear. They may even use or misuse Scripture or religious phrases to give the impression that they're not struggling with the loss. As opposed to a healthy context for acceptance, these individuals are often using denial to avoid pain. While this denial may alleviate short-term pain, it has the effect of merely slowing or delaying the necessary grief process.

Imposing a Context for Acceptance on Another Person

In my counseling office, trauma survivors tell me some of the comments others have made in an effort to provide comfort. While these friends and acquaintances generally mean well, their words commonly have the opposite effect of what is intended. One of the more frequent examples is when, immediately following a loss, a friend or loved one quotes Romans 8:28: "And we know that God causes all things to work together for good to those who love God, to those who are called according to His purpose." While this verse is true, and while it's a wonderful verse to use in many circumstances, it's not always helpful to quote it to a person who's just lost a child, for example. Instead of providing comfort, the result may be increased pain for the parent.

This second danger occurs when a helper—usually a friend, minister, or counselor—imposes his or her own framework upon the person who has undergone the trauma or loss. Often, helpers do so in an attempt to answer the "Why" questions of the survivor. At other times, imposing a context for acceptance seems to serve the function of reducing the helper's own anxiety as he or she grapples with the tremendous hurt and pain experienced by many survivors.

While a helper may truly have a context for making sense out of another person's pain, imposing that framework on the hurting individual is rarely the best course of action. Doing so may result in a couple of things. First, the imposed context increases the guilt feelings of the victim. The victim feels badly that he or she is not "rejoicing in the Lord" or seeing God's handiwork in trying times. This guilt, when added to other components of the struggle, makes it more difficult for the victim to progress. Second, the helper and the victim may become engaged in an argument about how the world works. The helper might attempt to explain the victim's struggles while the victim presents his or her own perspective. A clear biblical example of imposing a context for acceptance occurs in the book of Job. Job's friends are intent on explaining why Job is encountering trials, what he's done wrong, how God works, and what Job needs to do. The friends begin their time with Job, providing the comfort of their presence (Job 2:11–13), but they soon attempt to impose their context for acceptance upon Job, with the result that their helpful attempts devolve into a nonproductive argument. Job expresses his frustration and calls his friends sorry comforters who bring windy words (Job 16:2–3).

The period immediately following a trauma or loss is not the time for the helper to persuade the victim to adopt a certain context for acceptance. Nor is this a time to argue about theology or to correct a person's thinking. If an ongoing, long-term relationship occurs following a trauma, many occasions will arise for discussing theology, wrestling with the "Why" questions, and dealing with issues surrounding the nature of pain and suffering. In terms of the victim's context of acceptance, however, the best thing to do is provide support and allow survivors to develop their own context for making sense out of the struggles. When the individual forges his or her own understanding, there is less likelihood of short-circuiting the grieving process or of the person adopting someone else's understanding in an effort to please or placate the helping individual. Because the context for acceptance is such a powerful part of the recovery process, caregivers would do well to proceed with prudence, keeping in mind the mistakes of Job's friends.

Feedback Loops

As discussed, there are two possible pathways one could follow after experiencing trauma or loss. One pathway involves effectively coping with trauma or loss, and productively going through the grieving process, resulting in the development of a context for acceptance. The second pathway involves ineffective coping and often means a person becomes stuck in the grieving process, or perhaps altogether abandons attempts to grieve and adjust. Each of these pathways has a feedback loop to the start of the process. This means, in essence, that how individuals cope—effectively or ineffectively—affects how they deal with life in the future.

Constructive Feedback Loop

If individuals cope effectively, their context for acceptance shapes how they will face the future. In effect, the person's context for acceptance and related growth creates a type of lens through which the person interprets the world and by which the person makes decisions (see fig. 5.9). This feedback loop helps explain why some individuals go through trauma or loss and emerge stronger, more capable, having a deeper, richer relationship with God. If individuals encounter other stressors, crises, losses, or traumatic events, they have a framework for making sense out of what is happening, they commonly know how to cope, and, if necessary, they have an idea of how to grieve in a healthy, productive manner. Sometimes in counseling I encounter a person who's faced numerous losses and trauma, and yet the person seems poised, wise, and at peace, even in the midst of the difficulties. Most often, these individuals have worked through the grief process, have developed a clear context for acceptance, and are using this framework for coping with current life difficulties.

Figure 5.9. Constructive Feedback Loop

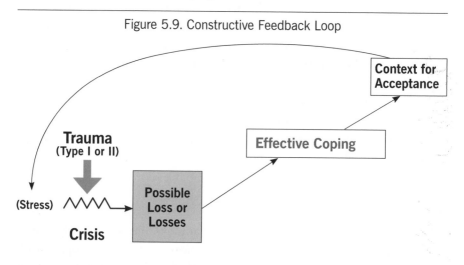

Problematic Feedback Loop

Individuals who cope ineffectively, or fail to complete the grieving process, also have a feedback loop (see fig. 5.10). Whereas the loop described above facilitates healthy functioning, this loop represents what happens when a person fails to cope productively.

Figure 5.10. Problematic Feedback Loop

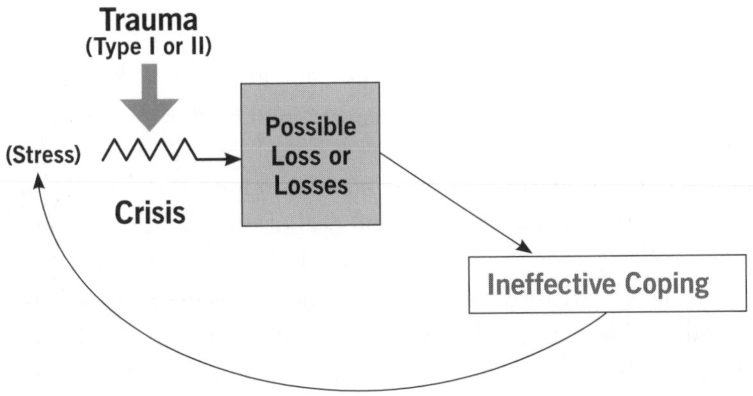

Ineffective coping, or unresolved grief, most commonly results in a severe depletion of energy. This puts a person in a precarious position when he or she experiences subsequent stressors or crises. If a person is low on energy, it's difficult to face many typical life stressors. Similarly, if a person experiences a crisis, but is already depleted, it will be more difficult to navigate the new crisis.

If individuals do not resolve traumatic experiences, they are ill prepared should they encounter other traumas. When a person has unresolved issues, trauma can have a layering effect, making it even more difficult for the person to cope with the second trauma or with any subsequent trauma.

When repeatedly traveling through the problematic feedback loop, a couple of things are likely to occur. First, it would not be surprising to find this person suffering from Post-Traumatic Stress Disorder (PTSD). Recurring trauma that goes unresolved can have serious consequences in this regard. Second, these individuals are likely to develop and function from a victim mentality. The person who develops a victim mentality feels consistently hopeless and helpless. This person fails to see any impact he or she has on the world, instead functioning from an external locus of control. They attribute the cause of events to factors occurring outside themselves, failing to recognize their responsibility in matters. In essence, these individuals feel like life happens to them and that they have little control over what takes place or over their ability to respond to events in their world. Persons functioning from a victim mentality are ill equipped to cope with the world in a productive manner.

CONCLUSION

The model in this chapter is designed to provide a map of sorts, which depicts the relationship between crisis, trauma, loss, and grief. There does appear to be a pattern to how these experiences take place, and to how humans commonly respond to these experiences.

While individuals seem to respond in a somewhat uniform manner during the initial periods of these experiences, a good deal of variation can be found in how people cope long-term. Some individuals adjust effectively, make sense out of even the toughest circumstances, and eventually grow to help others as a result. Other individuals do not fare as well. They may never enter the grieving process, or they may begin, but get stuck. Failure to progress can be draining physically and emotionally and leaves a person poorly equipped to face future struggles. In extreme cases, failure to progress can result in emotional paralysis, a victim mentality, or a general inability to live life to the fullest.

Helpers, both counselors and ministers, can make use of this map to understand where individuals are in the overall process and, ultimately, where they need to go. Helpers can also use this model to plan specific interventions to aid those who are hurting. It is to these interventions—considering when and how to provide the best help possible—the next chapter now turns.

CHAPTER 6

INTERVENTION STRATEGIES, PART 1

Stress, Crisis, and Trauma

Working with individuals who have experienced a crisis or trauma can be both rewarding and overwhelming. When a caregiver sits with a person or family who's in the midst of tragedy, the hurt is generally palpable. But what is the best way to help those who are in pain? Where does a helper begin? Are there things to avoid, ways of relating to the hurting person that might be more harmful than helpful? Is helping in the immediate aftermath the same as helping in the weeks, months, and even years that follow? Knowing how to render aid, recognizing what is needed, and having strategies for intervention are essential for those who desire to minister to individuals in crisis. In chapter 6, we consider intervention strategies for stress, loss, and trauma. In chapter 7, we will turn our attention to interventions for the grief process. This includes consideration of what to do when a person is satisfactorily progressing through the grief journey, and also how to proceed if a person gets stuck at some point in that same journey.

A STORY OF INTERVENTION

I HAD JUST FINISHED MY LAST counseling session on a Wednesday evening. I was sitting in the church office, completing some necessary paperwork when a man poked his head into the office. "Can you tell me how to get to Wedgwood Baptist Church?" he asked. I gave directions to the man, but inquired why he was looking for that particular church. As he hurried out the door, he told me that there had been a shooting at the church, and he was a reporter for a local news station on his way to cover the event.

Wedgwood Baptist Church was not only the church home of many of my friends and students, it was located a short distance from my home. I quickly returned to my house, turned on the television, and watched aerial news coverage of the church surrounded by police, fire, and rescue vehicles. The camera zoomed in to show wounded individuals being attended by paramedics, with some being placed in CareFlight helicopters. I recognized one of the wounded as Kevin Galey, the minister of counseling at the church and one of my Ph.D. counseling students.

I called Ian Jones, a fellow counseling professor, and we briefly discussed our wisest course of action. We agreed we should go to the scene and attempt to cross the police barricades in order to offer what help we could. We arrived at the barricade and, as expected, we were stopped by a police officer. We explained who we were, counseling professors from Southwestern Baptist Theological Seminary, and we showed the officer our Licensed Professional Counselor identification cards. He let us through the barrier, and we made our way into Bruce Shulkey Elementary School, situated across the street from the church. There, the first responder personnel had located their operations. For the next several hours we did what we could to assist those working with the traumatized church members.

In the time period immediately following the shooting, the investigating officers knew that a gunman had entered the church and made his way along a corridor leading to the sanctuary. He killed and wounded several church members along this part of the church. He then entered the sanctuary, which was full of hundreds of teenagers and youth workers. They were holding a "Saw You at the Pole" worship service in conjunction with the "See You at the Pole" prayer time that had taken place throughout the city before school that morning. The shooter walked up and down the aisles of the worship center, firing several rounds, wounding and killing more individuals. He also threw a pipe bomb toward the front of the auditorium. Police later learned that after several minutes of terrorizing those in the sanctuary, the gunman sat down near the back of the auditorium, put his gun to his head, and took his own life.

As police officers arrived on the scene, they initially thought that there might be more than one gunman. Also, police officers had concerns that other explosives may have been placed in the vicinity of the sanctuary. As the wounded and nonwounded were removed from the building, no one was allowed to reenter due to the unstable nature of the situation.

Church members were brought from the church grounds to the elementary school across the street. Individuals continued searching for missing family members and friends and were obviously relieved as they located loved ones. As time went by, however, some individuals realized that relatives or friends were unaccounted for and could possibly still be in the sanctuary.

I recall looking around the school that evening, noticing all the different people doing the best they could to provide help. Some police officers and fire personnel worked on the investigation, as others provided security to the school and around the crime scene. Other individuals and church leaders worked on reuniting families and on gathering and disseminating information as it became available. Chaplains and friends sat with those who had still not located family members. Others coordinated plans for the ongoing support for the church, for the shooting victims, and for all those immediately affected by this tragedy. A local grocery store sent trays of food to those remaining in the school.

About 1 A.M., after several hours of talking and praying with those who had been in the sanctuary, my colleague and I sat down to map out an intervention strategy for what our role would be, both in the immediate future and in the days ahead. Running a large counseling center out of the seminary, we had the ability to provide assistance for the church and for the community. Similarly, because our program had 250 masters and doctoral level counseling students, we knew we had many resources for providing help.

We decided that, early in the morning, we would open our counseling center and function as a launching pad to send our counselors into local churches and schools, as well as into any other community entity that requested help. Early the next day, after providing brief training to many of our students, we began receiving the first of many phone calls with requests for counselors to help children, teenagers, and adults deal with this event, which was having a profound effect on the whole city.

Over the next few days, Dr. Jones and I met with the staff at Wedgwood as they developed plans for ministering to the congregation. We sent counselors to the next several worship services and youth gatherings to be available for anyone needing help. We worked with the youth group in a variety of different ways, providing support, as counselors met with the teenagers so directly impacted. We created ongoing counseling groups and provided individual and family counseling for teens and parents who were involved in the shooting. We provided support for SWBTS students who were members of the church, many of whom were in the auditorium during the shooting. We directly ministered to many family members of those wounded or killed in the shooting.

Even today, as I look back on the weeks and months that followed the Wedgwood shooting, I recall a time of incredible need. The event had an impact on not only the church, but on other youth groups who had teens in attendance at the worship service, local middle and high schools who had teenagers either wounded or killed, and other area churches whose teenagers had friends in the Wedgwood youth group, many of whom were holding their own "Saw You at the Pole" celebrations. Fort Worth fire and police personnel talked of the scope of the event and how even the first officers on the scene had friends in the church. Southwestern Seminary had students and graduates killed and wounded, and held the funerals for many of the victims. A warm, late summer evening in September, which started out as a worship celebration for hundreds of teenagers, turned tragic for the entire city.

While an event like the Wedgwood shooting is not common, it does lead to questions of how best to help when any traumatic experience occurs. Whether a tragedy is large scale, such as this one, or much smaller, involving only a single individual, how can counselors, ministers, and lay individuals best assist those experiencing a crisis, trauma, or loss? What are the most appropriate intervention strategies?

The previous chapter provided a crisis model, or a map of the relationship between crisis, trauma, loss, and grief. Understanding this relationship sets the stage for knowing how to intervene when an individual experiences one or more of these. A helper who can read crisis situations and recognize where hurting individuals are located in the model is in a position to provide the most effective help. Part of this help is knowing how and when to intervene. What are the key intervention points and what should caregivers do when they recognize the manner in which individuals are affected by difficult circumstances? This chapter discusses three key intervention points related to helping in times of stress, crisis, and trauma.

INTERVENTION POINT 1:
HELPING WHEN LIFE IS STRESSFUL

The first intervention point may not be obvious, but it's important, nonetheless. Also, this intervention point is generally more related to prevention than to treatment. When a helper addresses the first intervention point, the impact of crisis or trauma can be attenuated.

Even if an individual is not experiencing adverse circumstances, life is often quite stressful. The demands of daily living produce a strain on us all. As mentioned, stress itself can result in a crisis, and relatively all crises generate stress.

The first key intervention point, then, is helping people deal with stress (see fig. 6.1). This includes helping them recognize and address stress, as well as providing support as they attempt to cope effectively. If individuals cope effectively, they're in a better position to deal with crises or trauma, should they occur.

Figure 6.1. Intervention Point 1

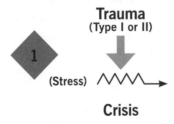

Recognizing Stress

Some people get so accustomed to the fast-paced life, they're unaware of the stress it produces. Some only become aware, in fact, when they suffer burnout or a stress-related medical condition such as heart disease or high blood pressure. Helping an individual recognize adverse stressors is a beginning point in his or her effective coping. If a person fails to recognize these stressors, he or she is unlikely to take appropriate steps to deal effectively with the negative effects.

Recognizing stress involves becoming aware of common, everyday stressors, of the stress associated with life cycle changes, and of unexpected stressors. All of these types of stressors can impact functioning, and, if too many of these occur simultaneously, problems often result.

Common stressors are produced by what is expected of a person during a typical day. These include fighting traffic to get to work, then rushing to meet a deadline set by a demanding boss. Other common stressors involve staying at home with three preschoolers, one of whom is running a fever, having an air conditioner in need of costly repairs, or dealing with an aging parent or in-law. Most individuals in modern day America face numerous daily stressors.

Stress is also the outcome when an individual transitions from one life-cycle stage to the next. Getting engaged and married, having a baby, having a child graduate, retiring from the workforce—all are examples of life-cycle changes that produce stress. Even if the life-cycle change is desired—a couple is really excited about marrying, for instance—such changes produce a great deal of stress on all involved and may deplete the energy available for coping with other life stressors.

Stress also results when the unexpected takes place. Getting reassigned or transferred at work, having a pipe freeze and burst during cold weather, or experiencing ongoing mechanical problems with a much-needed vehicle all produce stress. These unexpected sources of stress can be especially problematic when combined with other stressors a person or family encounters.

Recognizing stress is essential to effective coping. In counseling, it's not unusual for me to meet individuals who are under a great deal of stress, but who seem unaware of their stressors and are oblivious to how they are affected by them. These individuals may know that they don't feel good, or that they're having difficulty functioning well, but they don't always recognize their specific stressors. A person who knows what his or her stressors are, who is aware of how the stressors impact functioning, is in a better position to plot strategies for coping with the strain produced by life pressures.

Addressing Stress

Some individuals may recognize they're experiencing stress, but unless they deal with it effectively, they'll continue to be negatively affected by it. Many of these individuals have difficulty taking steps to reduce the stress. Addressing stress includes making good decisions about how to invest time and energy, getting adequate rest, eating properly, taking time to relax, being in a right relationship with God, and being able to say no to certain opportunities. Life often presents more than the average person can realistically accomplish. Many life

126

opportunities may be good ones, even chances to help others. Some individuals are inclined to take on too much and have difficulty turning down opportunities to take on even more. Learning to be realistic and making wise choices about how to invest time and energy helps a person avoid the mediocrity that often results from having too much to do.

Helpers, both counselors and ministers, should assist individuals as well as *when* couples and families in being realistic about how to schedule time and energy. *we do* Aiding these individuals in identifying what is essential and what is optional *this:* may help them reduce unnecessary stress and increase their personal and relational productivity. Caregivers may also serve to hold individuals accountable when they make decisions about appropriate measures for reducing problematic stress.

Churches, especially, must be cognizant about unnecessarily adding to the stress faced by individuals and families. In many churches, it's possible to attend activities several nights each week. Even Sundays, the day of rest, have tended to become days of frantic activity in churches. Church leaders can help church members by being wise in their programming and planning, avoiding overburdening those individuals who are already involved in numerous leadership and ministry activities.

By looking ahead and by thinking preventively, caregivers have the ability to help individuals reduce unhealthy stress. When we aid them in this process, we increase their emotional and physical resources should these individuals encounter crisis or trauma situations. *So this can happen*

Providing Support During Stressful Times

On many occasions, helpers will not be functioning to prevent stress but will be responding when it becomes obvious that an individual or family is struggling with stress. When we notice individuals under pressure, support becomes essential. This support can occur in a broader, informal fashion, or in the form of a counseling relationship.

Informal support entails identifying the needs of the person or family and helping to meet those needs. Needs may include encouragement, or merely a listening ear as individuals talk about what is taking place for them. Needs, on occasion, may involve such basics as food and clothing. This type of assistance reduces stress for others and encourages them to keep moving ahead.

In instances when persons are under excessive stress, counseling may be warranted. In this more formal helping relationship, the counselor assists clients in identifying and addressing stressors, in decision making, and in establishing both short-term and long-term goals. If an individual has difficulty saying no or setting boundaries, a counselor may be able to encourage and support the person as he or she attempts to do so. The effective Christian counselor can also help the individual look at the spiritual components of stress, addressing how the stressors are helping or hindering one's spiritual journey.

A basic element of caregiving is ministering to those who are struggling with stress, thereby helping them cope more effectively. Hard things do happen in life, and equipping individuals to face stress also prepares them to better cope in the event of crisis or trauma.

INTERVENTION POINT 2:
HELPING DURING CRISES

A second intervention point occurs when a person is in the midst of a crisis (see fig. 6.2). Because crises are not uncommon, knowing how and when to help is essential for those who minister to individuals in crisis circumstances. Intervening at this point involves the caregiver's assessing the nature or dimensions of the crisis event, assisting hurting individuals as they cope in the midst of crisis, and providing support to them over the course of the crisis.

Figure 6.2. Intervention Point 2

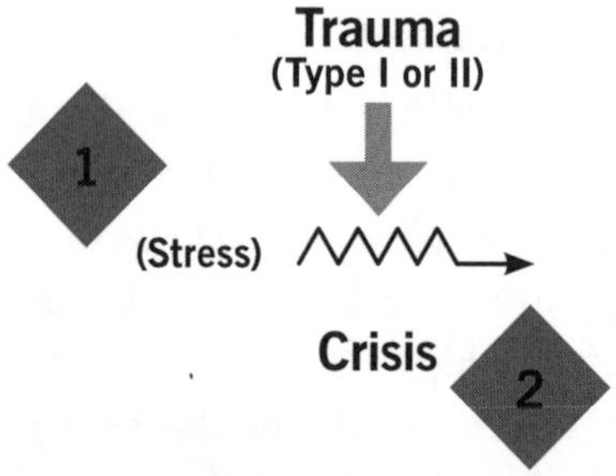

Assessing the Nature of the Crisis

From a ministry perspective, it's crucial for the caregiver to gain as much information as possible about what the person is encountering. As discussed in chapter 1, crises can be short-term or long-term, mild or severe, actual or perceived. Assessment involves an appraisal of the dimensions of the crisis event (rate of onset, severity, duration, and losses produced) as well as how equipped the crisis victim is to face the crisis (coping skills, perception of the event, available support, and number of associated stressors). Whether information is gleaned from the person experiencing the crisis or from others familiar with the situation, the helper is best prepared when he or she conducts a thorough assessment of the person's crisis. The specific nature of the crisis and how well- or ill-equipped a person is to cope will determine, to a great extent, the type of help to be offered. Determining the nature of the crisis and the elements involved is, then, the first step in dealing with the crisis.

Helping Individuals Cope During Crises

A key to helping during crises is aiding those affected as they attempt to cope. The specifics will depend, again, on the nature of the crisis.

If the crisis is sudden, and especially if it is rather severe in nature, those affected may be somewhat stunned. In many instances, people may have a number of physical needs. They may need assistance in accomplishing basic tasks such as getting groceries or seeking a place to stay for the night. Families might need help with child care or assistance with older relatives. When a crisis is sudden, those directly impacted often have difficulty assessing needs or making even simple decisions. Helping them develop an immediate plan of action can aid them through the early stages of the crisis.

If the crisis is more prolonged, some of the same physical and decision-making needs may be present. In long-term crises, too, people often need encouragement when they become weary. Knowing that others recognize the struggle and care about them helps individuals keep moving ahead through difficult times. When individuals are aware that someone else cares and that others are praying for them, that knowledge can be an invaluable source of encouragement and support.

Providing Support During Crises

Caregivers in the body of Christ should be actively involved in offering aid to hurting individuals who encounter times of crisis. This support benefits not only people surviving crisis events, but also serves to communicate the love of God in a very tangible manner.

One essential element in providing this support is being aware of resources that may assist those in difficult circumstances. The effective helper is acquainted with resources in both the church and the community. Such resources include medical resources; resources for housing, clothing, and food; resources for family crises (such as a crisis in marriage or with a teenager); and employment and legal resources. These resources may be geared toward helping an individual—as when a person unexpectedly loses a job—to larger resources following a natural disaster like flood, fire, hurricane, or tornado. It's even possible for an entity such as a church to develop a crisis or disaster response team to assist in times of disaster, a process discussed in more detail in chapter 12.

The wise caregiver is aware of available resources before help is necessary. If a helper waits until disaster strikes to address needs, that helper's effectiveness is reduced. If the helper or helping team has a plan prior to the time of need, they are more likely to meet the needs of hurting individuals and will reduce the possibility of burnout among caregivers.

Crises will happen, both to individuals and to families. In some instances, crises happen on a larger scale, involving multiple families, even entire communities. Intervening in times of crisis involves understanding elements of crisis situations, aiding crisis victims to cope with what has occurred, and providing support for those encountering times of crisis. Knowledge abut crisis events is helpful. Desire to help is crucial. Preparedness for helping is essential.

INTERVENTION POINT 3:
HELPING FOLLOWING TRAUMA

Many large-scale crisis events of the past several years have devastated individuals, communities, and even countries. One positive outcome of some of these circumstances is a greater understanding of how to work with individuals immediately following a disaster. Intervening following trauma is essential to effective crisis ministry (see fig. 6.3). When a traumatic event takes place, caregivers can utilize interventions for those involved, which have the potential to reduce the negative impact of the trauma and to help the victim more quickly return to healthy functioning.

Figure 6.3. Intervention Point 3

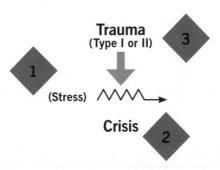

The CISM/CISD Approach

In 1997, George Everly and Jeffery Mitchell authored the book *Critical Incident Stress Management,* which set forth a comprehensive program of addressing large-scale crisis and trauma events. The purpose of their work was to develop a model that was, "an integrated and comprehensive multicomponent programmatic approach to the prevention and mitigation of crisis states and subsequent critical incident (traumatic) stress."[1] Their approach has been widely utilized in the field of disaster mental health and offers a useful framework for providing effective intervention following a traumatic event.

One specific component of the overall approach designed by Mitchell and Everly is called Critical Incident Stress Debriefing (CISD) and has a purpose of helping a group of trauma victims decompress following a crisis event. The elements of the debriefing are beneficial to utilize, as well, with individual trauma survivors in a counseling or ministry setting.

The model developed by Mitchell and Everly is not designed to be a substitute for long-term counseling. Rather, it is crafted for use in the hours and days that follow a traumatic incident and serves as a type of psychological first aid to trauma victims. In my counseling with individuals who have suffered trauma, this approach, when done well, has the ability to affect the *trajectory* of the individual's recovery. Initial intervention following trauma does not necessarily produce recovery on its own, but it helps the individual get started along the path to recovery. Identified below are some of the key elements of the CISD model with information about how to use these in a counseling or ministry setting.[2]

---

1. Everly and Mitchell, *Critical Incident Stress Management,* 11.
2. Those interested in focusing on crisis ministry or counseling should give serious consideration to taking a CISM course. Such courses are offered by the Red Cross, the American Association of Christian Counselors, or the International Critical Incident Stress Foundation.

Facts

The beginning point in intervention following trauma is inviting the individual to relate the facts regarding the trauma event. The primary importance of starting with facts is its being the least intimidating aspect of the trauma event for the survivor to recount. While some of the facts may be painful to discuss, starting here tends to be more nonthreatening than some of the other elements that will follow.

When working with an individual following trauma, I ask the person to tell me the story of what happened, usually encouraging the person to start just prior to the actual event. I might ask, for instance, "What were you doing that morning, before the event happened?" I then ask, "How did you first know something unusual was happening?" or "When did you first notice that something was wrong?" A woman who'd been robbed, for example, might tell me where she'd been heading and for what purpose, and then the first thing she specifically recalls about the robbery. I listen to the facts of the story, gleaning details about what occurred. It's essential to allow the person to talk as much as needed. The helping individual must be cautious not to talk excessively, but rather to focus on listening and briefly reflecting what he or she hears the survivor saying. Even if the helper does not agree with some of the facts, this is not the time to correct the one telling the trauma story.

When using the CISD approach in a group setting, the helping facilitator invites the group to walk through the facts of what occurred. The facilitator needs to be sensitive not to push anyone who chooses not to talk, allowing all to have the freedom to speak or to remain silent. Groups can be very powerful sources of support and help in the recovery process, and if the trauma occurred in a group setting, this type of debriefing produces many benefits. Often, in the facts stage of the group debriefing, individuals gain new pieces of information that may assist them in the overall recovery process. In some respects, the whole group works together to relate the larger story.

Thoughts

After an individual has taken me through the facts of the story, I next ask him or her to revisit the story, and this time to tell me what they recall *thinking* in the midst of the trauma event. Again, the sequencing is important. Asking the survivor to relate thoughts or feelings first tends to be intimidating, and the trauma survivor might hesitate or balk. If, however, the helper has listened well to the facts of the story, the survivor is more likely to feel comfortable in discussing the more personal components of thoughts and feelings about the event.

When individuals relate what they were thinking, their thoughts generally represent efforts to make sense out of the extreme circumstances. This was evident following the Wedgwood church shootings. Many of the young people and adults believed that the shooting was part of a skit. One individual who was wounded first believed he'd been hit by a paintball, not by a real bullet. As the gunman was shooting, a small group of middle-school boys, thinking they were witnessing a skit, stood up, waved their arms, and shouted, "Shoot me! Shoot me!" After exiting the auditorium, one young adult saw the police helicopters circling overhead and still thought that the church had rented the helicopters as part of a skit. In all these instances, individuals had difficulty processing what was occurring; their brains could not make sense out of what their eyes were seeing.

As a person relates his or her thoughts, the caregiver may notice the first signs of faulty beliefs about the event, or even types of magical thinking related to the event. Sometimes this comes in the form of the survivor taking responsibility in some way for the incident, even if he or she had nothing to do with it. The survivor, too, might second-guess his or her actions or choices. A man who'd been in a traffic accident may tell the helper that, because he went through a yellow light two blocks before the accident site, he caused the wreck to happen. If the trauma is extreme, a person's thoughts may be even more unusual or bizarre. In counseling, survivors of incest have told me how many tiles were on the ceiling of the bedroom or how many tassels hung from the lamp next to their bed. These types of thoughts are to be expected and seem to be the brain's way of attempting to process information taken in under extreme duress. Because the caregiver's primary task is listening and allowing the person to tell the story, it's not necessary to correct or challenge faulty or bizarre thinking at this point. The most useful thing a helper can do is to provide a supportive atmosphere in which the survivor feels safe enough to talk about the trauma event.

Reactions or Emotions

The third element involves asking trauma survivors to discuss their reactions to, or feelings about, what has happened. We've moved from the safest area—facts—through a more difficult area—thoughts—to an even more difficult area—the emotions that occurred during and following the trauma event.

In response, most trauma survivors identify emotions that they experienced during the event, such as fear, horror, panic, or strong anxiousness. They may discuss emotions that have emerged since the event, like anger, sadness, frustration, helplessness, or hopelessness. Survivors may disclose embarrassment at things they did or did not do surrounding the critical event. They may talk about an absence of emotions, emphasizing how numb they feel. Some individuals are quite aware of their emotions while others need prompting, or some may need assurances that it's safe to discuss their emotions. At times, a person may have an awareness of an emotion, but may need assistance in labeling it. Leading the survivor to discuss emotions calls for patience and sensitivity.

Allowing the person to talk about emotions, though, is critical. Even in the absence of physical wounds, trauma survivors almost always sustain emotional wounds. Often, the person may be ashamed of his or her emotional responses and embarrassed to talk about such matters. It's essential, then, that the helper allow the person to proceed at his or her own pace. The person has to feel safe to discuss any thoughts or emotions he or she may be experiencing. It's often the unwarranted shame a person feels that blocks the early phases of the recovery and grieving processes. Thus, helping a person verbalize these elements is essential early in the healing journey.

If a person does not identify certain emotions, the helper needs to gently inquire about them. It might be the person has experienced certain emotions, but feels the need to censor this information. I might ask, for example, if the survivor has any feelings of guilt over the events. As mentioned earlier, survivor guilt is a common outcome produced by traumatic circumstances. I try to gauge if the person is experiencing this type of guilt, and if so, how extensive it is. If the individual has not identified anger during the discussion of emotions, I inquire if they are, indeed, experiencing anger. Individuals tend to believe that certain emotions are acceptable and others are unacceptable, immature, or un-Christlike. This belief may necessitate the helper's gently prompting the trauma survivor to identify and talk about such emotions.

After we've discussed emotions for a period of time, I ask clients a question that is essential to the recovery process: "In all of this that happened, what has been most difficult, or the worst part?" This question invites the trauma survivor to put into words what continues to be the most difficult element of the entire experience. As a result of this question, the caregiver often gets a glimpse into what is bothering the survivor most about his or her ordeal.[3]

---

3. Everly and Mitchell, *Critical Incident Stress Management*, 86.

A survivor might give a response such as,

- "The most difficult part was that I just couldn't think. Everything seemed to be spinning and I had no idea of what to do. I've always prided myself on being a person of action, and I just stood there watching. I just let it happen."
- "The most difficult part has been replaying the accident over and over in my mind. Every night as I go to sleep, I see the other car coming toward me, then I can hear my wife screaming."

When a caregiver asks about this most difficult element, he or she needs to be prepared for answers that reveal the excruciating emotional pain that the survivor may be experiencing.

- "The hardest part has been wondering why God abandoned me. Where was He when I was being abused? Did He care? When I prayed, as a child, asking Him to not let it happen again, why didn't He answer me?"
- "The part I'm having a hard time getting past is the smell. I was pulling my grandmother out of her burning house and it was hard to breathe. I could smell the smoke, but then I think I could smell burning flesh. I can't get the smell out of my mind, and I feel nauseous every time I think about it."
- "The most difficult part is knowing I can never have my baby back again. I had read the books that said not to let her sleep on her stomach, but I just didn't think about it. I went in to get her after her nap and she was limp. I don't think I'll ever be able to forgive myself."

No matter how extreme the person's answer is, the caregiver must remain nonreactive. Remember, the task at this stage is not correcting the person's thinking—it is allowing the survivor a safe place to verbalize the difficult aspects of the ordeal. If the survivor identifies the central most component of what is bothering him or her, it will propel the person along the road to dealing with the trauma event in a healthier, more productive manner.

In a group setting, the facilitator invites the group to discuss emotions and asks the participants to identify the most difficult parts of their experiences. As with an individual survivor, these can be painful for the participants to discuss, as well as difficult for the helper to hear. The value in a group setting, however, is that individuals come to realize that they're not alone—others have some of the same thoughts and feelings. This sense that others understand can be most beneficial for the healing of the group members.

As mentioned, hearing the worst part of a person's trauma event can be quite difficult for the helper. It may even result in what experts identify as secondary trauma or vicarious trauma, which will be discussed in greater detail in chapter 13.

Discussing Symptoms

After allowing the survivor to talk about facts, thoughts, and emotions, the CISD model then encourages the survivor to identify specific symptoms that he or she has experienced since the trauma event. The purpose of symptom identification seems to be twofold. First, it allows the helper to hear how the trauma event has affected the survivor. It provides, in essence, a gauge for assessing the extent of the trauma or wounding experienced. Second, it aids the survivor in the valuable process of realizing that others experience similar kinds of symptoms—that the survivor is not abnormal, strange, or crazy because of how he or she has been affected.

Perhaps the best method of discussing symptoms is to have a symptom list that identifies common results of trauma (see Symptoms of Trauma, appendix A). When talking with clients about symptoms, I let them know that God has designed humans to behave in certain ways following extreme events. I tell them that, in some ways, all people react the same, and in other ways we act differently. All individuals, for example, experience symptoms following trauma. This is how our bodies and minds attempt to cope with extreme circumstances. Two individuals can, however, go through the same trauma event, but have markedly different symptoms.

Then I give them the Trauma Symptoms List that identifies cognitive, emotional, behavioral, spiritual, and relationship symptoms, as discussed in chapter 2 (see appendix A). The list also allows clients to identify whether a specific symptom occurred immediately following the trauma, emerged after a period of time, and whether or not the person is currently struggling with certain symptoms. I generally allow the person to scan the list and place a check by any symptoms they may have experienced following the trauma event. As we go over these, we usually discuss each symptom briefly.

In listening to the person identify symptoms, the caregiver must attend to two key concerns. First, the helper must be aware of any self-harm or suicidal thoughts the trauma survivor may be experiencing. Self-harm thoughts are one of the items listed on the symptoms sheet, thereby providing a natural opportunity to discuss whether or not the person is suicidal. If the person does seem to be struggling with thoughts of self-harm, the helper must take appropriate steps to ensure the person's safety. Second, trauma events can sometimes have such an extreme impact, an individual will experience symptoms that require attention of a medical specialist. If, for instance, an individual struggles with a heart condition or hypertension, that person may need to seek medical consultation. Similarly, a person who has diabetes may have adverse effects if he or she has difficulty eating properly following trauma. Thus, helpers must be alert for any conditions that might call for medical attention.

Identifying Resources

The last component of the CISD model is helping the survivor identify available resources. Caregivers can help survivors identify whom they already have available as sources for support. This may include immediate family members, other relatives, friends, fellow church members, or coworkers. I ask survivors to specify who, in their circle of support, tends to be safe and who may not seem safe. Generally, survivors have no trouble identifying those with whom they feel safe.

On occasion, a caregiver will work with a survivor who does not have adequate support. Support may be absent entirely, or it may not be currently accessible. In some instances, the survivor's sources of support were also involved in the trauma and thus are not in a position to help. In that case, the caregiver needs to be aware of other resources that may be available to the survivor. These include counseling resources, church resources, or resources in the community. Providing an individual with these resources for ongoing assistance is essential in the overall recovery process.

When discussing resources, I help the individual leave the session with an action plan regarding what to do next. Because one of the common symptoms of trauma is difficulty planning or making decisions, it's imperative that the helper aid the survivor in identifying a few basic steps or a simple plan of action.

The helper should inquire about follow-up. Is there the opportunity to touch base with the survivor in a couple of days to see how he or she is doing? Follow-up is possible in some instances, but in others, helping is a onetime encounter. If the helper is making referrals to a counselor or medical special-ist, it's best to put in writing the pertinent names and phone numbers to give to the client.

Allow Survivors to Talk, Talk, Talk

A typical response of those who've been traumatized is the need to talk about the event. Although some individuals shut down and do not talk, many feel compelled to talk about their traumatic experiences, often telling the story repeatedly. One of the most beneficial things a caregiver can do is allow the survivor to talk about what has taken place as much as he or she needs to.

Talking seems to serve the purpose of aiding the survivor in making some initial sense out of what has happened. It may give a person a feeling of having some control over what feels very much out of control. Talking also decreases the likelihood that the wounds go underground, existing only in the survivor's unspoken thoughts and memories of the event.

Friends and family members can grow impatient with a survivor's need to recount what occurred. They may believe that the survivor needs to move on, needs to quit dwelling on the past, or needs to quit focusing on the negative aspects of the event. If those close to the survivor express beliefs such as these, and if it results in the survivor not talking, the outcome is generally the oppo-site of what the loved ones ultimately desire. The recovery process is hindered.

Helpers, then, should invite survivors to talk and then listen to them in a supportive and caring way. Simple reflective statements help the survivor ex-plore the dark corners of the event. Praying with and for those survivors who are amenable also provides comfort to them. All of these elements that facilitate the hurting person's verbalizing his or her thoughts and feelings about a trau-matic experience are powerful parts of early recovery.

Normalizing the Aftermath

Another central feature of dealing with trauma survivors is normalizing the experience, the symptoms, and how the survivor is responding to the extreme events. Almost all trauma survivors I've talked to in counseling tell me, at some point, that they feel crazy. The way the person is responding to the trauma is usually foreign to how that person has functioned prior to the trauma event. Other survivors struggle with emotions, thoughts, and even with their spiritual functioning. All of this has the effect of leaving the survivor wondering if he or she is mentally unstable.

Clients are greatly relieved to know that what they're experiencing is not unusual, and, in fact, that it seems to be how God designed us. Normalizing the symptoms tends to reduce the guilt and anxiety survivors feel about how they're responding. Letting them know there is a progression or a process to recovery enables them to be patient. Reducing the anxiety that a person is damaged or crazy thus facilitates the healing and recovery process.

Because normalization is such a crucial part of trauma counseling and ministry, helpers must, as much as possible, understand the nature of trauma, how it impacts individuals, and what a normal course of recovery looks like. Helping clients understand what is typical can be invaluable to healing.

Conclusion

Stress, crises, and trauma all have the ability to negatively impact individuals, marriages, and families. Knowing how to intervene in times of stress results in strengthening individuals when they face other difficult times. Successfully intervening when an individual encounters a crisis or traumatic event reduces pain, feelings of isolation, and the sense of struggle, enabling a person to cope and move ahead with life. We now turn our attention to other intervention strategies. How can we best help when a person is grieving? How should we attempt to minister if a person seems to be stuck in the grief process, if the person demonstrates symptoms that suggest that he or she is not progressing in the grief journey? The next chapter considers intervention strategies related to both appropriate and problematic grief.

CHAPTER 7

INTERVENTION STRATEGIES, PART 2

Facilitating the Grieving Process

Whether an individual experiences a traumatic event or undergoes a significant loss, a successful recovery involves effectively traversing the grief process. Counseling and ministry interventions help individuals effectively cope with losses by providing care as these individuals adjust to the losses and grieve accordingly. Sometimes, however, an individual will become stuck; for various reasons, the person ceases to progress along the grief journey. When this occurs, intervention involves helping those who are hurting to enter or reenter the grieving process, with the ultimate goal of their moving toward more effective means of coping. Each of these two interventions is explored in this chapter.

INTERVENTION POINT 4: FACILITATING HEALTHY GRIEVING

Following a significant trauma or crisis, many individuals desire to fully recover from the losses sustained. They may recognize the necessity of grief and of the overall process associated. Other individuals are less clear about what is needed or of how to act or feel in the aftermath of a personal tragedy. The task for the counselor or minister is to help facilitate the grieving process and thereby aid the person in effectively coping with what has taken place (see fig. 7.1). Intervention tasks in this portion of caregiving include helping the person tell his or her story, identifying symptoms of grief and components of the grief process, determining how the person grieves, identifying and mobilizing support for the grieving individual, helping the person face and deal with spiritual components of what is occurring, aiding individuals in developing appropriate rituals for grieving, and providing assistance for planning and decision making in the period following the loss. We now consider each of these tasks in more detail.

Figure 7.1. Intervention Point 4

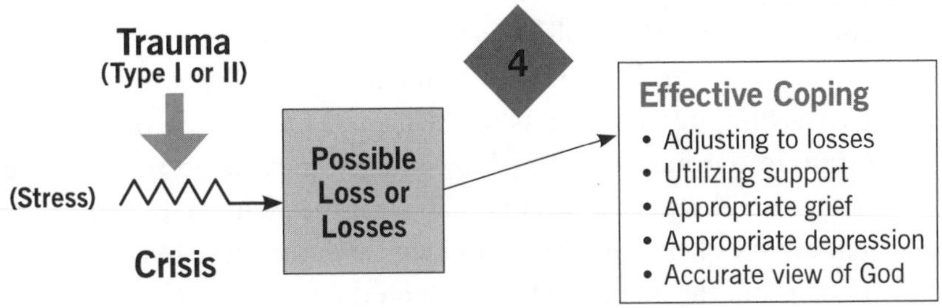

Helping Individuals Tell Their Stories

The beginning point of working with individuals in the grieving process is helping them relate the story of their loss. Whether the loss is due to trauma or a more general type of loss, like the death of a loved one, the story is beneficial in a couple of important respects. First, the story provides information to the caregiver, allowing him or her to have a clearer picture of the nature of the loss and of the resulting grief. Everyone's story is unique, and because each person responds differently to losses, the story is the beginning point for the helper to connect with, understand, and ultimately, minister effectively to the hurting person. Second, telling the story also benefits the hurting person. Often, the hurting person will not have related the entire loss story to anyone. Merely recounting the story in the presence of a caring, supportive individual is a powerful component in the healing process.

When I work with people following loss, I ask them to tell me their stories, in much the same manner as I do following trauma events. I ask them to tell me the facts of what occurred and the details of what they recall of their loss event, their thoughts about their losses, and then any emotions they've dealt with as a result of their losses. If the losses are the deaths of loved ones, I ask clients to tell me how they learned of their loved one's death, as well as thoughts and emotions associated to that time. I allow them to tell their entire stories and let them know I'm actively listening. It is essential that I understand details of what has taken place, because in succeeding sessions, my clients and I will return to their stories many times.

Bringing a Picture

When grieving involves the death of a loved one, I generally ask the survivor to bring a picture of the deceased person to one of our first sessions. If the survivor agrees to bring a picture, I encourage the person to choose a photograph that is particularly representative of the deceased loved one. In most cases, the survivor will be more than willing to bring a picture; often, clients immediately have a picture in mind. It's not uncommon for the survivor to bring several pictures showing different facets of their loved one. When the client brings the picture to our next meeting, I encourage the client to tell me about the loved one, what this person was like, and what the picture represents about the person. I ask the client what I need to know about the loved one if I'm to most fully understand the impact of the death on the hurting person.

Pictures are powerful representations of the loved one. Not only does the picture aid the caregiver in knowing the impact of the loss on the survivor, the discussions surrounding the picture tend to facilitate the early grieving process. The caregiver should realize, however, that when a person brings a picture to a session, it will often evoke memories of the loved one and strong feelings of sadness associated with the loss. The helping individual must be aware of the emotions the picture can evoke and must also be supportive of the hurting individual as he or she reminisces about the loved one.

Making a Loss Timeline

If, in meeting with a grieving individual, I recognize that he or she is dealing with multiple losses or grief events, it's important that I understand the nature and sequencing of these events. Oftentimes, an individual focuses on the most current loss or the most painful loss, not recognizing how other losses may also be contributing to the grieving process. When an individual has experienced numerous losses, I generally have the person make a timeline or a history of significant loss events. This timeline of losses helps me see the sequence and spacing of losses, and also allows the hurting individual to gain a perspective on the number of losses that may be having an impact on him or her. Wright advocates working with hurting individuals to create a timeline, which identifies the range of losses the person has experienced, including a description of the loss, the date each loss occurred, and the intensity of the loss.[1]

---

1. Wright, *New Guide to Crisis and Trauma Counseling*, 65–66.

Scaling Losses

If an individual has experienced multiple significant losses, I ask that person to scale the impact of the losses. Simply put, I ask the person to rate, on a scale of 1 to 10 (with 10 being the most powerful), how much each loss is affecting him or her. Scaling allows me to have a clearer read on how the losses are influencing the person, information that is not necessarily evident by just having the person tell his or her story. Part of my reason for using scaling is that I've made faulty assumptions in the past, thinking that the most current loss was bothering a person most, only to discover through scaling that an earlier loss was much more significant. If a person reports past losses, it also sets the stage for identifying how the person tended to grieve over these earlier losses, as we will discuss later in this chapter.

Asking for and listening to the story, then, is the essential starting point in the helping process. The caregiver must be patient, supportive, and caring, and must allow the hurting person to do the vast majority of the talking. Caregivers must refrain from the often powerful temptations to correct the story, to cheer up the hurting person, or to try to fix the problem. Unlike Job's friends, helpers should avoid explaining how the world works to the one suffering the loss. Support and caring go a great distance in establishing a safe, trusting relationship in which the hurting person is allowed to grieve.

Identifying Symptoms of Grief

Grief, like trauma, produces certain symptoms. These symptoms tend to be more pronounced when the loss is great, as in the death of a loved one. Some people are able to recognize the connection between certain symptoms and their grief, while others seem to be unaware of how these are related. Some individuals even seem disconcerted that they're experiencing various symptoms as they grieve. Having individuals identify how the grief is affecting them cognitively, emotionally, and behaviorally is beneficial in the early grieving process. This may be accomplished through the use of a Grief Symptoms sheet (see example in appendix B), used in much the same manner as when discussing trauma-related symptoms with a trauma survivor. Identification of symptoms may also be accomplished by asking hurting individuals to describe how their grief affects their functioning. The helper listens as they do so, prompting them about certain symptoms they may fail to mention.

As with trauma survivors, a great value in discussing grief symptoms is normalizing the impact of grief on the survivor's mind and body. At this point, it is often beneficial to refer the hurting person to some of the numerous Scripture passages or Bible figures who deal with grief. As mentioned above, some who experience grief are troubled by the symptoms, some even concluding that such symptoms are a sign of weakness, lack of faith, or even an indication of mental instability. Normalization of symptoms as a reaction to loss helps remove these often unspoken concerns and provides support to the hurting person.

For some individuals, it may be appropriate to refer them to written resources that talk about loss or grief. Grief-related resources that discuss common symptoms help the grieving person recognize that the presence of symptoms is not unusual. The caregiver should keep in mind, however, that many grieving individuals do not have the energy to read lengthy or detailed information about grief. The helper must exercise caution when making recommendations of this nature, lest a further burden is added to an individual's grieving process.

On rare occasions, when a person is grieving, symptoms may require medical attention. If, for instance, a person is experiencing chest pains or having difficulty breathing, the person should contact a family physician for a medical workup. If a client expresses any kind of self-harm thoughts following a significant loss, the helper must take appropriate steps to ensure the hurting person's safety. If a caregiver is unsure of what these steps may be, consultation with a licensed counselor will provide information about assessing risk and about necessary actions to take if there is clear risk. If a person is struggling with self-harm thoughts, referral to a professional counselor is generally a wise move.

Determining How the Person Grieves

As discussed, some elements of grief are similar for everyone, but some facets are very personal and individual—each person grieves in his or her own way. Helping in the grief journey, though, involves identifying how the person grieves. This information is beneficial to the caregiver as it shapes the type of assistance provided. It's also useful to the grieving individual as it can assist that individual in understanding what is occurring as well as provide guidance as the hurting person navigates the grief journey.

There are an unlimited number of elements to how individuals grieve. A few of these include whether a person grieves privately or publicly, the role of friends in grief, whether the grief is experienced cognitively or emotionally, whether or not a person desires help as he or she grieves, and specific time frames when coping is easier or more difficult. The helper can watch for clues about each of these and can work with the grieving person to assist him or her in discovering the unique manner in which grief occurs.

Public Versus Private

Some grieving individuals do not want to be around other people. For many, struggling with grief in the presence of another person is intimidating and complicates an already difficult process. Other grieving individuals want contact with loved ones and friends. They're comfortable grieving publicly. For these individuals, being in close proximity to others helps them progress in the grief journey. The caregiver can assist a grieving person in identifying whether it's preferable to grieve publicly, privately, or both. Granting permission to the grieving person to express hurt in the setting where the person is most comfortable can be a great benefit.

The Role of Friends

Friends and other supporters often make a significant difference in helping a grief-stricken individual. Knowing that others care and are supportive is often crucial to recovery from a significant loss. By the same token, the behavior of some well-meaning friends may actually hinder the grief process.

A caregiver should work with the grieving person to identify friends in the person's world, and whether or not these friends would help or hinder the grief process. The helper can find out from grieving individuals what role they desire friends to play. Some grieving individuals want friends readily available. In these instances, regular contact with friends facilitates the grief journey. Others may want friends to check in at certain intervals to see how the hurting person is doing. Still others in the midst of grief want friends to allow them time and space. This may mean friends are available if the grieving person requests something from them.

Sometimes just clarifying the role of friends and other supporters greatly benefits the hurting person. The hurting person may need assistance in communicating to friends what role they are needed to play. This could occur in the form of a direct conversation with friends or it may be in a letter sent to the hurting individual's friends. The caregiver may role-play such interactions with the grieving person or may read a letter before it is sent to friends. On some occasions, a hurting person may agree to have a counseling session with the helper and some key friends to discuss the best methods of helping the hurting person grieve. In my experience, when friends know what is needed or desired by the grieving person, they are more than willing to do whatever is requested. Often, friends do not know what is needed and the hurting person may not know how to communicate needs to friends. Clarifying needs with both the hurting individual and with friends assists the grief process.

Cognitive Versus Emotional Responses

Some individuals experience a range of emotions with grief. Others are more restricted in their emotional expressions and may function more cognitively, desiring to make sense out of the loss. The wise helper recognizes a person's approach to grief, whether it is more cognitive or emotional. Providing support in line with how the person grieves helps facilitate the process.

Some grieving individuals that a caregiver encounters have received numerous faulty messages about grief. They may view any expression of emotion as a sign of weakness or even as a lack of faith. Men, especially, may struggle with emotions. Being taught in American society that "big boys don't cry" and that "men are tough" may make it difficult for males to recognize or feel certain emotions. Other individuals grow up in families where certain emotions are off-limits. Anger and sadness are two of the most common emotions that are often considered wrong or bad. Because these two emotions frequently accompany grief, if a person doesn't feel permitted to be sad or angry, his or her grief process tends to slow or stop.

Those working with grieving individuals need to be attuned to personal and family messages about emotions and whether or not these emotions are acceptable expressions of grief. Granting the person permission to experience emotions, noting biblical references to a range of emotions, and making a person feel safe if they do experience emotions are all part of helping that person grieve.

For some, the struggle takes place on a more cognitive level. They may wrestle with questions about the loss, about how they're experiencing the loss, and even about the overall grief process. Allowing these individuals safety to talk, explore, question, and even to doubt is generally necessary as they progress in the grief journey.

The helper allows the person, whether functioning from a cognitive or affective perspective, to express him- or herself and provides the structure and the encouragement for them to do so. Because most individuals experience both cognitive and affective components to grief, the helper should be proficient in facilitating each of these.

Wanting Help Versus Valuing Independence

Following a significant loss, some individuals need and value the help of others. When friends and neighbors offer to bring meals and care for the lawn of the grieving person, that person sees it as helpful and beneficial. Other individuals may see it as intrusive and as treating them as if they were weak and incapable. Whereas one person may struggle to keep the yard following a loss, another may see yard work as a welcome outlet that helps facilitate coping.

Identifying whether an individual desires independence following a loss or whether he or she needs to temporarily rely on others can prove of great benefit to the grieving individual. On some occasions, the caregiver will aid grieving individuals in identifying what they need to do for themselves and for what, specifically, they need assistance. Once hurting individuals have clarified where they need assistance, the helper can aid them in communicating these needs to friends, or can direct them to church or community resources that are able to offer such assistance.

Identifying Specific Times When Grief Is Problematic

One of the most important tasks a helper can accomplish is to help the hurting person in identifying the pattern of grief: When is it more intense? When does the intensity lessen? What are the most difficult situations to encounter? Identifying patterns of how grief tends to ebb and flow can be of great value in working with a grieving person. To help identify times when grief is more intense or problematic, I often utilize the Holiday/Anniversary Checklist (see appendix C), which allows me to tell times of the day, week, or year that are more difficult for the grieving individual.

I commonly ask a grieving individual if certain times of the day are more difficult. This might be waking up in the morning and first remembering the loss. It might be in the evening when a person has a daily reminder of loneliness. It may be at nighttime when the hurting person dreams of a lost loved one.

Similarly, I inquire about times in the week that are more problematic. For some, work is a welcome relief from grief, whereas for others, the inability to concentrate or function productively is a constant reminder of the loss. Some individuals find that going to church alone is a stark reminder of the loneliness they experience.

Identifying times of the day, week, or month that are potentially tricky or difficult allows the helper to work with the individual to craft plans for coping.

If an individual has trouble in the evenings, it may help him or her to get together with friends or take an evening class at a local community college. If Sundays are difficult, the hurting person may ask a friend to transport him or her to church. When a person is hurting, it may be a good time to read a certain psalm or another comforting Bible passage or to spend time in prayer. Caregivers can help the person identify methods of coping, which can be implemented at specific difficult times and can aid in dealing effectively with those times.

As discussed earlier, the helper must be especially aware of holidays and of particular markers that are clear reminders of the loss. A caregiver should attempt to determine which holidays or anniversaries may be difficult for an individual. As with so many other components of grief, there's a great deal of variation in how persons can be affected by holidays. One of my counseling clients was dreading the upcoming Christmas holiday but was looking forward to Thanksgiving. At the same time, another grieving client dreaded Thanksgiving, but had no concerns about Christmas. While each person reacts differently, holidays commonly serve as reminders of pain and loss that a person has experienced.

In working with counseling clients, I try to be cognizant of relevant holidays or anniversary markers that might impact them. I bring up the issue of holidays several weeks prior to the occasion, with the intent to assess how well equipped or how anxious the client feels as he or she looks ahead to these times. This assessment allows me to work with the client to develop specific plans for making it through holidays and anniversaries.

While paying attention to when things are more difficult is an essential component of effective helping, it's also important to be aware of times when the hurting person seems to feel better. A hurting person may inform the helper that he or she feels better when exercising regularly, for example. Another individual may dread going to church, but feels better when doing so. One client of mine hated to express emotions such as sadness, and really disliked to cry. This client noticed, however, that when he felt the need and allowed himself to experience the emotions related to grief, he felt better. He described the result as a sense of relief, followed by feelings of peace. Knowing that he felt better when he expressed emotions permitted us to discuss ways he could allow himself to do just that.

Caregivers who are involved in working with grieving individuals must recognize the range of ways that people experience grief. Identifying how grief occurs for a person and providing support when things are difficult are essential to facilitating the grief journey. Not doing so risks hindering or stopping the larger grief journey.

Identifying and Utilizing Support

An essential component of helping those who grieve is assisting them in identifying and making use of available support. The grief journey is difficult, and individuals usually feel isolated as they struggle following loss. While support of loving friends and relatives will not make the pain disappear, it may make the pain more bearable.

A helper can aid grieving individuals in recognizing sources of support. I ask the individual to identify those who might be able to help as he or she grieves. Most often, the individual will identify relatives, friends, neighbors, or fellow church members. The grieving person may have stories of how certain individuals have already provided useful assistance.

Some individuals are adept at accepting the support of others. Some, however, have difficulty accepting help. At times, a grieving person may need encouragement to accept the support of others, of allowing others to sustain the grieving person in difficult times. If a hurting individual can accept the support of others, he or she may have a smoother recovery process.

At times, though, individuals in the life of a hurting person, despite best intentions, cause more problems than they solve. These could be persons who are nosy, wanting details that hurting people are not ready to divulge. These may be persons who evoke feelings of guilt, questioning why the grieving individuals are still struggling. These could be religious friends who offer simplistic, unhelpful platitudes or try to explain what has happened. Often, grieving individuals need assistance in buffering themselves from such acquaintances. I often coach clients to develop short, succinct phrases they can use with such individuals. The hurting person may say, "This is hard, but I'm doing okay right now," or "I'm coping as best I can; I'll be sure to let you know if I need anything." Simple phrases such as these allow the hurting person to be polite but to keep a safe emotional distance between him- or herself and the well-intentioned but unhelpful friend.

On many occasions, support of friends, family, neighbors, and church will be enough to help the grieving person travel through the process. In some cases, however, a grief support group or more formal counseling might be a highly useful course of action. Many churches and communities offer grief support groups, and such groups allow individuals to gain information and grieve in the company of others who've experienced similar losses. Some groups, for example, are designed for widows and widowers. Others help people deal with the grief associated with divorce. Still other support groups assist individuals and families who have experienced the impact of cancer or some other terminal illness.

Grief groups for children and teenagers can be especially beneficial, as they are often led by people with expertise in helping children and teens grieve and adjust. Groups can be powerful sources of support, allowing a person to see that others are experiencing similar reactions to losses and the related difficulties.

Occasionally, a helper will encounter a person who has very little support following a loss. Some individuals may be estranged from family members and may have few friends who could potentially lend support. Other individuals lack the social skills for developing social networks, which can be so helpful in times of crisis or tragedy. Still others may have loving, caring families but live such a great distance away from them that the family is of little support in the person's day-to-day functioning. The skilled helper should, then, be knowledgeable of whether a hurting person has a support network, be cognizant of alternate sources of support, and be proficient at accessing such support on behalf of hurting individuals. Any caregiver who spends much time dealing with grieving persons must develop his or her own support networks that can be activated or utilized to aid those in the grief process. The network may involve churches offering grief support groups, as well as having in place a process of counselor referral for grieving individuals. It may involve specialized training in working with those who encounter grief. It will surely involve talking to others in the local church and in the community who are potential sources of support. In essence, often the main task of the caregiver is to weave together a safety net for the hurting person. In doing so, the helper greatly increases the likelihood that the hurting person will move through the grief process in a healthy, productive manner.

Assessing and Exploring Spiritual Resources

An ongoing helping relationship with a grieving individual becomes an excellent opportunity to assess and explore a person's relationship with God. Whether or not the hurting person has accepted Christ as Savior, the caregiver must be aware of the individual's spiritual status and level of spiritual maturity.

If the person is a believer, his or her understanding of God, sense of God's role in the loss, and religious practices and beliefs should be a regular facet of counseling discussions. When counseling a believer who's suffered a loss, I listen carefully, and gently probe in an effort to assess how that person views his or her relationship with God. I'm careful, in the early phases of the counseling relationship, not to explain what I think is happening (remember Job's friends), or even to correct questionable theology. I focus on being supportive and caring as the believer journeys through grief. After we've established a clear, working relationship, however, I'm generally more open in asking questions about the person's faith and attempting to determine whether it's a source of help or if the believer is struggling with some part of his or her religious belief system. When I meet with believers, we frequently consider Scripture passages, stories of Bible figures, or discuss matters related to their overall relationship with Christ. I may even ask them to do some assignment between sessions that involves a particular Scripture passage, Bible figure, devotional reading, or prayer activity. Any activity of this nature is designed to help individuals clarify their general understanding of God and, more specifically, the role God plays in the losses they've experienced.

On occasion I counsel with a person who does not profess a relationship with Christ. I exercise caution in how I deal with these individuals about spiritual matters. While I always talk with clients about spiritual matters at some point in our counseling relationship, timing is a crucial determiner of when I do so. If I mention God too soon, a client may flee the therapy relationship and I forfeit any opportunity I may have to work with the individual. If I wait too long, I might miss a wonderful opportunity to share some element of the good news with the client. Many of those clients are amazingly open to consider spiritual matters. These clients are often pondering life and death, ultimate purpose, meaning of life, and such matters when they've experienced a significant loss. I don't believe this openness invites my telling them everything I know. Praying for the guidance of the Holy Spirit in these instances, however, I try to be sensitive to the situation and to appropriate times and methods of talking with them about matters of faith.

Helping the Grieving Person Cope

Another important facet of working with grieving individuals is guiding them in the process of coping with what has taken place. This guidance can have a very immediate component, such as helping them make short-term decisions,

Hands
+
Feet

or providing assistance with aspects of daily functioning. It may also have a more long-term component, including identifying future plans and goals.

Guiding the client in daily functioning includes inquiring about such matters as grocery shopping or paying bills on time. I've worked with clients on developing "to-do" lists of daily tasks. A counselor friend of mine had a grieving client who was struggling to stay current with his bills. The counselor had the client bring the bills to the session, and the counselor and client worked together to make the appropriate payments.

A grieving person's coping can be specifically related to certain decisions. A widow may need to make some financial decisions following the death of her husband. Another person may need to decide whether to stay in a current location or move closer to other relatives. Some decisions involve such matters as their visiting a gravesite on a trip home or what to do about purchasing a headstone. All these types of decisions are important to discuss in counseling. Questions, though, that specifically relate to the deceased individual and to the grief journey should be handled carefully. Remember, no two people grieve alike. The counselor needs to ask him- or herself, "What's in the best interest of this specific client?"

Some grieving persons want to make sudden, extreme changes. I've seen individuals begin dating and get married within a short time following the loss of a spouse. I've seen others quit jobs or careers, change churches, or drop out of meaningful activities. The desire for sudden change is understandable, but often precipitous changes produce unexpected and even unwanted consequences. While it's not the helper's job to advocate for or against changes an adult client wants to make, it is prudent to encourage the person not to make rash decisions.

Honoring the Memory of a Deceased Loved One

As an individual travels through the grief process, one of the biggest struggles the person faces is how he or she can move on with life, but continue to honor the memory of the loved one. Accomplishing this is one of the most crucial tasks in the overall recovery process, but one that often keeps people locked in the grief journey. If a person starts to feel better, he or she may immediately experience guilt, believing he or she is somehow dishonoring the memory of the loved one. At the same time, however, a grieving person often acknowledges that the loved one would want the survivor to move on, to get on with life. This dilemma is not easily resolved, and it often persists for months as a person deals with the grief.

To help individuals with this particular dilemma, I have them identify specific ways they can honor their deceased loved one. I ask them to develop ways of moving on with life while intentionally incorporating the good things about their loved ones as they travel forward.

Commemorating a lost loved one may include specific rituals performed in memory of the deceased person. This might mean putting fresh flowers or season-appropriate decorations on the gravesite. It might mean joining some organization in honor of the loved one. Many parents who lose a child to an accident or illness will join organizations in which they can work to alleviate a particular societal problem—drunk driving, for instance. Gathering with relatives and friends and relating stories, both serious and humorous, about the deceased loved one is an excellent way to honor his or her memory. I often ask a grieving person to list the characteristics that they most admire about the deceased loved one. When the grieving person finishes the list, I ask which characteristic they would like to more incorporate into their own life in honor of the loved one. If the deceased person was brave, for instance, I ask the client where they may be able to express courage in order to honor their loved one. Honoring the memory of the deceased loved one frees the hurting individual to move ahead with life without the sense of guilt that often accompanies progress.

Listening for the Context for Acceptance

As I help a person deal with the grief that results from loss, I listen for a developing context for acceptance. There's no specific timetable for this to occur, but it's not unusual to hear elements of it as a person progresses in the grief journey. In a counseling session with a young widower, he told me, "What I'm going through is difficult, but I can see many ways that God was providing for me, both prior to and following the death of my wife." This particular comment did not mean the individual had completed his journey through grief. There would still be many difficult days ahead for him. He was, however, beginning to notice and express a clear sense of God's care through his most difficult times. It is this type of recognition of the bigger picture that suggests the development of a context for acceptance that will be of help to him as he continues to grieve.

As individuals begin to recover from loss, I continue to provide support. Instead of meeting every week, we may meet every other week, then once a month. As time passes, I see these people adjusting, growing, and moving ahead with life and with relationships. When I notice these types of markers, I know that my work with the person is approaching completion and that their journeys with grief are nearing the point where they can continue without my assistance. While the grief journey may persist for quite some time, it will generally be less painful as the person reaches a point of having hope and of desiring to move ahead with life.

Final Thoughts About Healthy Grieving

One of the complications in helping a person successfully work through grief is that it's difficult to determine when a person has arrived, when the person has completed the grief process. In the early days, grief can be intense and unmistakable. Later, it's more intermittent, becoming less powerful over time. This can lead to the question, "When will I be over the grief?"

I believe that a person can progress through the grief journey and successfully resolve the hurt and pain that accompany grief. This doesn't mean, however, that the person will reach a point where he or she never feels grief, where it's gone completely. Grief seems to occur something like ocean waves. At first, the waves are big, strong, and unmistakable. Later, as the person works through the grief, the waves tend to rise and fall, sometimes in an almost rhythmic pattern. Late in the process, the waves are much smaller, although still there. Even if individuals recover well, they may still experience periods of grief long after the loss occurred. Following the death of a loved one, for instance, a person may travel successfully through the grief process, but may still feel pangs of grief even years later. This is not unusual and does not mean the person has failed to grieve. Generally, if the person has worked through the grief, he or she will deal with these unexpected waves in a healthy, productive manner. Christian caregivers can be aware that even if a person recovers from loss, feelings of grief may arise long after sustaining the loss. Sensitivity to this possibility and support for individuals will help them in the overall process of dealing with grief.

INTERVENTION POINT 5: WORKING WITH INDIVIDUALS STUCK IN THE GRIEVING JOURNEY

It's not uncommon for a caregiver to come across a person who has not successfully worked through the grief process. This encounter may take many forms. The person may contact a caregiver, seeking help, realizing he or she is stuck. Other individuals may confide that they have a general sense that they're not doing well or that something seems wrong in their lives, not recognizing their struggle as related to trauma or loss. Still others may seek help for some issue completely unrelated to grief, but the helper recognizes the connection of the unresolved grief to the person's presenting concern.

In each of these instances, the task is the same: helping individuals enter or reenter the grief process and aiding them as they progress accordingly (see fig. 7.2). At this intervention point, the goal is to determine if a person is, indeed, stuck—assessing whether or not he or she needs to grieve losses; if so, identifying why the person is stuck; and launching the individual in the direction of effective coping. We'll also briefly focus on what to do if the person's rewards for remaining stuck are greater than the benefits that result from active involvement in the grief process

Figure 7.2. Intervention Point 5

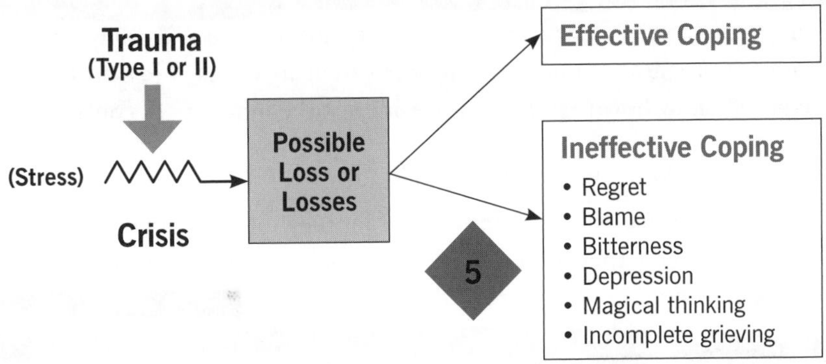

Making Accurate Assessments

When a caregiver senses that a person may not be progressing through the grief process, it's necessary to make a thorough assessment to determine whether or not this is the case. Assessment should concentrate in a couple of specific areas.

Assessing the Person's Loss History

If a person seeks out a minister or counselor, he or she may clearly identify losses experienced. Other individuals are less aware of the connection between specific losses and their current struggle. If this seems to be the case, I ask the person to briefly walk through his or her history and help me understand key events in his or her life. As the individual does this, I listen for losses. Some are apparent, such as any death of a loved one. I pay attention not only to concrete losses, but try to identify other events that might not be identified as losses or may be more abstract or ambiguous in nature. I attempt also to determine whether losses were less significant or had a more far-reaching impact on the client. I can generally determine impact by having the person scale the impact, as discussed earlier. The goal in this part of the assessment is getting an accurate read on what has taken place for the person and how it has affected him or her.

Assessing Grief Related to Identified Losses

Once I've identified the client's losses, I attempt to discover whether the client ever grieved the losses. Some clients have sustained numerous losses but have never grieved them. It's not unusual to find a person who has even experienced a tragic, extensive loss, but has never grieved. Other individuals have begun the grieving process, but for one reason or another have not progressed. They may have become stuck in their attempt to cope and adjust to the loss. Information gained from assessing the extent to which a person has grieved helps me know how to proceed as we address the individual's concerns.

Identifying Why a Person Is Stuck

Individuals become stuck in the grief journey for a variety of reasons. Some individuals know they're stuck, resulting in a great deal of frustration to them. Others may not even be aware of the need to grieve. Determining what brings individuals to a point where they're not progressing is pivotal in knowing how to help them move ahead.

Fear

Some persons fail to grieve due to fear associated with loss and with the grief process in general. Many clients have told me that they're afraid to start grieving for fear that they'll never be able to stop. These individuals feel as if they're standing on the edge of a cliff and afraid to take the step over the edge—they sense that if they take this step, they'll fall into a bottomless pit. When I hear this, I let them know that this is a common fear related to grieving. I also let them know that the fear of what grieving will be like—the fear that they'll start falling and won't be able to stop—is usually greater than the reality.

Other clients may fear expressing emotions or looking weak if they grieve. Some fear a general loss of control. Still others may fear some kind of punishment from God if they grieve. The latter can be a productive area to listen for and explore magical thinking, as discussed earlier.

It Feels Wrong to Grieve

Other individuals become stuck because it feels wrong to grieve. Such individuals might envision it wrong to express emotions or thoughts about their losses, believing that they're being weak or are expressing an absence of faith if they grieve. If individuals harbor some prohibition against grieving, it usually comes from family, cultural, or religious messages about the wrongness of grieving. If a person believes grieving is wrong, it's productive for the helper to explore the messages the person may have received about grief. Pointing the person to the numerous Bible passages and stories in which grief is a part of life is beneficial in working with such an individual.

Grieving Is Painful

Some individuals fail to grieve because grief hurts. When this person approaches the grief process, the pain associated causes him or her to back away from the process. Thus the person becomes stuck. We live at a time in which many people do what feels good and avoid what feels bad. If a person tends to function out of this unfortunate framework, he or she will probably avoid the pain associated with grief. This individual may try to distract him- or herself from the pain through any number of activities, some of which are destructive. Other activities may be more honorable, but equally problematic in the long run. I've known individuals to distract themselves from the pain of losses through throwing themselves into work, academic pursuits, even into ministry. Other individuals may not try to distract themselves from the pain but may merely deny that the pain is present and that grief is necessary. Whatever the cause, the person is driven to reduce, deny, or distort the pain. Paradoxically, individuals often trade the alleviation of short-term, immediate pain for pain that appears at a later time.

Lack of Knowledge

Some individuals fail to grieve because they don't know that grieving is necessary. Thus, they go through life, doing the best they can, but after a significant loss, they may not be aware of the role grief plays in the overall recovery from loss. Other individuals may be aware that grief is necessary, but they may lack knowledge of how to grieve. In American society, few avenues are available where an individual can learn how to grieve. When individuals experience losses, they're most often left to figure out the grief process as best they can. We offer few classes or seminars for grieving individuals. Some people may acquire knowledge about grief through reading, through a friend who's experienced loss, or through some form of support group. Most individuals, however, have little information about grief and may become stuck due to an information deficit.

When I work with individuals who've experienced crisis, loss, trauma, or grief, I show them a map of how these concepts relate to each other, as presented in chapter 5. Counseling clients commonly refer back to this map, identifying where they are in the grief journey or noting progress they've made. The information about grief seems to be quite beneficial in helping people to move ahead following a loss.

Busyness or an Active Pace of Life

It's not uncommon for me to encounter a person who knows that grief is necessary, but has had difficulty grieving due to the busyness of life. Even though a person may experience a significant loss, he or she may not feel the freedom to slow down and ponder the meaning of the loss. Sometimes, individuals believe that if they slow down to grieve, they won't be able to keep pace with various life responsibilities, like work or educational pursuits. A mother of young preschoolers might have difficulty in slowing the pace of her life to grieve a loss. Similarly, a businessperson may lose his or her job if they don't keep up with demands in the workplace.

I encounter students who, during a semester, have experienced some tragedy such as the death of a parent or some other close relative. Students tell me that they can't afford to dwell on the loss or they won't be able to focus adequately to finish the semester. Temporarily delaying grief is not always a bad thing. Sometimes certain demands of life must be met. The problem occurs when a person continually endeavors to stay busy and never stops to grieve, or a person attempts to stay busy in an effort to avoid grief. It's possible to arrange one's life to function at such a pace that the person altogether avoids addressing sadness, pain, loss, or grief. When a helper encounters a person functioning in this manner, the individual is often stuck in the grief process.

The Belief That One Should Be Exempt from Grief

On occasion, I encounter a person who's stuck in the grief process, believing that he or she should be exempt from grieving. This person is often a member of the helping professions such as counselors, social workers, and ministers. The exemption belief even appears in counselors who specialize in working with trauma and grief. The faulty belief seems to run something like this: "Because I know about grief, I shouldn't have to experience grief." While knowledge of how the grief process works can be beneficial, it does not give a person a free pass to avoid the grief that comes associated with trauma or loss.

A variation on those who think they should be able to avoid grief are those who are constantly looking for a shortcut or a way to speed through the process. Again, I see this in many counselors and ministers. These individuals often express surprise at how much the grief hurts, even if they work with those who are grieving. They also tell me they know they need to grieve, but they want to do it as rapidly and efficiently as possible. When this occurs, I convey to these individuals that I know no shortcut to grief, and that everyone's timetable is different. Information of this nature generally helps individuals slow down and identify where they need to focus as they attempt to deal with losses.

Grief Fatigue

One of the most common reasons individuals get stuck as they attempt to grieve is that they become weary in the process, run out of energy, and eventually slow or stop progressing. Many are not avoiding, denying, or running from the grief, but rather their resources for coping have become depleted. Fatigue related to grief is easily understandable. Grieving takes time, effort, and a great deal of emotional and physical energy. Clients commonly tell me that they're tired of grieving and just want to be finished. When encountering individuals who are fatigued in the grief journey, caregivers must recognize the necessity of providing support, not just at the beginning of the journey, but throughout the entire process.

Individuals get stuck in the grief process for any number of reasons, and it's not unusual for a person to be simultaneously dealing with several of the elements identified above. Recognizing why a person is stuck is crucial to helping them move ahead.

Launching Individuals Toward Effective Coping

When individuals are stuck, whether they have never grieved or if they began and ran out of energy, the task is to launch them in the direction of effectively coping with losses and grieving in a healthy manner (see fig. 7.3).

Figure 7.3. Launching Toward Effective Coping

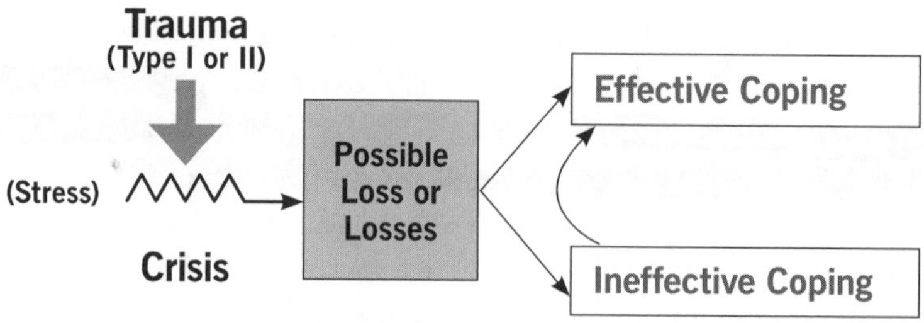

Modified Facts, Thoughts, Feelings Intervention

If an individual seems stuck, I do something similar to my initial intervention with those who have undergone a traumatic experience. I have the individual walk me through the facts, thoughts, and feelings of the trauma or loss events they've experienced. I have them do this whether the loss occurred in the recent past or if it took place years ago. I frequently encounter a struggling client who's never told another human about difficult things he or she experienced. Having individuals tell the story and listening in a caring, supportive manner serves the function of launching them in the direction of facing and dealing with the difficult situation. I still find myself amazed that individuals will talk of trauma events that happened decades before, and they'll still remember details, including sounds, smells, sights, thoughts, and emotions. Often, clients remember details that might seem unusual, like what they were wearing, what they had for supper, or what was on television at the moment a traumatic event took place. Talking about such things can help the individual begin to move ahead.

Giving Permission and Support for Grieving

After an individual tells me of a crisis, trauma, or loss from the past, one of the most powerful things I can do to help is give permission and support for grieving. I help them identify losses that resulted from the event, and I explain the need to grieve these losses. When individuals understand the connection between past events, losses, and the need to grieve, they're usually willing to do so. When I provide support for them in this process, it helps them move ahead to more effective means of coping.

Choosing to Remain Stuck

Occasionally, I encounter an individual who seems to remain stuck despite my best efforts to help. This sometimes occurs even when the person tells me that he or she wants to move ahead and doesn't want to stay immobilized in the grief. If I make several efforts to help the person progress, but he or she remains stuck, I ask myself, "Is this client experiencing a payoff for being stuck; are they receiving some benefit from not progressing?" In some instances, I even ask the client if they can recognize any benefit in remaining stuck.

I believe that some individuals enjoy being bitter and blaming others. Some have done this for so long that it becomes a way of life, even part of their identities. These individuals may become so accustomed to being depressed, hurt, or bitter, they have a hard time giving these up.

Other individuals become familiar and comfortable with being stuck. They know how to live their lives stuck in the grief. Although these individuals claim they want to move ahead, a helper senses that such people are ambivalent about moving ahead. A biblical example is seen in the children of Israel as they are freed from slavery in Egypt. Even though they had cried out to God to rescue them from slavery, when He answers their prayers, they spend time and energy thinking about and expressing a desire to return to Egypt. They even develop selective memories, recalling only how great things were back in Egypt (see Exod. 16:3 and Num. 11:4–6). The Israelites had developed an identity as slaves and desired a return to the comfort of a known way of life.

Those who've experienced loss and are facing the grief process may act in a similar manner. While they know they need to progress, they may be quite anxious about doing so and, as a result, resist all efforts of help. When I deal with individuals who seem to present this kind of ambivalence, I talk with them about the Israelites, using their story as a vivid example of human ambivalence and a tendency to remain in comfortable, familiar territory.

Support and loving encouragement are usually sufficient to help people progress. In other instances, information about the necessity of grieving and about how a person can move ahead will assist the stuck person to move in a productive direction. When individuals experience some success in this process, they are generally encouraged to keep growing, even when facing anxiety about grief. Thus, the caregiver serves a crucial role in helping the person make necessary gains.

CONCLUSION

For individuals to recover following a crisis or trauma, or when they have experienced significant losses, it's necessary for them to grieve the losses in order to adjust and to cope effectively. Those who do so tend to live productive, exemplary lives, often helping others who are struggling with similar circumstances. Other individuals, for a variety of reasons, do not seem to move ahead in a productive manner. Counselors and ministers are in strategic positions to help both groups of individuals face and deal with difficult experiences. One of the more rewarding experiences a helper can have is seeing a person go through the dark valleys of life, emerge from the other side, and look around for others to help through the darkness. For caregivers to know they have assisted a person through the darkest times gives satisfaction rarely paralleled in the helping professions.

CHAPTER 8

CRISIS COUNSELING AND THE MINISTER

Over the years, it's become increasingly common for me to receive phone calls from former students or acquaintances who are now serving in various church staff or church ministry positions. Often, these calls relate to difficult ministry situations involving individuals in their congregations. Sometimes these crises may be small in scope, with ministers informing me about what they've done in a specific situation and wanting to know anything they might have missed. On other occasions, the minister is facing a new challenge relative to a ministry crisis, and he or she is requesting guidance on how to proceed. Following are examples of crises encountered by various church ministry personnel.

A STUDENT MINISTRY CRISIS

DAVID WAS SERVING AS INTERIM pastor of a church in a metropolitan area on the other side of the state where he lived. One Wednesday, he received a phone call from one of the church deacons, informing him of events that were unfolding in the community of David's interim pastorate. A school coach had been accused of providing alcohol to several of the local high school's cheerleaders, as well as being sexually involved with them. When a law enforcement officer went to the coach's house to arrest him, the coach barricaded the door to his house and committed suicide. To complicate matters further, the coach, his wife and children, some of the cheerleaders, and several athletes were members of the church David was pastoring. The deacon asked David to meet with the youth group the upcoming Sunday prior to delivering the morning sermon. David called to discuss his plans for approaching this most unfortunate set of circumstances.

A SUDDEN DEATH

ANDREW PASTORED A SMALL CONGREGATION not far from my home. My wife and I had been in his church on several occasions, leading marriage and parenting conferences. His call came after dealing with a heartbreaking crisis for one of his young couples. The husband had just returned from military duty. He'd been sent overseas a few weeks after the couple's wedding. In his absence, his wife gave birth to their baby girl, and the husband saw her for the first time when he returned from active duty. Andrew received a frantic phone call from these young parents saying that the baby had died from SIDS. Andrew met with the couple on several occasions over the next few days, sitting with them, crying with them, and ministering to their needs. He encouraged the young couple to seek counseling for the loss of the child, for the husband's struggles related to his military duty, and for problems the couple were having in their marriage. The couple informed Andrew that they would talk to him but they wouldn't see a counselor. Andrew, in his usual caring fashion, provided the help he could, but called me to ask if there was anything else he should be doing. We discussed several steps for him to take in continuing to minister to this couple.

A SUICIDAL CHURCH MEMBER

BRAD WAS ONE OF MY FAVORITE former students, and I enjoyed our periodic phone calls as he began serving as pastor, first in a small church across the state, then in a large church closer to me. I appreciated his conscientious efforts to truly minister to hurting individuals and families in his congregation. Brad called me one day in the midst of a crisis situation. A prominent church member and owner of a large business in Brad's community was accused of having an affair. The church member became despondent, and his wife called Brad one night, saying that her husband was threatening to kill himself and that he left the house with a gun. Brad drove around the community and found the church member at a local park, sitting in his vehicle and holding the gun to his head. Brad spent the next several hours talking to the man and working to keep the man from ending his life. Brad was able to talk the man out of attempting suicide. He called me, asking what to do next.

ABUSE IN THE CHILDREN'S MINISTRY

STEPHEN WAS A FRIEND OF MINE WHO became pastor of a church in a neighboring state. Stephen was an incredibly caring person who would do anything for his church members. When he called, I could hear his concern as he related a difficult situation unfolding in his church. During a church activity, members of the youth group were helping provide child care, working with adults who were watching the younger children. One young teenager managed to get a small child by herself and sexually molested her. The child told her parents, who contacted police and then informed Stephen. Stephen was now working with two families who were devastated by the incident. The family of the perpetrating teenager was dealing with a child in the juvenile justice system. The other family was coping with the knowledge that their child had been molested. Stephen desired to minister to both families as best he could, as well as to the rest of the congregation, who were close to each of the families directly involved. We spent time discussing how he might proceed.

IMPORTANCE OF THE MINISTER

These stories are actual accounts of crises that occurred in church settings. In all of these instances, individuals and families were directly impacted by a crisis situation. Each of the churches involved also had to face and deal with the crisis. The ministers in the stories were all caring individuals, who sought to provide for parishioners in the best manner possible.

Most ministers are well aware of the amount of time that can be spent addressing crises. Sudden, unexpected events in ministry are often the norm. Those who survive in ministry develop proficiency in dealing with routine crises that are a part of every minister's week. On some occasions, ministers encounter individuals experiencing more extensive or extreme crises or trauma. These types of events may occur to a church member, to a family associated with the church, in the larger church body, or in the community where the church resides. The minister plays a crucial role in helping hurting individuals and is generally a person to whom others look when a crisis occurs.

Individuals, in fact, often seek help from a minister prior to seeking help elsewhere. Some ministers have received phone calls about a crisis even before medical or law enforcement personnel were notified. Both believers and non-believers often seek out a minister for guidance, counsel, support, and spiritual direction. Some individuals who request help from a minister, inform the minister that they have no desire or plan to look for help or support elsewhere—from a counselor, for example.

Because individuals see ministry personnel as a source of aid in times of crisis, it is essential that ministers know how best to help others. This includes having an understanding of how to respond, knowing about confidentiality in crisis situations, knowing when and how to refer a person to a counselor, and comprehending the importance of training others to be involved in crisis ministry in the church setting.

THE NEED FOR KNOWLEDGE AND TRAINING

Because ministers encounter a wide range of crises in the course of their work, they need to be knowledgeable about crises and have training in how best to respond when critical events occur. Ministers may take a number of measures to increase their effectiveness surrounding crisis circumstances.

Preparation Versus Reaction

Whether a person is a senior pastor or functions in some other ministerial capacity, he or she is likely to invest large quantities of time and energy responding to various crises. In a given week, crises may even consume the bulk of a minister's available time and energy. To be most effective, ministers must prepare to deal with crisis and trauma events instead of merely reacting to them.

Being prepared is advantageous in a number of ways. When a minister is prepared, he or she is more likely to increase the effectiveness of the crisis response or to act in a way that benefits the person or family experiencing the event. Effective preparation also reduces the likelihood of a minister's experiencing burnout from responding to crises. Burnout is much more likely if the minister is constantly reacting to crises and struggling to provide help. Preparation also diminishes the possibility of harming an individual in the caregiving process. Even a well-intentioned minister may respond in a manner that is not helpful to those in crises, but the knowledgeable, trained, and prepared minister is much less likely to do so.

Preparation for addressing crises involves several factors. First, knowing the nature of crises and trauma, how they occur, and how individuals are affected by extreme events helps the minister be ready when such events transpire. A grasp of this knowledge also provides the minister with confidence for offering help in such circumstances. Second, preparation involves knowing what sources of support are available to aid in the overall helping process. The prepared minister is aware of human and programmatic sources of support that may be available through his or her church, in other local churches, in the community, or even within his or her denomination. Third, preparation involves knowing where to refer individuals for ongoing counseling, should this be necessary.

Since crises do occur, the wise minister spends time expanding his or her knowledge and developing a plan of action for addressing difficult circumstances. Energy invested in such preparation provides a great return when a crisis or traumatic situation takes place.

Dealing with Expectations of Self and Others

In coping with extreme and demanding ministry situations, it's important to understand the nature of expectations—both from others and from oneself. Knowing how expectations function can aid the minister in making decisions throughout a crisis event.

Even in the best of times, people tend to have high expectations of ministers, especially of pastors. Parishioners often expect a minister to be wise, caring, kind, and knowledgeable. Additionally, the minister is expected to be good with all age groups, always friendly, financially adept, have a good marriage, and be a great parent. Expectations of ministers can be exceedingly high. In crises, expectations may even increase. The minister is expected to be available, to have answers, to provide hope, to know the right thing to say and do, and to be a comforting presence. Some parishioners may even expect the minister to be omniscient—to be at the hospital, for instance, even if no one has informed the minister of the crisis event. Ministers may be expected to fix things and to make the situation better, to do so without making mistakes, and to be stress-free in crisis situations.

Little wonder that ministers often feel ill-prepared to deal with a crisis, or not know how best to help. The gap between how equipped the minister feels and the expectations of those undergoing crises can, in fact, be quite large. As the gap increases, so will the stress experienced by the minister.

As others place expectations on the minister, the minister may also come to believe these same things about him- or herself. Ministers may believe, for instance, that they must know the right thing to say in all circumstances. They may think that they should be exempt from experiencing stress when a parishioner faces a crisis or trauma. Or ministers may believe they should not question or doubt their own ability. No matter how much help ministers provide, they may struggle, thinking that they should have done more. There's a danger that ministers may develop a super hero-type belief about their role in crises. Often the expectations of both parishioners and ministers can be unrealistic; the expectations then reinforce each other, creating an unfortunate standard that the minister will never be able to attain.

Ideally, ministers are of greatest help in crisis situations if they have reasonable expectations about what they can accomplish and what their role and responsibilities are during crisis events. If the minister is able to regularly communicate realistic expectations to other staff members and to parishioners, frustration is less likely to be added to the already complex nature of the crisis or trauma event.

Realize That Healing Is a Process

Often, ministers are involved in the initial crisis as well as with the immediate follow-up to a traumatic event. In the first contact with a person or family following a crisis, the minister may forget that recovery from any significant loss is a process occurring over time. A minister is of greatest benefit when he or she understands that recovery takes time and that support is necessary far beyond the first few days after an individual experiences trauma or loss.

The minister who has an overall knowledge of trauma events and how they impact individuals, who is aware of self-expectations as well as the expectations of others, who understands the nature of recovery from trauma or loss—that minister is in the best position to provide tangible help. A minister must avoid the trap of assuming he or she has seen everything or that there is nothing new to learn about crisis ministry. The effective minister will be prepared for helping in crisis events and must avoid merely reacting, always feeling two steps behind when crises occur.

CONFIDENTIALITY AND CRISIS EVENTS

In formal counseling, confidentiality is not only foundational to counseling success, it is a legal necessity. Lukens notes, "Confidentiality is crucial to an effective and trusting counseling relationship. Without it, most counseling relationships would never begin, and those that did would be unlikely to survive. Few ethical constraints within the field of counseling are as universally accepted as confidentiality.[1] Corey, Corey, and Callanan, experts in counseling ethics, note that confidentiality is composed of both ethical and legal components. "Mental health professionals have an ethical responsibility, as well as a legal and professional duty, to safeguard clients from unauthorized disclosures of information given in the therapeutic relationship. Professionals must not disclose this information except when authorized by law or by the client to do so."[2] But what role does confidentiality play in crisis ministry, since crisis counseling is somewhat different than formal counseling? Should a minister keep information given by a person in crisis confidential and should the minister ever intentionally break confidentiality?

A few years ago, while I watched the local evening news, an incident unfolded related to crisis ministry. A teenager had taken a weapon into an area school and had threatened several individuals. While no one was harmed, the situation was tense enough for the school district to call in crisis counselors to help students process what had occurred. As the crisis counselors left the building, members of the media waited to interview the counselors about the incident. One exiting counselor was identified by the news station as a youth minister in a local church. When the eager reporter asked the youth minister what was taking place inside the building, he related details of his counseling session with a female student who'd been confronted by the gunman.

As I watched, I wondered if the young lady was watching as well. If so, how did she feel about this youth minister telling the viewing audience her thoughts and feelings? I wondered if the youth minister had been trained in crisis counseling, or if he was an individual just desiring to be helpful. I wondered if the concept of confidentiality crossed his mind, and if he spoke with his crisis clients about it. I wondered if his disclosures of her thoughts and feelings would make her less likely to trust others in the religious community. I had no way, of course, to get answers to those questions, but the situation did highlight matters of confidentiality related to crisis events and the need for helpers to be informed about the basics in this area.

---

1. Lukens, "Essential Elements for Ethical Counsel," 44.
2. Corey, Corey, and Callanan, *Issues and Ethics in the Helping Professions*, 210.

What Confidentiality Does

Confidentiality helps create a safe atmosphere in which clients are free to talk openly about issues that concern them, about thoughts, fears, emotions, and even about hopes, dreams, and life direction. In counseling, confidentiality allows individuals to talk about matters they might otherwise have difficulty discussing. Assurance of confidentiality on the part of the counselor or minister increases client trust and invites individuals to talk freely about what concerns them.

While not always a part of crisis ministry, confidentiality is still a good idea. It gives crisis victims assurance that what they share will not be talked about elsewhere and allows them to explore and discuss dynamics of the crisis event. When I work with individuals following a crisis or trauma event, I assure them of confidentiality and briefly convey the limits to confidentiality, much in the same manner as when I'm in a formal counseling relationship.

Limits to Confidentiality

Although confidentiality is foundational to counseling and a good idea for crisis ministry, it is not absolute. Certain circumstances require a counselor to breach confidentiality: when a counselor believes a person is a danger to him- or herself or to another person; in instances of sexual or physical abuse of a child, teenager, older adult, or disabled person; or when a counselor is required by the legal system to disclose information given in the counseling session.

A counselor will, as a matter of course, go over these limits to confidentiality at the beginning of a *formal* counseling relationship, having the client sign a document stating that he or she understands the limits of confidentiality. Because much of crisis counseling is *informal* in nature, a crisis counselor will verbally convey issues of confidentiality and its limits to a crisis victim.

Specific guidelines about confidentiality vary from state to state in regard to duty to warn if an individual is in danger. Licensed counselors are required to be knowledgeable about guidelines for the state in which they provide counseling services. Such knowledge helps protect a counselor from legal challenges in regard to confidentiality. Ministers, as well, are wise to become informed about the guidelines for, and limits of, confidentiality in the state where they serve. This is especially true regarding the reporting of any sexual or physical abuse of children that comes to their knowledge, either directly or indirectly. Ministers are required to report knowledge of such events to state protective services. Failure to do so puts a church in a precarious legal position.

When discussing confidentiality, ministers should be careful of making promises that they cannot or should not keep. This is especially true for ministers to children and teenagers. A teenager at youth camp, for instance, might say to a youth leader, "I have something I want to tell you, but you have to promise you won't tell anybody about it." The eager youth worker may be tempted to make such a promise in the belief that he or she is helping the teen. If the youth worker makes this kind of promise, then the teen discloses some type of abuse, the youth worker is in a bind. In such instances, if a teenager requests secrecy of this nature, I usually reply, "You know, I can keep a confidence of just about anything, but in a few instances I can't. If there's some danger to you or another person, I have to report this to the right person. I can tell that you have something on your mind, and I'd really like to hear about it." In most cases, the teenager will talk, and the counselor or minister avoids being put in a precarious position.

MAKING COUNSELING REFERRALS

While ministers can provide much needed help to those experiencing crisis or trauma, most ministers do not have the time to carry an extensive counseling load. Knowing, then, when to refer a hurting individual to a counselor and knowing how to select a counselor are essential for the minister.

When to Refer

By virtue of their roles and positions, most ministers end up doing a certain amount of counseling as a part of their ministerial duties. As mentioned, many individuals seek out their pastors, student ministers, or children's ministers because of comfort and trust in those individuals. The minister must recognize, however, when it's best to refer a client or couple to a counselor for more extensive help. Here are some guidelines for knowing when to encourage a person to seek help from a trained counselor.

1. *When the minister's time is limited.* Because ministers tend to have extremely busy schedules, it may be hard for them to provide counseling to a large number of individuals. If an individual seems to require ongoing counseling that necessitates more than a few sessions, it's often appropriate to refer that individual for more formal counseling. Some ministers are forthright, informing those who seek counseling that if

they require more than two or three sessions, the minister will provide the person with names of counselors who can offer ongoing help.

2. *When the minister is not gifted in counseling.* All ministers can learn to do some basic counseling. Not all ministers, however, are gifted in effective counseling. The minister who has gifts and talents consistent with counseling hurting individuals will likely offer this type of care and will find it fulfilling and rewarding. Other ministers experience counseling as a strain or frustration, and possibly not the best use of their time and energy. The wise minister recognizes whether or not he or she has the spiritual gifts and abilities of an effective counselor. If not, then knowing how and when to make good referrals is essential.

3. *When counseling is complicated.* Sometimes counseling is straightforward; a person presents with a concern, and the steps to resolution are apparent, with the client being sufficiently motivated to take these steps. In other instances, counseling is complex, almost like a mystery to be solved. Some clients have unspoken needs and agendas that can drive the counseling sessions. It's not unusual, even for experienced counselors, to feel overwhelmed by what is taking place in a counseling session. If a minister senses that the complexity of a counseling case is beyond his or her training and experience, it's probably time to make a referral.

4. *When there is no change.* A minister might meet for several sessions with a client who's experienced a crisis, loss, or trauma, but finds that the person is not progressing. In some instances, the person may seem to be doing worse. While temporary regression can very well be part of crisis counseling, if the lack of progress is ongoing, it may be time to refer the client for professional counseling.

5. *If the client experiences self-harm thoughts.* If a client is experiencing anything more than mild self-harm thoughts, the minister would be wise to consult with a counselor who has experience in dealing with suicidal clients. If suicidal thoughts are extensive, it's time to consider making a referral.

How to Make a Referral

Some churches are fortunate. They have counselors serving the churches in some capacity and thus have easy access to them when people are in need of more formal counseling. Most churches, however, are not in this position, and ministry personnel will occasionally need to refer individuals for formal counseling. When making a counseling referral, there are several important questions to consider.

1. *Who sponsors the counselor?* Is the counselor employed by an agency, a church, or is he or she in private practice? If the counselor works for an agency, is the agency funded by the government or by any specific private entity? Answers to these questions will help the minister determine if the counselor must adhere to a certain approach, or if the counseling services provided entail institutional requirements or limitations.

2. *What is the counselor's spiritual orientation?* How does the counselor approach and address spiritual issues and concerns? Is the counselor a believer? Are spiritual matters a regular part of counseling sessions? From what perspective does the counselor approach spiritual concerns? Ministers should look for a counselor to whom they feel comfortable sending members of their congregation or ministry arena.

3. *Is the counselor licensed or certified?* A counselor's licensing or certification provides information about the counselor's training and affiliations. In most states, licensure is a more thorough and strenuous process than certification, and while a license does not guarantee quality of counseling, it means that the counselor has met certain educational, testing, and training standards. If the counselor is licensed or certified, by whom has this been done? Be cautious, as a number of diploma mills grant educational degrees and licensing certifications. Some of these are even religious in nature. It's not a bad idea to ask other professionals in your congregation if they recognize the licensure or certification held by the counselor, and what the licensure or certification signifies.

4. *What is the counselor's training and specialization?* For referring a survivor of crisis or trauma, the ideal counselor will have training, experience, or specialization in crisis counseling. Ask the counselor about his or her background, and if he or she has training in trauma, crisis, or grief counseling.

5. *How long has the counselor been practicing in the community?* As with licensure, length of practice does not ensure quality, but it can be an indicator of a counselor's overall success record. If the counselor has not been in practice for any length of time, it might be wise to inquire about background and where he or she is from. <u>Be cautious of anyone who's made several different moves in a short period of time.</u>

6. *What is the counselor's reputation?* A counselor's reputation is a crucial factor in making referrals. This is a question best asked not of the counselor, but of those who have had contact with the counselor. What do others say about the counselor? What do other professionals say about him or her? Within a congregation, there are usually individuals who know of a counselor's reputation. Schoolteachers, social workers, law enforcement personnel, or other counselors may provide information about how the counselor is viewed by fellow professionals. Inquire from others who've made referrals to the counselor or from former clients of the counselor. These individuals may be able to provide information about the counselor's approach and effectiveness.

7. *What does the counselor claim about his or her accomplishments?* Avoid any individual who claims a 100 percent success rate or any type of miracle cure. At best, counseling is hard work for both the client and the counselor. Reputable counselors will be reasonable and measured in claims they make about counseling outcomes.

Some Additional Thoughts on Making Referrals

Hopefully, over time, a minister will develop relationships with counselors and will feel comfortable referring those in need to these trusted individuals. Ideally, one of these counselors may even be willing to serve as a consultant to the minister in some of the crisis counseling provided by the minister. A wise minister will attempt to build such relationships before they're needed. If a minister has already done some of the footwork, obtaining answers to the questions above, he or she can more easily make a referral when it becomes necessary. When a referral is necessary, it's usually too late to do a thorough search for a good counselor. Once again, being prepared is better than reacting.

CONCLUSION

Ministers carry a heavy burden of responsibility for those under their care. In the best of circumstances, ministry calls for personal maturity and growth, leadership, and a minister's willingness to attend to those whom God has placed under his or her purview.

Scripture paints the picture of the minister as a shepherd, or one with the task of providing for the needs of the flock—protecting them, leading them, and having responsibility for their well-being. Regarding Jesus' story of the lost sheep in Luke 15, Geldenhuys states, "The shepherd considers no trouble, sacrifice and suffering too great to find the lost sheep and bring it back. In spite of all hardships during the long search among the forests, cliffs and gorges, the shepherd continues to seek until he has found the lost sheep."[3] In a similar manner, the minister must seek out and care for those experiencing crisis situations or difficult circumstances. Ministers who are trained and prepared for a range of different crises are in the best position to make a difference, to provide meaningful help, and to be a leader to those in the flock who are in great need of a shepherd.

---

3. Geldenhuys, *New International Commentary on the Gospel of Luke*, 402.

CHAPTER 9

CRISIS MINISTRY AND THE COUNSELOR

A COUNSELOR'S STORY

ON DECEMBER 26, 2004, AN undersea earthquake occurred just west of Sumatra, Indonesia. It triggered a series of powerful and destructive tsunamis that crashed into the shorelines of Indonesia, Sri Lanka, Malaysia, Thailand, and East Africa, killing almost two hundred thousand people and leaving thousands of others missing. At the time of the tsunamis, Julie and her husband, Phil, were missionaries living in Indonesia, where the couple had served for several years, working in student ministry. In addition to her missionary duties, Julie was working toward the completion of her master's degree in counseling. As the couple awoke that morning, little did they realize that they would occupy front row seats to one of the largest disasters in modern history—the tsunamis that devastated entire regions of Southeast Asia.

Phil was sent to Aceh, a focal point of destruction. There, he ministered to those who suffered most directly and set up a base camp for volunteers who would arrive in the weeks and months to come. Julie stayed in Jakarta, debriefing missionary personnel and crisis counselor nationals who were exiting the regions most devastated by the tsunamis. The couple talked by phone each evening, supporting and encouraging each other in the midst of this international tragedy.

Two years after her involvement in this disaster, Julie sat down with me and talked about her experience, what she saw, and what she learned. The situation, she said, was extremely chaotic, and it was difficult for caregivers to know where to begin to help. While many volunteers arrived on the scene, other individuals were present with less than noble intentions, looting local shops and stealing items off of dead bodies. Unsanitary conditions endangered tsunami victims and volunteers alike. Due to the chaos and destruction, the tsunami survivors were very transient, making any type of meaningful follow-up care virtually impossible.

Julie spoke of the ongoing images of destruction seen on television. Because there was no limit on what could be broadcast, grisly scenes of death and destruction were repeatedly played for all to see, reinforcing the existing layers of trauma. Julie was especially struck by the amount of ambiguous loss; even eighteen months after the tsunamis, people were still awaiting confirmation about whether relatives were deceased or just missing.

From a counseling standpoint, Julie also had a number of observations. Counselors wanted to help everybody, and they tended to feel guilty no matter how much help they provided. She observed that, in larger crises, counselors should be aware of their limitations, realistic about what they can accomplish, and able to say no to areas where they may not be of the most benefit. Counselors should be cognizant of their own need to debrief, to have someone to whom they can talk about what they're seeing and experiencing. She noted the necessity for counselors to have training in crisis counseling, although she knows that no amount of training really prepares a counselor for what's required in providing help following a large-scale disaster. Most of all, Julie stressed the need for counselors to recognize that what they accomplish is the result not of their own efforts, but of God working through the counselors to help those in difficult circumstances.

INTRODUCTION

Counselors frequently encounter clients who are struggling with crises, trauma, loss, or grief. Not all counselors, however, are trained in crisis counseling. This chapter provides information about distinguishing between general counseling and crisis counseling: What makes crisis counseling a specialized focus in the therapy field? We then turn our attention to common mistakes a counselor might make in attempting to provide crisis counseling. Knowing the characteristics or qualities of an effective crisis counselor assists individuals in determining if they should pursue a focus in this field. And last, we will consider specific needs in the larger crisis counseling field.

GENERAL COUNSELING VERSUS CRISIS COUNSELING

Counseling generally entails instances of crisis counseling. Clients often seek out counselors following a crisis or trauma experience. On other occasions, a client may undergo a crisis or loss while in therapy. Successful therapists must become adept at dealing with difficult circumstances faced by clients. Although most counselors deal with client crises, several aspects of crisis counseling differ from a general counseling practice.

Differences in Intensity

First, crisis counseling tends to be more intense, requiring a different set of approaches. In general counseling, a client who is familiar to the therapist may be relaxed, and even cheerful following a good week. A counselor can also relax, maybe even look forward to seeing how the client has fared the previous week. Crisis counseling necessitates counselor alertness and the need for strong skills in assessing client symptomology and safety. Crisis counseling sessions are regularly quite intense as individuals struggle with frustration, confusion, pain, and uncertainty. Crisis counseling frequently calls for rapid decision making on the part of the counselor.

Differences in Counseling Location

Another difference between general and crisis counseling is that the latter is more likely to require the counselor to be on-site in certain instances. Whereas some agencies may require general counselors to do in-home visits with clients or client families, counselors usually do all their work from a specific office or in a specific location. Conversely, crisis counselors often go to the scene of a tragedy and may work with individuals during or immediately following a disaster. For days after the Oklahoma City bombing, chaplains, CISD-trained counselors, and other disaster mental health professionals worked with survivors, victim families, first responders, and with those involved in the ongoing rescue efforts. Similarly, after the bombings of the World Trade Center towers, many counselors were on-site in the days following September 11. Commonly, crisis work is chaotic, even dangerous. Doing counseling in the familiar surroundings of one's office is quite unlike working with people at the scene of a disaster.

Social Work Function of Crisis Counseling

The fields of social work and counseling have long been related. All counseling has some elements of social work, and many social workers provide a range of counseling services. Generally, however, counseling involves working directly with a client, whereas social work involves helping individuals or families navigate social systems within society. Crisis counseling often requires the counselor to serve in some social work capacities. The effective crisis counselor needs to be knowledgeable of a variety of community resources and must have skill in helping clients access and utilize these resources. An example is the client who lost all her belongings in an apartment fire. A crisis counselor may need to help the woman find shelter, clothing, food, and even medical care. The crisis counselor commonly assists clients in knowing how to deal with insurance companies, federal agencies, and even banks and credit card companies. The crisis counselor is often involved in much more than just listening to the client's concerns, and frequently must function in a social work capacity when helping the survivor of a tragedy.

Length of Sessions

Most often, general counseling is done in fifty-minute sessions. Week by week a client comes to his or her sessions, which start and end at designated times. Crisis counseling may occur in this manner, but often it does not. A great deal of crisis counseling is a onetime encounter between the crisis victim and the counselor. If the counselor is on-site, this encounter may transpire in a brief exchange or it may occur as both counselor and crisis victim are eating a hot meal. Generally, initial crisis intervention counseling is done in a single session; the counselor meets with a person one time, but commonly never sees the person again. Crisis counselors must, therefore, be able to work in single sessions. This involves the challenging task of connecting with the person, helping the person talk about what is concerning him or her, making rapid and accurate assessments about how the person is doing, and offering concrete, tangible ongoing help, if necessary. Often, the crisis counselor does not have the luxury of time and must function rapidly and efficiently, while simultaneously appearing calm and relaxed in order not to make the crisis victim anxious about time pressures.

When to Meet with Clients

In general counseling, the counselor meets with clients at the appointed time and will vary scheduling only if there is some true emergency. Crisis counseling necessitates scheduling flexibility on the part of the counselor or a greater ability to meet at the convenience of the client. Following the Wedgwood shootings, I received a number of phone calls from those directly involved who asked to meet with me. Some of these individuals felt initially as if they were doing okay and didn't need to talk to a counselor, but eventually did make the decision to call and ask for help. Thus, in the first several days after the shooting, I met some individuals and couples after regular work hours and on weekends. Counselors involved in crisis ministry can rarely fit crises into a prescribed schedule.

The counselor who chooses to become more involved in crisis or trauma counseling needs all the skills practiced in general counseling, but must also be flexible, calm, and able to function in the face of chaos, confusion, and intensity. Recognizing basic differences between general counseling and crisis counseling allows a counselor to decide about his or her suitability to function as a crisis counselor.

COMMON COUNSELOR MISTAKES

Because crisis counseling is different from general counseling, therapists run the risk of committing certain errors when assisting clients. Counseling approaches that fit a general counseling clientele do not always serve the needs of those in crises. Several common counseling mistakes are identified below.

Believing That Everyone Needs Crisis Intervention

Some inexperienced counselors seem to think that all trauma survivors are in need of counseling. On occasion, counselors may attempt to foist counseling services on people who may not need it. As more and more counselors have become aware of crisis intervention methodology and undergone some amount of training, counselors may begin to circle like vultures, following large-scale tragedies, wanting to "get in on the action." These individuals seem indiscriminate about whether or not counseling is needed or wanted, and the general sense seems to be that every crisis or disaster survivor needs counseling. As discussed, however, two individuals can go through the same traumatic experience but be affected quite differently. One person may have enduring emotional scars, while the other person comes away from the same experience relatively symptom-free.

While being available to help, counselors mustn't force themselves into situations where they're unwanted or unneeded. On one occasion, an agency contacted me about bringing counselors to do a crisis intervention debriefing for their employees. The crisis event, though, had occurred two months prior. The agency arranged for the intervention and mandated that all employees attend, even though all employees had not been involved in the trauma event. Some employees were even new to the agency. We conducted the debriefings, but because of the time lapse between the event and the debriefings, because all employees were required to participate, and because of the variance in how individuals were affected—all combined to make the effort somewhat futile. The person in charge at the agency, though, believed that everyone would benefit from the debriefing, which proved not to be the case.

Attempting to Take Away the Survivor's Pain

In general, counselors are caring people. Compassion for hurting individuals is, in fact, part of what leads a person to the counseling field. Counselors want to help people move from struggles to solutions, aiding clients as they strive to function more effectively, and helping clients reduce the emotional pain that necessitated counseling.

The counselor's desire to help alleviate pain can, though, actually hinder the effectiveness of crisis counseling. In the days or weeks following a significant trauma or loss, clients' emotions are raw, and the struggles are readily apparent. Because counselors are caring individuals, they may endeavor to reduce or remove the client's pain, that is, the counselor is uncomfortable with the client's pain, and thus attempts to alleviate the pain in order to reduce the counselor's own anxiety. These attempts may include trying to cheer up the client, distracting the client, or offering simplistic solutions or platitudes.

Counselors should recognize that their role is not to cheer up a client, but rather to walk beside the client in the midst of that person's pain and struggle. The counselor must avoid the mistake of trying to alleviate personal anxiety by getting the client to feel better.

Attempting to Rush Clients Through the Recovery Process

About a year after the Wedgwood shootings, I overheard a comment by a person in the counseling profession. He stated that those who'd been in the sanctuary had now had enough time to recover. This person added that anyone still struggling was doing so as a result of sin, not as a part of the grief journey. Not only was this counselor misguided, but if he truly believed in a specific time period for recovery, he might encourage those suffering trauma to rush through the recovery process.

Counselors may be tempted to hurry clients through the recovery process for a variety of reasons. Like the counselor mentioned above, it may be due to theological or psychological misunderstanding of the nature of recovery. Another counselor might rush clients due to the counselor's own impatience or because of the counselor's need to have people progress at a certain rate. A counselor who practices from a strict brief-therapy framework may be tempted to work with a trauma survivor in a set number of sessions, pushing for the client to finish therapy, perhaps prematurely.

Some clients do make rapid progress following a crisis event. If the event is not severe, if the client has adequate coping skills and good support, the client might make a speedy recovery. More commonly, however, and especially with severe trauma, the counselor must be patient, work at a pace at which the client is comfortable, feels safe, and at which the counselor avoids overwhelming the client by moving too briskly.

Mistaking Temporary Relief for Recovery

Following trauma, and especially if a person is grieving a loss related to a significant trauma event, the recovery process involves times when the client feels better and times when the client feels worse. It's not unusual for the client to experience many of these ups and downs, much like riding a roller coaster. Clients may believe they've finished the grieving process because they temporarily feel better. Counselors must be cautious, avoiding becoming too excited about their clients' apparent progress or too concerned if clients have a difficult week. Counselors who lead clients to believe that they are "over the worst" may contribute to clients' feeling quite dismayed when they encounter the next period of struggle. Often, counselors can predict that the journey will have better days and worse days, encouraging their clients when things go well, but continuing to provide support when things are difficult.

Understanding or Attempting to Treat Trauma from a Unidimensional Perspective

A temptation in working with trauma survivors is to approach help from a one-dimensional perspective. After a trauma event, a person may go to his or her family physician and describe what he or she is experiencing. The physician might then prescribe medication for anxiety or depression, without assisting the person in exploring what occurred and how the person is reacting. In this instance, the physician is operating from a biological or medical perspective.

In a like way, a counselor may tend to understand trauma from a single perspective. One counselor may consider only the cognitive component of what the person is going through and what the person thinks and believes about the event. Another counselor may focus on what the person is feeling, looking only at the emotions related. Another counselor may attempt to reduce the client's struggle to the realm of spiritual matters, seeing the person's anguish or grief symptoms as a lack of faith. Other counselors may focus on everything but the spiritual component, completely missing how the client has been affected spiritually. To be most effective, a counselor needs to understand that trauma impacts a person on many levels, and the best approach to recovery takes into account the person as a whole.

Trying to Make a Client Fit a Certain Model of Recovery

Some counselors try to make a client fit a particular model of recovery, most often that of Kübler-Ross. In 1969, Elizabeth Kübler-Ross posited her ideas about the stages of grief in her book *On Death and Dying*. In it, she identified five stages of grief: denial, anger, bargaining, depression, and acceptance. On more than one occasion, I've talked with counselors who believe that all grieving individuals must pass through these stages in order, even suggesting to the client that he or she will experience these specific emotions in this particular sequence, a claim that Kübler-Ross does not make.

There's a danger in taking any particular model or theory and trying to make all clients fit the framework. This also holds true regarding the model of crisis intervention set forth in this current volume. It must serve only as a map or guide for a general understanding of what happens to people in difficult circumstances. The wise counselor understands individual variation, that not everyone functions the same following grief or loss. Thus, the wise counselor will listen carefully to the client, dealing with the client as an individual and avoiding imposing any model of functioning on a client where it does not fit.

Exempting Themselves

One last mistake a counselor may make is the "counselor exemption." I've had the opportunity of working with a number of counselors who've had some kind of significant crisis or loss. When counselors as clients come to see me, they often believe that, because they have knowledge of how humans are affected by crisis events, they should be exempt from going through struggles related to their own crises. When this occurs, I point it out to the counselor/client, and we discuss how having knowledge about the impact of crises does not inoculate a person from the effects of crises or from the symptoms produced by traumatic experiences. Counselors who come as clients are often impatient, though, wanting to hurry the process or find some shortcut. While knowledge may help a person work through the pain, it does not exempt one from the pain.

CHARACTERISTICS OF A CRISIS COUNSELOR

All counselors do some amount of counseling involving clients in crisis situations. Some counselors, however, may feel called to specialize in ministering to those in crisis. Because crisis counseling is different from general counseling, what characteristics should a person possess in order to specialize in crisis counseling? Listed below are several.

Training

As with any area of counseling specialization, a counselor must be trained in crisis counseling. This training should include developing knowledge of how individuals are affected by crises and trauma, and the most effective interventions. Because the crisis counseling field is still actively growing and expanding, counselors who've received some training must be willing to stay abreast of growth and new information related to crisis, grief, and trauma, updating their training through continuing education and through reading of new developments in the crisis counseling field.

Awareness of One's Own Loss History

In nearly every training seminar I lead on crisis counseling and ministry, someone approaches me following the presentation. This person talks about a personal traumatic experience or loss that came to mind as we were discussing trauma-related matters. Often, these persons are veteran counselors who've worked with clients for many years. Occasionally, it's apparent that the pain from the traumatic experience or loss is very real and very clear. Sometimes counselors tell me that they do not think they have worked through the loss that they've identified. While a counselor doesn't necessarily have to be in perfect emotional shape to work with others, a counselor should be aware of his or her own loss history and of how the counselor's experiences might affect work with clients, especially in providing crisis, trauma, or grief counseling. If a counselor is unaware of the personal impact of a trauma or loss, he or she may not be in the best position to aid others who are struggling. Similarly, the counselor who has undergone a specific type of trauma or loss must exercise caution not to superimpose his or her personal experience onto the client. Wrestling with one's own loss history and attempting to understand how it impacts one's counseling will aid the counselor as he or she works with others in any portion of the grieving process.

The Ability to Be Nonreactive in the Face of Grief and Loss

In any type of counseling, the counselor must learn to be relatively nonreactive when clients disclose difficult information. Clients often relate information about horrible events or about difficult and painful thought processes. Such disclosures are generally accompanied by raw and strong emotions including anger, sadness, grief, confusion, and even despair. If a counselor reacts to a client's disclosure, it may produce further feelings of shame in the client and reduce the likelihood of future disclosures. Thus, the crisis counselor must not react in a manner that might escalate or exacerbate the crisis. The crisis counselor must possess the ability to remain calm, to self-sooth in the face of strong emotions, and must be able to think clearly during intense moments in a counseling session. The effective crisis counselor functions in a calm and low-key manner, which provides the client with a sense of safety and stability—ingredients important to the client's ability to regulate emotions and his or her willingness to talk openly about what has happened.

The Capacity for Tolerating Chaos

Any crisis counselor who goes on-site following a large-scale disaster must be willing to function amid general chaos. If a counselor is at the scene of a tragedy, there are regularly questions about who's in charge and about the chain of command. If multiple agencies are present, there's often confusion about how these interface with each other and about the specific responsibilities of each entity involved. A crisis counselor must be able to function when things are unstructured, disorderly, and confusing. The counselor must be clear about his or her role and must be willing to function within the framework of the overall crisis intervention effort. Crisis counselors must be flexible, able to change directions, not easily flustered, and able to make decisions in high-stress environments.

Knowledge of Laws and Licensure Guidelines

A counselor is responsible for knowing licensure regulations and legal guidelines for his or her area of practice. A crisis counselor must be aware of such guidelines and should have a sense of how these apply to crisis situations and crisis counseling. Because trauma victims often have thoughts of self-harm, the counselor must know when and how to work toward the client's safety. The counselor must understand issues such as confidentiality and dual relationships, and must function according to any licensures or certifications under which he or she is sanctioned to provide services. Because each state tends to differ regarding regulations for confidentiality and duty to warn, it is imperative that a crisis counselor be aware of the guidelines and also be willing to follow ongoing legislation or court decisions that produce changes in these guidelines. A crisis counselor must develop the ability to read crisis situations and ensure he or she is functioning ethically in every instance.

The Capability of Interacting with Other Professionals

An effective crisis counselor must possess the ability to interface with other professionals and agencies in order to maximize support to clients. Crisis counselors must be able to make referrals to medical doctors, psychiatrists, and to hospitals. The ability to communicate and network with other professionals increases the likelihood of helping certain clients. Counselors should also know how to interact with pastors, youth ministers, teachers, and school counselors. An awareness of community agencies allows the counselor to access a range of resources for certain clients. If a counselor is able to access resources in various agencies and help clients navigate red tape, which is often a part of agency life—these abilities are of great benefit to many clients.

Due to the nature of counseling, all counselors will provide some amount of crisis counseling, helping clients plot a course through difficult circumstances. Counselors who desire to specialize in crisis counseling, however, should evaluate their calling, their gifts and talents, and their personalities in light of the specialization's unique requirements.

NEEDS IN THE CRISIS COUNSELING FIELD

Because crisis counseling is a growing field, many needs exist. A great deal of the field remains unexplored and uncharted, calling for individuals who will investigate and map the territory. Needs in the field include more Christian counselors developing expertise in crisis counseling, researchers to continue gaining information about how trauma and loss affect individuals and how best to help victims, and counselors trained in crisis counseling to interface with those in ministry to offer help to hurting individuals.

The Need for Expertise in Crisis Counseling

Many individuals begin or spend their early years in the counseling profession working in agencies, hospitals, or in settings where the work is hard, comprised of long hours, often performing thankless tasks. Counselors, thus, tend to move in the direction of having more control over schedule, clientele, and type of counseling. Counselors also may become comfortable in a particular counseling setting and with the type of clients seen.

Becoming an expert in crisis counseling, however, necessitates that a counselor take risks, be involved in difficult cases, and possibly move out of the comfort of the counseling office. The field desperately needs counselors who are willing to function in just such a manner.

While the secular crisis counseling field has grown rapidly over the past decade, Christian counseling experts are rare. H. Norman Wright, a pioneer in the Christian counseling field, is one of the few individuals who have intentionally focused on crisis, trauma, and loss, spending a good portion of his life preparing counselors and ministers to help others in crisis circumstances. Other writers from the pastoral ministries areas have attempted to provide pastors and other ministers with basic crisis counseling training. Many others are needed to develop specialization and to train caregivers in the concepts and intervention strategies of crisis ministry and counseling.

The Need for Research and Understanding of How Crisis, Trauma, and Loss Impact Individuals, Families, and Communities

In the human relations field, researchers attempt to develop methods of obtaining accurate information about how individuals function in a variety of situations. Researchers provide information about, for example, effective parenting, what makes marriage work, and how divorce affects children. Gaining information about those who experience a traumatic event, however, can be much more difficult. When a person has just experienced some extremely critical life event, it's ethically questionable to ask that person to provide information to a researcher, or to fill out a questionnaire so a researcher can develop information about the impact of trauma. Thus, gaining information about the nature of trauma is not a simple task. The field stands in need of researchers who will develop creative, ethical methods of generating information and furthering our understanding of how individuals respond to crises, trauma, and loss. Along similar lines, what are the best methods of intervention following extreme events, and how can researches reliably test such approaches? The traumatology field is wide open for individuals who can generate sound, reliable research.

In addition to the need for general research in the field, a need exists for Christian counselors to further our understanding of the interaction between traumatic events and an individual's spiritual functioning. How does trauma impact a person's faith and his or her relationship with God? Similarly, how does a person's spiritual functioning mitigate the impact of trauma? Most of the formal studies conducted in the field come from secular researchers who aren't interested in or are wary of the spiritual dimension of individual functioning during and following crisis or trauma. What role does prayer play before, during, and following trauma? What is healthy faith in difficult times, and how can a person develop faith of this nature? Are there elements of religiousness that are unhealthy, that hinder a person's response to trauma? What role does a supportive faith community play, and what must this community do to be most helpful in times of crisis? These and many other similar areas are in need of careful examination and understanding.

The Need for Counselors to Interface with Ministers in Providing Crisis Care

Many ministers distrust counselors and the counseling profession. Further, over the last several decades, the counseling profession as a whole has done more than its share to alienate the religious community. Other ministers have an uneasy truce with counselors, perhaps finding one trusted counselor while generally distrusting the field. Some ministers unquestioningly trust the counseling profession, or anyone credentialed in the field. This, too, is perhaps unwise.

Counselors must look for ways to interface with ministers and to work in concert with them to provide help for those who are struggling. Many individuals who encounter a crisis will not turn to the counselor first, but will come to the minister. Ministers can become overwhelmed by the crisis ministry demands of their positions, but don't know where to turn if they have questions or when they need support.

Counselors must look for ways to bridge the gap that often exists between ministry and the counseling profession. Doing so includes attempting to understand crisis events from the minister's perspective, the needs of the minister when he or she has a parishioner in a crisis situation, and how the counselor can be of most help to the minister. Counselors may also endeavor to be available for periodic consultation, helping with questions about referrals or providing support if the minister faces a difficult counseling situation. Counselors must respect the minister's role and function in the life of church members, seeking to support the minister in the various tasks to which the minister has been called. A counselor and minister working together provide a powerful team in crisis situations, whether they occur on a small scale with one individual's crisis, or on a much larger scale when many are affected in a church body or in the community.

CONCLUSION

Not all counselors should focus their efforts in crisis counseling. Some counselors are best suited for other venues and do well to spend their time and energy accordingly. There are counselors, however, whose calling, gifts, interests, and skills lie in the area of helping people both during and following the most critical of circumstances. Those who are so gifted must develop these gifts, skills, and talents, keep abreast of the crisis counseling discipline, and network with other professionals and ministry personnel in the field in order to provide the best care to those who are hurting. Whether on scene in a large-scale disaster or in the counseling office, crisis counseling is a much needed component of crisis ministry.

CHAPTER 10

Children and Crises

Mark's Story

Mark was eleven years old when his family attended a large festival in their city. This annual family outing was one of Mark's favorite activities, and he liked the food, music, and games that were all part of the springtime gathering. While the family was enjoying their activities, a few large raindrops began to fall. The rain became more persistent, accompanied by hail. Even being accustomed to springtime storms, the event participants began heading for their vehicles. Before most of them managed to take cover, the hail became the size of oranges.

What began as a fun family outing now turned dangerous. Families scrambled for any cover they could find. One family made it to their car and opened the doors, only to have several individuals jump in the car with them. Another family attempted to squeeze under a window air-conditioning unit outside a nearby building. The hail damaged roofs, shattered windshields, and was even powerful enough to perforate the fiberglass hoods of many automobiles.

Although Mark and his family made it to safety, they were understandably shaken. A few weeks following the event, Mark's mother approached me about her son and the struggles he was facing. She told me that Mark had become quite anxious and seemed afraid to be away from his parents. This was especially true during storms, but Mark would even panic when clouds gathered on the horizon. Mark's mother wanted to know what was wrong and how she could help.

JESUS AND CHILDREN

One of my favorite images of Jesus is presented in Mark 10:13–16. I can see Jesus as He plays with the children brought to Him by His followers, sitting on the ground with kids all around Him. Surely one was sitting in His lap. Another may have been poking Him. One might have been saying, "Jesus, look at me!" as the child attempted a cartwheel. One was probably telling Jesus an important story, maybe about her dog. Jesus was comfortable with children and the children loved Jesus. The disciples, on the other hand, were troubled. Perhaps they were concerned that people were misusing Jesus' precious time, and that He had more important things to do. The disciples rebuked the parents, attempting to free Jesus from these little ones.

Mark 10:14 makes clear Jesus' response: "But when Jesus saw this, He was indignant and said to them, 'Permit the children to come to Me; do not hinder them; for the kingdom of God belongs to such as these.'" According to Salmond, the Greek word translated *indignant* in the NASB conveys both wrath and grief.[1] Jesus was angry with the lack of care shown by the disciples toward the children and grieved that the disciples had so misunderstood His message that they would hinder anyone from coming to Him, even those who appeared to be insignificant. Jesus used this event to instruct His followers about the importance of childlike faith. After this teaching moment, Jesus continues to interact with the children. Verse 16 states, "And He took them in His arms and began blessing them, laying His hands on them."

Jesus noticed and valued children, taking time even in the midst of His adult world to talk and play with them. Jesus' care of children demonstrates the importance of not overlooking or ignoring children, or treating them as unimportant. Sometimes following a disaster or crisis event, children get overlooked or brushed aside, as the disciples attempted to do even in Jesus' day.

CHILDREN ARE DIFFERENT FROM ADULTS

A child might experience the same traumatic event as an adult does, but the child will process the event in a manner markedly different from the adult. Children feel the same fear and anxiousness as adults do, but they may not show it. For children, the emotions related to a crisis or traumatic incident are

---

1. Salmond, *The Century Bible*, 244.

often overwhelming. Children feel emotions but do not always have labels for them or the capacity to put into words what they're experiencing.

Similarly, a child does not possess the same perspective of an extreme event that an adult may have. Children often struggle to make sense out of what happened, why it happened, and whether or not it will happen again. Whereas an adult can reason through many difficult circumstances, a child may not be able to do so. One example of this happened after the shooting at my church, described in the introduction. On Wednesday following the shooting, I drove my children to church for their evening mission activities. As we approached the parking lot near where the shooting took place, they became noticeably frightened, saying, "Dad, we can't go in the parking lot!" From my adult perspective, I knew that it was safe to enter the parking lot. Church members were probably safer than usual, in fact, because of the additional security personnel patrolling the church grounds. To my children, however, the once safe church parking lot was a scary place. They didn't have the ability to view the traumatic event from a larger perspective.

Children also differ from adults in what is traumatizing. Many of the same things that traumatize adults will be traumatic to children as well, including natural disasters, sudden death of a family member, or a personal accident or injury. Children, however, have other types of experiences that can also be traumatic. Any kind of physical or sexual abuse is traumatizing to a child. This type of experience is even more complex when a parent, one who should be providing for the child's safety, is the abuser. Children often experience severe or prolonged illness differently than adults do. An adult has the capacity to understand more of what is occurring, but illnesses, doctor appointments, medical procedures, and hospitalizations are often confusing and frightening to children. When parents divorce, children may experience the entire ordeal as traumatic. In the past, divorce was considered to be more of an inconvenience to a child, and what was thought to be in the parents' best interests must also be good for the child. Many researchers, though, are beginning to understand the long-term impact divorce has on children, and the impact looks more like a trauma than a temporary difficult period.[2] Thus, children and adults experience trauma through many of the same types of events, but children are traumatized by experiences that may not have an impact on adults in the same manner or to the same degree.

---

2. Brooks and Siegel, *The Scared Child*, 83–84.

A fundamental way that children differ from adults in how they interpret and respond to crisis events is the immature nature of their thought processes. Children do not process information about the world in the same manner as teenagers or adults. Understanding how children think is a part of comprehending how children respond to extreme and traumatizing events.

✳ CHILDREN'S THOUGHT PROCESSES ✳

Jean Piaget was a Swiss psychologist who spent most of his career studying the cognitive processes of children and teenagers. Although more current research on brain functioning has expanded Piaget's work, most developmentalists view Piaget as a pioneer in helping teachers, child-care workers, parents, and psychologists understand how children see and interpret the world.

Piaget believed that children pass through different stages of cognitive development. Each of these stages is marked by certain ways the child attempts to understand and make sense out of the world.[3] The first three stages occur during childhood and are identified below.

Sensorimotor Stage

The sensorimotor stage occurs in the first two years of life. During this stage, the child's main cognitive task is connecting sensory input or stimuli to motor activity. Thus, a young child will drop his spoon off the high chair, entertained by the fact that the spoon falls to the floor and makes a certain noise. As any parent knows, if the parent picks the spoon up and returns it to the child, the child will generally drop it again. This specific activity can take place for a prolonged period of time, and, more than likely, the parent will tire of the activity before the child does. This repeated cycle of behavior is actually very important to the child's cognitive development. The child is learning the connection between sensory events and motor skills.

Preoperational Stage

From the ages of two through seven, a child functions in the preoperational stage. In this phase, children perform basic problem-solving operations and communicate in an increasingly effective manner. Children's play and interactions in this stage are generally overt. When a child plays house, for example,

---

3. Berger, *Developing Person Through the Life Span*, 43.

the child comments on every movement he or she makes, often directing others in the activity, as well. A common phrase during the preoperational stage is, "Let's pretend . . ."

While those in this second stage are more advanced in their cognitive abilities than an infant or young toddler, children make strategic errors in their thinking process. Younger preschoolers will attribute lifelike qualities to inanimate objects, a process called animism.[4] A young child, for instance, might believe the moon is following the family's car or might sing a song to the Christmas tree.

Children in the preoperational stage are also egocentric in their thinking. A young child has difficulty thinking from another person's perspective. When my two older children were in preschool, my wife and I sometimes needed to take two vehicles to church. One time, my daughter and I were following behind my wife and son as we drove to church. I asked my daughter who was in the car in front of us, and she replied, "Mommy and Micah." I then asked, "Who's in the car behind Mommy and Micah?" Typical of a preschooler, my daughter was unable to think from any perspective outside her own, and thus, she did not have an answer.

One other cognitive error of preoperational children is a general inability to think about two properties of an item. If I have two rows of M&M's, for instance, both with seven pieces of candy, but have the first row spread out longer than the second, a younger child will tend to choose the longer row when asked which one he or she would like to have. Even if I explain that both rows have seven pieces of candy, counting them for the child, the child will still tend to choose the longer row. Younger children have difficulty focusing on more than one property of an item, and the longer row looks like it has more.

These errors in thinking in the preoperational stage become extremely important in understanding how children perceive and attempt to understand traumatic or crisis experiences. Unable to process all the information, a child often misperceives or misinterprets what has occurred. According to Brooks and Seigel, "Because preschoolers' understanding of the world is limited, they are able to grasp only bits and pieces of information about a traumatic situation. They then fill in gaps with their imagination."[5] Young children tend to make cause and effect connections that do not really exist, often believing they are responsible for events that are not actually in their control.

---

4. Santrock, *Life-Span Development*, 228.
5. Brooks and Seigel, *The Scared Child*, 16.

Concrete Operational Stage

Piaget's third stage of cognitive development is that of concrete operations, and generally occurs between the ages of seven and twelve. In this stage, children's thinking becomes more sophisticated. One major characteristic is the ability to internally manipulate symbols of language. Another characteristic is the ability to group items in more than one category at a time.[6] Older school-age children do not tend to play the "Let's pretend . . ." game, but rather use their imaginations to create entire stories or play sequences. Children in this age range do not commit many of the cognitive errors made by younger children. They can perform more sophisticated problem solving, but children in the concrete operations stage tend to have difficulty seeing a range of possible solutions to a given problem. Their thinking is inclined to be concrete, and they do not easily grasp more abstract concepts.

While school-age children are growing to be more sophisticated in their cognitive abilities, they are still susceptible to certain difficulties. Because they understand more, they have an increased awareness of their vulnerability.[7] They may realize that parents cannot always protect them and that bad things can happen. Because school-age children can process information internally, they may withdraw from others. School-age children understand more of what has occurred and they do not make errors in thinking that younger children are prone to make, but they still may not know how to understand emotions they experience and how to communicate with others about what is going on for them following a traumatic event.

HOW CHILDREN EXPERIENCE CRISIS AND TRAUMA

As with adults, all children are unique in how they are affected by and how they respond to extreme events.[8] The response of a specific child depends on the child's personality and on his or her developmental stage. The child's ability to cope is influenced to a great extent by support the child receives before, during, and following the traumatic event.

Traumatic events tend to produce feelings of helplessness and vulnerability in children. The world is no longer a safe place. In many instances, the child

---

6. Kelvin Seifert, Robert Hoffnung, and Michele Hoffnung, *Lifespan Development*, 2d ed. (Boston: Houghton Mifflin, 2000), 273.

7. Brooks and Siegel, *The Scared Child*, 18.

8. Wolfelt, *A Child's View of Grief*, 6.

comes to realize that the big people in the world, namely parents, cannot always protect him or her from harm. In some instances, the parents have caused the harm, which adds much to the child's confusion and sense of susceptibility. These feelings of helplessness and vulnerability produce anxiety in children, and a child may express this anxiety in a number of ways.

Apparent Unawareness

In some instances, a child may appear unaware of, or unfazed by, extreme events. On occasion, a parent tells me that a child seems to feel no impact from a significant loss, even the loss of a parent or a close grandparent. This apparent lack of awareness is often due to a couple of processes. First, strong emotions that accompany any extreme event or related loss are generally overwhelming. Children have difficulty experiencing strong emotions for a sustained period of time. A child may be noticeably sad following a death, but may suddenly shift and begin playing with friends or toys, behaviors that can be confusing to adults. To parents or other adults, it may appear as if the child is unaware, is not affected, or does not care about what has occurred. The likely reality is that the emotions are so overwhelming that the child shifts away from the uncomfortable emotions to more familiar and comforting activities.

A child may also appear unaffected because the child doesn't know how to articulate the emotions or anxiousness he or she feels. The child feels things, but cannot put the swirl of thoughts and emotions into words. When invited to talk about a traumatic event, a child may decline or may state that the event did not bother him or her. In most trauma situations, the child is affected, though, and feels emotions but doesn't yet have adequate verbal skills for coping. Supportive, patient care by adults is essential on these occasions.

[handwritten margin note: when a child appears to be unaffected by a death]

Through Play

According to Landreth, "Play is the singular central activity of childhood, occurring at all times and in all places."[9] Children play in almost every circumstance or surrounding. Thus, a child often deals with traumatic experiences through play. Play serves the functions of discharging emotions, allowing the child some control over outcomes, and buffering the child from some of the horrors of a difficult event.

Following natural disasters, adults may notice that neighborhood children

---

9. Landreth, *Play Therapy*, 7.

spend hours re-creating the tornado or hurricane or flood. A child who suffers numerous illnesses may play doctor or hospital. Children who have experienced a robbery may re-create the event, wanting to be the police officer, or finding some way to prevent the bad person from hurting the family.

The child's play becomes, then, an essential part of coping and of working through the confusing and painful circumstances. At times, adults may be frustrated with children, thinking they're being frivolous or uncaring, not realizing how important play is to a child's overall effort to cope.

Regression

One of the exciting things about parenting is watching children progress to new developmental stages. Seeing a child take his or her first steps, learn to read, or play a first soccer game is thrilling to a parent. Conversely, watching a child revert to an earlier stage of functioning can be frustrating and disconcerting. Following traumatic events, children often appear to take steps backward.

Subsequent to any type of trauma, many children are clingy and demand attention from parents. Even a rather independent child may want to be held or rocked. The child might have trouble with any kind of separation from parents and may not want to go to church or school. These types of fears are often seen at bedtime, when a child does not want to sleep alone or expresses a desire to sleep with parents. The child may want the parent to check and double-check that all doors are locked and may want the parent to look in closets and under the bed for anything that could be dangerous.

Regression also takes other forms. A young child may wet his or her pants or revert to thumb sucking or crawling.[10] A child of any age may suddenly start wetting the bed, even if the child has not had an accident of this nature for years. A child may request help with tasks he or she has already mastered, such as tying shoes or getting dressed.

While a child's regression can be quite disconcerting to parents, it's a fairly typical effect of a traumatic event or of a significant loss. A parent's calm assurance and support often helps the child regain a sense of stability and security.

Emotional Expressions

As do adults, children may experience both sadness and anger following a trauma or loss, and may, indeed, express open anger and sadness. Both sadness

---

10. Fitzgerald, *The Grieving Child*, 132.

and anger, however, may also be expressed in ways that make it harder to determine what a child is feeling. Anger may surface in the form of frustration, with a child bursting into tears when having difficulty with some task or activity. Sadness may be articulated through withdrawal, lack of energy, or through a lack of interest in a favorite activity. Because children have difficulty recognizing and understanding the strong emotions that follow difficult circumstances, they are generally confused and frustrated by what they encounter.

Following a traumatic event or significant loss, children also commonly experience guilt and self-blame. Because children's thought processes are not mature, they often blame themselves for events over which they have no control. A child may believe that he or she caused a family automobile accident or that because the child misbehaved, he or she contracted a serious illness.

One of the most common examples of guilt and self-blame occurs when parents divorce. It's not uncommon for a child to believe that he or she is the cause for the parents' breakup. These particular feelings are often exacerbated if the child overhears parents arguing about parenting matters pertaining to the child in the time period leading up to the divorce. In some instances, the child may also believe that by being good, the parents will get back together. When reconciliation does not occur, the child often experiences confusion in addition to sadness and frustration.

Behavioral Expressions

Following an extreme event, a child may attempt to cope through his or her behavior. Whereas reading a child's emotions can be difficult, an adult may clearly see the impact of trauma or loss through what a child does.

While some children become passive and withdrawn following trauma, others act out. Some children become aggressive toward siblings, other children, and even parents. Other children test limits, misbehaving at home, at school, and even in church. A formerly compliant child may challenge a parent, refusing to follow even reasonable rules.

Often behavioral changes are seen in the disruption of a child's normal routines. As do adults, children may have trouble eating and sleeping following a crisis or trauma. Many children have disturbing dreams and nightmares, and a few may experience night terrors, from which a child awakens terrorized by images of a trauma event.

Some children exhibit risky behaviors following traumatic events, engaging in dangerous play, for instance, with no regard to personal safety. A young child I knew, following the death of his mother, would regularly leap off of various high places, such as stairs, playground equipment, and anything else he could climb. This was not characteristic of him prior to his mother's death, but it's not unusual behavior for a child suffering a significant loss.

When school-age children experience trauma, schoolwork often suffers. The child may have difficulty concentrating. If his or her family continues to be in crisis, parents may not be physically or emotionally available to help with schoolwork or projects. Declining grades are often an indicator that a child is struggling in the wake of a loss or trauma.

Helping Children Cope

When a child experiences a traumatic event, there are many ways in which adults can assist the child's coping and adjusting. Parents, relatives, and other adult caregivers are vital to helping the child adjust, and their sensitivity is essential to the child's coping effectively.

Strive to Maintain a Routine

Children function best if they have routines or stable, familiar patterns for activities. Routines provide the child with a sense of security and safety. Following a traumatic or crisis experience, though, a child's routines are often disrupted. This is especially true if a parent dies, if parents divorce, or if the family faces certain types of natural disasters. If parents are victims of the traumatic experience, it may be difficult for the family to maintain any type of routine.

Adhering as closely as possible to normal routines serves to comfort children. In the case of certain disruptions, the family may need to develop new routines, even including the children in deciding some elements of the routine. Attempting to maintain normalcy aids the child, reducing his or her feelings of being adrift during difficult times.

Provide the Child with Physical Contact

Physical contact with parents or adults is comforting, following a traumatic event. When parents hold a child, hug the child, and express affection toward the child, the young one feels reassured and soothed. An exception is if a child has experienced sexual abuse or some types of physical abuse. Abused children still need physical contact, but this should not be done in a manner that reminds the child of the abuse.

Allow the Child to Play

As mentioned, play is an essential part of any child's world, and especially so following a trauma or loss. Play allows a child a breather from strong emotions, helps the child gain control when things seem quite out of control, and helps the child discharge emotions. Play is not a sign of disrespect following a loss, such as the death of a relative. Play is a crucial part of the child's attempt to cope and adjust.

Help a Child Gain Mastery over the Environment

Traumatic experiences tend to produce feelings of lack of control and vulnerability. Adults can look for ways to help children gain some measure of mastery over the environment. This might include putting a nightlight in a child's room or giving the child a flashlight. Allowing a child to give input into nonessential family decisions, having the child draw a picture, or working with the child to rebuild something damaged during a trauma event are examples of activities that might reduce feelings of helplessness.

Avoid Parentifying the Child

A parentified child is one who is pulled into an adult role or must assume adultlike responsibility. Following traumatic events or losses, children can be compelled into positions of adult duties. An older child may end up cooking dinner several nights a week or serving as the primary babysitter for younger siblings.

I've heard people tell fairly young children something like, "With your dad gone, you're now the man of the house. Your mother will really need your help now." In other instances, a parent may look to a child as a friend and confidant, conveying to the child information that is more appropriate for adult relationships.

The main problem with children being parentified is that they're not emotionally ready for what is asked from them. While a child may have to perform extra chores, and a child and parent may develop a close relationship following divorce or death of the other parent, the young one still needs to be allowed to be a child. Ideally, following trauma or loss, parents, relatives, and other adults should allow children to continue to be children, by not pulling them into roles for which they are not prepared.

COMMUNICATING WITH CHILDREN FOLLOWING TRAUMA

A crucial element of helping a child cope is communicating with the child about the events that have taken place and about how the child is doing. Because children do not view traumatic events in the same manner as do adults, communication can be somewhat tricky. Parents and other adults should be talking to children after extreme events and encouraging children to talk. Parents should listen for both what the child says, as well as for what the child does not say. If a child doesn't say anything about a traumatic event, it doesn't mean he or she isn't thinking about it. When a child is not talking, parents can gently ask questions, or talk about some component of the event, even if the child does not respond. Parents should be aware of giving nonverbal messages that indicate to the child that it's not okay to talk about difficult circumstances. Other communication guidelines are as follows:

Listen to Children

If a child experiences a traumatic event, adults should listen to the child, both when he or she talks about the experience and in general conversations. Listening involves paying attention with one's eyes as well as one's ears, as a child will often communicate through behavior. If a child is not talking, asking the child about thoughts and feelings might facilitate communication.

Be Truthful with Children

It's tempting to soften the blow to a child by not telling him or her the truth about what has happened. While this might avoid short-term discomfort for the adult, in the long run, it will be confusing to the child. It's possible to tell the truth in a gentle way while providing support to the child.

Do Not Tell the Child More Than the Child Needs to Know

Whereas it's essential to be truthful with children, there are details of traumatic events that a child does not need to hear. Parents should be discerning about what is appropriate for children to know. Following the September 11 bombings in New York City, my wife and I discussed how much of the event and related news coverage to expose our children to. With our two older children, we discussed many facets of the bombing—who was responsible, what it meant to our country, and even plans for family safety should there be a disaster closer to home. We tended to keep our two younger children sheltered from many aspects of the news reports, especially from the repeated images of the buildings collapsing or people jumping out of the upper floors. A child's age, level of maturity, and personality serve as guides for how much information to disclose.

A child may, though, get information from sources outside the family. Following a community disaster, a child may hear disturbing details from school peers, neighbors, or through the media. If this happens, parents can listen for the child's concerns, talk factually with him or her, and reassure the child in a supportive manner. There may be an instance when a parent chooses not to let a child have exposure to the media or be around another child who possesses more information than is beneficial.

Answer Questions

Children often will ask many questions about a tragic event. A child can benefit not only from being allowed to ask questions, but also from being encouraged to do so. When children ask questions, adults get a feel for what those children are thinking and how they view or interpret events. Parents should answer questions as best they can, being honest and attempting to answer at the child's level of readiness. When parents answer questions, they help undo many faulty conclusions children may draw about circumstances based on lack of understanding of an event or based on magical types of thinking.

Avoid Making False Promises

On some occasions following a traumatic event, a parent or adult will tell a child that, "Everything is okay. Nothing else bad will happen." While this is an understandable response designed to reassure a child, in some crisis events the situation continues to deteriorate. Following a robbery, parents may be tempted to tell a child that something of this nature will never happen again. Perhaps the better way to handle this is to describe to the child the steps that parents are taking to ensure the child's safety. The family who was robbed might talk to the child about changing locks or getting a watchdog. Where a fire occurred, the family might talk about and practice escape plans, equipping the child with a plan should a similar event ever recur.

*giving children resources - action steps - for what they will do.

CHILDREN AND COUNSELING

Even after a difficult or traumatic event, not all children need counseling. Many children will make it though a crisis or recover from the blow of trauma with the help of loving, supportive adults who are a part of the children's world. Safe, familiar adults, especially parents, are usually the best source of helping children cope.

In some instances, however, a child will benefit from counseling or from counseling-related services. Listed below are some situations when a parent may consider taking a child to counseling.

When Parents' Emotional Resources Are Diminished

Crisis or trauma often strikes an entire family. When this occurs, a parent or parents may not have the capacity to provide the child with the emotional support he or she might need, and the child might benefit from seeing a counselor. Counselors working with a family or with any particular member of a family should be cognizant of children in the family and of whether or not the parents are able to provide for the physical and emotional needs of children. The counselor may need to work with the family to access counseling help for children.

When the Child Struggles with Self-harm Thoughts or Behaviors

It's not as common for children to engage in self-destructive behavior as it is for teenagers, but it does happen. If a child is talking about harming him- or herself, or if the child engages in any kind of self-harm behavior or gestures, it's necessary to find a counselor for the child.

Persistent Struggles in School

It's not unusual for a child's academic and social functioning to be negatively affected by a traumatic event. In many cases, this difficulty is temporary, and the child returns to his or her normal functioning. If the child experiences a prolonged period of academic struggle, if his or her grades drop noticeably, or if the child has a conspicuous increase of peer-related problems, it can be helpful to seek out a counselor.

Ongoing Regressive Behavior

While some regressive behavior is normal, if the problem persists over a prolonged period, it's time to locate a counselor. If the regression, such as bed-wetting, seems to have any physiological basis, talking to the child's pediatrician is also a wise step.

Any Extensive Trauma

Seeking a counselor is prudent anytime a child experiences a severe trauma. If a child is in close proximity to trauma, if the child's life is threatened, or if anyone around the child loses his or her life, the child may benefit from counseling. Instances of abuse, especially when the abuse has occurred on multiple occasions, call for locating a counselor who specializes in treating sexual or physical abuse.

When seeking a counselor for a child, the ideal is to locate a therapist with expertise in working with children. Many therapists focus on adults and do not have training in, or knowledge about, counseling children. A children's counselor will have experience in addressing a variety of struggles faced by children and is in a position to provide the best care.

Therapy with children may involve more traditional methods of having the child talk about concerns, or it may take the form of play therapy. Play therapy is used especially for younger children who have difficulty expressing themselves verbally. In these instances, the process of play becomes the therapeutic avenue for helping the child work through emotions related to a tragedy or loss.

Children's therapy may also take place in a group setting. Many agencies and churches offer groups for children that focus on grief, coping with divorce, or learning skills for relating to others. Groups can be valuable in that children hear peers talk about their experiences, such as dealing with divorce or death of a loved one. Children learn from peers and can serve as support to peers, as well.

As for adults, it is essential that the child feel safe with the therapist and that the child-therapist relationship be a good fit. An effective therapist should communicate with parents, not so much the specifics of what a child talks about or does in a session, but to provide an overview of how the child is doing and where counseling is heading. The combination of supportive parents and a skilled counselor can be very helpful in aiding a child's recovery following difficult experiences.

FRAGILE, YET RESILIENT

Children are fragile. Crises, traumatic events, and significant losses can wound a child, impacting his or her emotions, beliefs about the world, conclusions about the child's worth, about the trustworthiness of adults, and even about the nature of God. I regularly deal with adults in counseling who refer to events from their childhoods that shaped their lives for years after. Trauma in childhood can leave emotional scars that are challenging to overcome.

At the same time, children are remarkably resilient. Many, many children experience harsh circumstances, losses, abuse, and even extensive trauma, and not only survive, but thrive as they move through adolescence and into adulthood. While I see people in counseling who struggle, I also see many others who are thriving. Many of these individuals experienced extreme life circumstances during childhood, but are doing well in adult life. They have strong marriages, are good parents, and are often leaders in church and community life. They do well in school and have close relationships. I'm regularly amazed at how resilient children can be.

I love the story told in Luke 2:41–50, in which Jesus' family loses Him. Having traveled to Jerusalem for Passover, the family returns toward Nazareth in a large group following the celebration. Both parents probably assumed Jesus was with the other parent, or with some relative. When they discover Jesus is missing, they hurry back to Jerusalem to find Him. *The search takes three days!* Having made my own share of parenting mistakes, I can imagine the thoughts that went through Mary's and Joseph's minds, and the lively parent conversations between them during the search. They finally locate young Jesus, who seems quite perplexed that they would have missed Him. Mary does that great mom thing, saying, "Why have you treated us like this?" (Luke 2:48 HCSB). Jesus' parents made mistakes, and yet Jesus was unaffected.

Children are both fragile and resilient. Caregivers and adults who work with children must recognize the importance of the love and care given to children following a crisis or traumatic event. Failure to do so can result in years of struggle. Effective caregiving, on the other hand, helps facilitate the child's ability to cope.

CHAPTER 11

ADOLESCENTS AND CRISES

TIM'S STORY

FIFTEEN-YEAR-OLD TIM LOVED TO GO skiing each Christmas break. Between Christmas and New Year's, his mother would take Tim and his older brother James for a week of fun in the mountains. Tim's parents were divorced, but his mother loved the outdoors and had made the ski trip an annual vacation since her sons became teenagers. This particular year, the snow started falling heavily as the two boys and their mother drove up the mountain toward the ski resort. At a certain spot, all vehicles were required to pull to the side of the road and put chains on their tires before proceeding up the hill. Tim and James jumped out of the car, laughing and sliding in the snow. They were veterans at getting the chains on the tires and could do so quickly. As they were putting the rear driver's side chains in place, a car slid out of control and careened toward the boys. Tim managed to jump out of the way, but the car struck James, injuring him severely. Although onlookers helped and notified rescue personnel, James died a few hours later.

A few weeks after the accident, Tim's mother brought him to counseling. Tim was withdrawn, depressed, and not doing well in school. Tim repeatedly saw mental images of the accident, and he felt guilty for not rescuing his brother from the crash. Tim was even experiencing some hallucination-like symptoms that had not been present prior to the accident, and he was worried that he was going crazy.

Counseling with Tim entailed helping him talk about the accident, about his relationship with his brother, and about the losses he'd experienced as a result of the accident. Involving Tim's mother in periodic counseling sessions assisted in providing stability and gave her strategies for both understanding and reaching out to her son. While Tim had withdrawn from family and friends, he was willing to talk in counseling, which allowed an outlet for him to deal with his emotions and to process what occurred. Tim and his mother consulted a physician to monitor the hallucinations—the doctor concluded that the trauma played a part in Tim's symptoms, which eventually subsided over time. Tim left counseling after several weeks, not completely recovered, but in a much better position to continue grieving and adjusting to the loss of his brother.

ADOLESCENCE AND THE BIBLE

The Bible does not speak directly to the life phase known in American culture as adolescence. The Bible does, however, contain many stories and direct passages that relate to youthfulness. Some passages teach the young how to grow and mature; others highlight some of the problems and the promise associated with youth.

The book of Proverbs was written, in part, to help guide those who are young. Proverbs 1:4 identifies one of the main purposes of the book: "To give prudence to the naive, to the youth knowledge and discretion." Each of the first six chapters of Proverbs begins with encouragement for the young person to heed the words of the more experienced individual, and to function not according to the follies of youth, but learn to have wisdom and prudence. The writers of Proverbs acknowledge the tendency of youth to be impulsive, immature, and in need of guidance.

Many Bible figures appear in the pages of Scripture when they are young. In the Old Testament, Joseph is seventeen when he's sold into slavery after telling his brothers that, in his dream, they all bowed down to him (Gen. 37:1–11). When David offers to fight Goliath, Saul says, "You are not able to go against this Philistine to fight with him; for you are but a youth while he has been a warrior from his youth" (1 Sam. 17:33). When God calls Jeremiah, the prophet replies that he is too young. God responds, "Do not say, 'I am a youth,' because everywhere I send you, you shall go, and all that I command you, you shall speak" (Jer. 1:7). In the New Testament, Paul tells Timothy, "Let no one look down on your youthfulness, but rather in speech, conduct, love, faith and purity, show yourself an example of those who believe" (1 Tim. 4:12). Many individuals speculate that Mary was a teenager when the angel told her she would give birth to the Messiah (Luke 1:30–33). While there are challenges in being young, the examples of each of these notable figures demonstrate that God often chooses to work through individuals despite their youthfulness.

THE TEEN YEARS

Being an adolescent is kind of like walking up a path etched into the side of a mountain—a vertical rise on one side, a steep drop-off on the other. It can be simultaneously exhilarating and frightening. In the mountains, the view is great, and having made the climb lends a sense of accomplishment. It's possible, however, to step off the path and to tumble down the side of the mountain. Such a tumble can be frightening and painful.

Like the mountain hiker, most teens enjoy a number of positive experiences. They acquire new talents and abilities, often finding areas where they surpass their peers. Teens develop physical strength and have a great deal of stamina. Independence produces a thrill, allowing the teen to go new places and try new activities. Relationships with the opposite sex are often exciting. Even sleeping until noon on Saturdays or in the summertime can be a source of great joy.

The teen years can also be frustrating, scary, and troublesome, much like the hiker sliding down a steep mountainside. Life often seems out of control. Feelings of anger and rage may suddenly emerge, then vanish. Teens agonize over their appearance, wondering if they're attractive or ugly. Embarrassing moments produce excruciating pain. Some teens feel isolated, believing no one understands or cares. Many teens know the feelings of being excluded or being the source of peer ridicule and derision.

Teenagers often find themselves suspended between two worlds—not quite adults, but definitely not children. Thinking, behavior, and emotions often range dramatically between these two worlds. At times, teens are quite mature and reasonable. On other occasions, they act self-centered and childlike, if not childish.

The adolescent years are a unique and challenging phase of development, and those who work with teens following crisis or trauma events must understand some of the distinct features of how teens are affected. To comprehend this specific developmental stage, it's important to understand some of the changes that take place for adolescents, how teens interpret difficult events, and how trauma affects teens. Last, a helper must know how to relate to adolescents following a difficult event.

Important Changes During Adolescence

Perhaps the most characteristic marker of the teen years is rapid growth with accompanying physical and emotional changes. A parent buying shoes for a teenage male may discover that six weeks later he's outgrown them. Teens not only grow physically, but change emotionally and cognitively, as well. These rapid and extensive changes have a great impact on how a teen experiences a crisis or trauma event and have important implications for those assisting the adolescent. Some of the key areas of change for adolescents are identity formation, puberty, and cognitive growth and development.

Identity Formation

One of the main tasks of the adolescent years is developing a sense of identity. A person's identity is a clear and consistent awareness of whom one is. This sense, when fully developed, tends to be stable across time and in various situations. A younger teen in the process of developing a sense of identity often experiences a great deal of flux in how the teen sees him- or herself. One week, the teen may dress like the cool kids. The next week, the teen may try to look like one of the athletes. This may be followed by trying to look punk or preppie, then again trying to look like one of the cool kids. Veteran parents, and others who work with youth, know not to get too upset by a teen trying on identities like he or she tries on clothes—it's all part of the process of determining identity.

As adolescence progresses, most teens begin to develop a clearer sense of self. They discover talents and skills, find what they enjoy doing, identify and adhere to a specific set of values, and generally form a peer group that shares their interests and value systems. When a teen develops a sense of self that is relatively stable from month to month and in many different situations, the teen has achieved a sense of identity.

Noted author and child development expert David Elkind believes there are two pathways adolescents travel in the attempt to develop a sense of identity.[1] The first is the pathway of integration, where teens are able to distinguish their thoughts, feelings, and experiences from those of other individuals while simultaneously discovering how they are similar to others. This integration is integral to the development of a sense of identity. Teens who function by an

---

1. Elkind, *All Grown Up and No Place to Go*, 18–22.

integrated sense of self are more future-oriented, can delay gratification for long-term pursuits, and do not have to rely on others in making decisions. In short, they function by a clear sense of personal identity.

The second pathway is one of substitution, whereby instead of differentiating from others, the adolescent appropriates thoughts, beliefs, and emotions from others, resulting in a patchwork self. Elkind believes that teens who develop a patchwork self are more easily influenced by others, have more difficulty with impulse control, and tend to be focused on the present. Regarding the patchwork self, Elkind states, "A young person who has constructed a sense of self in this way has no inner sense of self to fall back on for guidance and direction. Such individuals are easily influenced by others, both because they have no inner gyroscope and because they have developed the habit of following others rather than making their own decisions. Each new situation is a fresh challenge, and they are always looking for external direction—which may not be forthcoming. Adolescents with a patchwork self are vulnerable to stress because they must always look to others for coping strategies."[2]

Identity development is thus a central task of adolescence, and it may be affected when a teen experiences a crisis or trauma. Depending on the severity and extent of the event, identity development can be delayed or even halted. Faulty beliefs resulting from a traumatic event may be incorporated into what the teen believes about him- or herself. Those working with teens in a crisis or trauma situation must, then, be alert to the impact an extreme event can have on the process and outcome of identity development.

Puberty

Early in adolescence, teenagers experience a period of rapid growth and sexual development that marks progression from childhood to the teen years. Crucial changes include development of primary sex characteristics—the parts of the body that have to do with reproduction—and secondary sex characteristics, which include changing body shape and getting taller. Females experience growth of pubic hair and breast development; males experience growth of pubic and facial hair and a deepening voice.

Puberty is also characterized by significant hormonal changes. The hypothalamus alerts the pituitary, which sends signals to the adrenal gland and ovaries or testes to increase hormone production, which results in the growth

---

2. Ibid., 22.

experienced by teenagers. In addition to physical and sexual changes, hormones contribute to emotional development. According to Berger, hormones play a role in the rapid emotional shifts and emotional extremes a teen may experience. She states, "Although these hormonal effects are lifelong, they are more erratic and powerful, and less familiar and controllable in the years right after puberty begins."[3]

Puberty and the associated changes are also linked to a teen's feelings of self-worth. The young person who develops early in the teen years may be seen as more mature than his or her counterpart who develops later. The teen who develops later may struggle with a lack of self-confidence and can be the object of peer derision. All of this impacts how the teen sees and feels about him- or herself. When combined together, the rapid hormonal changes, a teen's rate of development, and how the teen feels about these changes make for a potentially complicated journey.

Like so many other experiences in the adolescent years, puberty can produce joy and anxiety, happiness and pain. If a teen experiences a crisis or traumatic event, the effects of the trauma are layered on the already complicated processes of physical and sexual development. A teen who is naturally prone to mood shifts and extremes can be overwhelmed by the emotions associated with traumatic experiences, making coping even more treacherous.

Cognitive Development

Yet another key area of development during the adolescent years is growth in the brain and associated cognitive alterations. Comprehending changes that take place in cognitive development is pivotal to an overall understanding of how trauma impacts a teenager.

Piaget, the Swiss psychologist identified in chapter 10, was a pioneer in studying how children and teenagers think. He was one of the first to describe a significant shift in cognitive processes between childhood and adolescence. Older children can perform basic problem-solving tasks and generally avoid the cognitive errors of younger children, and teenagers are often much more sophisticated in their thinking and reasoning abilities. Piaget referred to adolescence as a time of formal operations, marked by the ability to think abstractly, to reason more effectively and efficiently, and to see more than one solution to various problems. Most parents of teens have experienced their

---

3. Berger, *Developing Person Through the Life Span*, 343.

child suddenly becoming very lawyerlike in arguing for what he or she wants. The teen remembers facts and dates, and spots loopholes from a mile away. Many teens argue as a means of entertainment, appearing to get a thrill out of their newly developed cognitive abilities.

Recently, technological advances such as PET scans (positron emission tomography) and MRIs (magnetic resonance imaging) have allowed researchers to map the brains of teenagers. The results provide much more detailed information about what takes place in adolescent brain development. Prior to the 1990s, the general belief was that a person's brain changed dramatically in early childhood and that the major phases of brain development were complete prior to adolescence. According to Bradley, researchers now understand differently. He states, "While it is true that 95 percent of the brain is developed by the age five, *the most advanced parts of the brain don't complete their development until adolescence is pretty much over.*"[4]

Key brain changes occur in the corpus callosum, the prefrontal cortex, and in the nerve cells within the brain. During adolescence, the corpus callosum, or the band of nerves that connects the two halves of the brain, grows dramatically. The growth in this brain structure allows the halves of the teenager's brain to communicate with each other, which becomes significant in decision making.[5]

A second major area of change in an adolescent's brain occurs in the neurons, or nerve cells residing in the brain. During the teen years a young person's brain cells experience rapid growth, connecting with many other brain cells. When teenagers perform certain cognitive or physical activities, these connections between nerve cells grow stronger and more efficient. Connections between brain cells that are not used eventually shrink and disappear, a process known as blossoming and pruning.[6] A teenager's brain is actually being rewired through these processes. Additionally, the nerve cells in the brain are undergoing a development called myelination. Myelin serves as a type of insulation that allows messages to be transmitted more rapidly along each nerve cell. As a teenager's brain undergoes this particular change, the teen is able to think and perform many tasks more quickly and efficiently. These specific changes in the brain's nerve cells actually produce a great deal of the erratic behavior common to the teen years.

---

4. Bradley, *Yes, Your Teen Is Crazy,* 6 (italics in the original).
5. Ibid.
6. David Walsh, *Why Do They Act That Way? A Survival Guide to the Adolescent Brain for You and Your Teen* (New York: Free Press, 2004), 32–33.

One other area of brain development occurs in the prefrontal cortex, or the area of the brain responsible for the higher or executive functioning of the brain. According to Bradley, not only does this specific part of the brain do most of its maturation during the teen years, but it is responsible for such functions as emotional control, impulse restraint, and decision making.[7]

Contrary, then, to earlier beliefs, the adolescent is undergoing extensive changes in brain structure and in cognitive abilities. These changes impact how the teenager views and interprets events, how he or she attempts to cope, and what the teen concludes about the world. When trauma strikes during these crucial developmental processes, the blow can be far-reaching.

CHANGES IN ADOLESCENCE: IMPACT ON GENERAL FUNCTIONING

A couple of my friends and I took our sons to a hockey game a few years ago. Our sons had all just entered middle school and were beginning their growth spurts. During one of the intermissions, the arena allowed children down on the ice to pick up hockey pucks as a part of a promotional activity. Sitting high above the ice, I watched our sons enter the rink. Three toothpicks wearing size eleven tennis shoes, the boys walked out on the ice, attempting to keep their footing, something not easy for them to do even on non-icy surfaces. Watching, I was cognizant that this simple activity was somewhat representative of adolescence: the boys were aware that others were looking, and they were attempting to look cool and nonchalant, each doing his best not to fall on his face in front of the crowd.

Adolescence is a tricky stage of life, involving changes in every area of development. But how do these changes, described above, impact adolescent functioning? What do these changes mean for everyday living? Understanding how adolescent development impacts daily functioning is a crucial component of grasping how these changes impact a teenager during periods of crisis or trauma.

Egocentrism

During the teen years, adolescents often return to egocentric functioning. It's not uncommon for teens to sense themselves as the center of the universe

---

7. Bradley, *Yes, Your Teen Is Crazy*, 7.

and to have difficulty being empathetic or seeing things from any perspective besides their own. A teenage girl, for instance, might ask to borrow her mother's hairbrush, only to scream at the mother later in the day when the mother wants to borrow the daughter's hairbrush.

Teens function by the imaginary audience, that is, the sense that they're on center stage and everyone else in the world is watching them, paying close attention to every move they make. This is why a teenager often feels so self-conscious, shy, or embarrassed, even about things that didn't bother the teen when younger. Because of the imaginary audience, adolescents tend to be preoccupied with what others think about them.

Functioning from an egocentric perspective, a teenager tends to feel that his or her world is unique and that others do not understand what the teen is experiencing. Phrases like, "You don't know what it's like!" and "You didn't have to deal with the things I have to deal with!" are common and are generally directed toward parents. Like so many other aspects of the teenage world, the egocentrism experienced by teens can be exciting (Everyone is watching me) or disconcerting (No one really cares about me).

Impulsive Behavior

Sooner or later, teens, especially younger ones, will do or say something that appears strange to an adult. My twin daughters recently went on a middle school mission trip. When they returned, we heard story after story that made me thankful for other individuals willing to travel across the U.S. with younger teens. One middle schooler decided to make the five-day trip without bathing. Another poured large quantities of salt in everyone's drinks at a nice restaurant. Still another covered his new, expensive tennis shoes with layer upon layer of duct tape; the shoes had to be cut off his feet at the day's end. If an adult were to ask any one of these teens why they did these things, the answer would be the famous line, "I don't know."

Many of the changes teenagers experience contribute to this impulsive behavior. Teens can act without thinking, make rash decisions, and often have difficulty seeing consequences or long-term effects of choices they make. While teens may clamor for adult responsibility, their spasms of impulsiveness necessitate adult supervision until they begin to demonstrate consistency and stability in their behavior. Further, a teenager's tendencies toward impulsiveness can be exacerbated in times of crisis.

Help them
think through

Risk-taking

Risk-taking behavior is a common characteristic of the teen years, influenced by the numerous changes adolescents undergo. This tendency toward risk taking may be mild—expressed in adventurous activities like extreme sports—or it may be more dangerous, like using drugs and alcohol, or engaging in unsafe driving or risky sexual behavior.

According to Berger, teens are inclined to live by the invincibility fable, or the sense that they can't be harmed by things dangerous to other humans.[8] Teens believe that they're not vulnerable or that bad things can't happen to them. This belief contributes to various kinds of extreme behavior and unnecessary risk taking.

Taking unnecessary risks is not just limited to troubled teens. Walsh states, "All sorts of kids take foolish risks. It happens often enough that most people think of teenage risk taking as a part of growing up. But sometimes we're caught off guard. When good kids—the honor students, the class presidents, the kids who play sports, hold down after school jobs, and follow the rules—when they get themselves into dangerous or destructive situations, we often don't know what to think of it."[9]

As teenagers move into early adulthood, gain experience with life, and encounter real consequences of taking risks, many come to be more reasonable about their choices. While in the teen years, however, risk taking may produce thrills, or it may generate outcomes more costly in nature.

Errors in Thinking

While teenagers are much more sophisticated in their thinking and problem-solving abilities than are younger children, teens still make errors in their thinking processes. Although teenagers' brains are being rewired for more complicated thought processes, they lack the practical experience that helps them make wise choices. Identified below are several notable types of errors teens make in cognitive processing.

1. *All-or-nothing thinking.* Teenagers tend to view the world in extremes of good or bad, right or wrong, all or nothing. A teenage boy may come home one day, announcing that his math teacher really likes him. Later

---

8. Berger, *Developing Person Through the Life Span*, 368.
9. Walsh, *Why Do They Act That Way?* 55.

that week, however, the teen may state that this same teacher hates him. One parent can be the good guy one day, but the bad guy the next. A love interest may be without flaw for several weeks, but the worst person in the world when the relationship goes bad. Often there seems to be no middle ground. Many teens become interested in social causes as they travel through adolescence, seeing these causes as good and right.

2. *Drawing conclusions from limited evidence.* Most parents have heard their teens draw extreme conclusions from limited information. "My English teacher hates me," the teen announces, walking in the door from school. "How do you know?" asks the mother. The teen gives a vague answer about trying to ask the teacher a question before class and the teacher's not responding. The teenager concludes that the teacher dislikes him. Similarly, another teen may declare, "Nobody likes me." When the parent tries to determine what's going on, the parent finds that the daughter was snubbed by her current love interest. In both these instances, the adolescent takes limited information and draws a conclusion of questionable accuracy.

3. *Fair and unfair thinking.* Adolescents are often preoccupied with what seems fair or unfair. Sometimes this is directed outwardly—the teen champions an underdog in a larger social matter. More commonly, the teen, fueled by egocentric thinking, evaluates and makes proclamations about what seems fair or unfair in the teen's immediate world. The teenager may remind parents of unfair treatment related to what took place for other siblings: "It's not fair; Mary didn't have to be in at ten." Fair/unfair discussions are often directed at schoolteachers and administrators: "It's unfair we have to wear uniforms!" Fair/unfair statements can be aimed at anything that doesn't fit with what the teen wants to do: "It's unfair that I have to take out the trash! What about Steven? You never make him do anything!" When adults hear the word "unfair," it most often does not refer to a larger cosmic equity but that something isn't going the way the teen wants it to.

In each of these examples the adolescent's cognitive processes, ability to reason, and conclusions about events is affected by the significant and extensive changes the brain is experiencing. These changes, although necessary for eventual adult thinking, result in various errors in how the teen views and interprets the world.

CHANGES IN ADOLESCENCE:
IMPACT DURING CRISIS OR TRAUMA

According to Brooks and Seigel, extreme events can have a profound impact on teenagers. They state, "Adolescents, or 'almost adults,' are an inherently erratic bunch, and their responses to trauma reflect their nature. They have a grown-up grasp of the reality of the traumatic situation, but their reactions can swing wildly from that of a mature adult to that of a young child. One minute they're asking what they can do to help out, and the next minute they're acting recklessly."[10]

The fact that teenagers experience rapid growth and development over a period of several years has important implications for how they experience crisis, trauma, and loss. Several key areas affected by trauma events are identified below.

Misperceiving or Misinterpreting Situations

The rapid brain development and maturation of teens affect the manner in which they perceive or interpret events, which, in turn, affects their coping with trauma or crises situations. With the tendency toward extreme thinking, even smaller events may feel like crises. Breaking up with a boyfriend or girlfriend, making a low grade in a class, even struggling with acne can appear to be a crisis. In the immature thinking of teens, any kind of embarrassment or frustration seems unending and teens can believe that things will always feel distressing. Because of their tendency to misinterpret events, some teens live lives of perpetual crisis.

When a teen does, in actuality, experience a trauma event, immature thought processes contribute to the teen's struggles to cope effectively. Following a natural disaster, an adolescent may panic, thinking he or she will never see friends again, or believing that things will never return to normal. Teens also have a tendency to fill in the gaps in the aftermath of trauma, developing faulty conclusions about why an event happened or what the event means. Because the teen may be in the process of identity development, the teen might be inclined to draw faulty conclusions about his or her own value, worth, performance, or future.

---

10. Brooks and Siegel, *The Scared Child*, 19.

Struggling with Emotions

In the best of circumstances, most teenagers tend to experience emotional extremes and rapid mood swings. When a teen goes through a traumatic event, these emotions are often exacerbated and magnified. Following trauma, a teen can feel hopeless, helpless, and despondent. Unlike most adults, a teen is not always able to reason through some of the emotions and does not have the life experience that allows him or her to view the situation from any objective reference point.

With teens, even regular life events can feel emotionally devastating, and these feelings are magnified following trauma. Teens may conclude that no one really understands, and they can be prone to internalize these feelings, becoming withdrawn or depressed. Some teens act out their emotions, taking out frustration on people or objects around them.

One of the dangers with the emotional component of trauma is the risk of teenagers acting impulsively and engaging in self-harm or suicidal behaviors. In a 2002 survey of teenage behavior conducted by the Centers for Disease Control, 28 percent of teens between the ages of fourteen and eighteen reported feeling sad or hopeless, 19 percent seriously considered attempting suicide, and 9 percent attempted suicide, with males being five times more likely to complete the suicide.[11] Anyone working with teens following trauma events needs to be alert to the increased likelihood of such feelings and behaviors.

Behavioral Impact

A crisis or trauma event can have an impact on a teenager's behavior. A teen may withdraw from family or friends, preferring to spend time alone listening to music or watching television. Another teen may cling to a boy- or girlfriend or to a particular group of friends. Some teens deal with trauma by seeking control over various situations, striving for perfection in school, for instance. While teens can be naturally impulsive, trauma might amplify erratic or risk-taking activities. A teen may begin or increase drug or alcohol use, or may engage in self-harm behaviors or gestures. Those who work with teens know that many engage in cutting behaviors, scrapping or cutting into the skin on their arms or legs in an effort to cope with painful emotions and experiences.

Because teens don't always understand what is taking place internally following traumatic or extreme experiences, they often have difficulty communicating what they're thinking or feeling. Adults may have to observe an adolescent's

---

11. Berger, *Developing Person Through the Life Span*, 394.

behavior after a traumatic experience in an effort to determine how a teen is coping. Any types of dramatic shifts in behavior or a teen's suddenly participating in dangerous activities are generally indicators that the trauma is affecting the teen in a negative manner.

TYPES OF TRAUMAS

Adolescents are susceptible to a wider range of trauma and crisis events than are children. They also face many of the same ones adults may experience, although they are lacking adult maturity and perspective when attempting to cope. Teenagers have several particular areas of vulnerability to traumatic events.

Death of a Family Member

Any death can be difficult to navigate, but this is especially true for teenagers if a parent or sibling dies. Perschy notes the difficulty following such a death, commenting, "The emotional turmoil that follows the death of someone close can be unnerving for even the most secure teen. The scariness of the intense mood swings makes some teens question their sanity. The guilt for wishing for the quick death of a pain-stricken parent can weigh heavily on a teen. The intense anger at medical personnel, meddling relatives, and at the person who has died defies logical thinking."[12]

If a parent dies, the teen may struggle not only with the general sense of loss, but may feel abandoned by the parent. Death of a sibling often produces feelings of guilt over not having been nicer to the sibling. The loss of a beloved grandparent leaves a teenager feeling empty and sad.

Death of a Friend

It's unusual for a child to lose a friend to death. This possibility increases, however, in adolescence. Teenagers begin driving, may use or abuse drugs or alcohol, sometimes engage in risky behavior, and the suicide rate among teens is much higher than among children. It's not unlikely that a teenager could suffer the tragic death of a friend. Whereas adults may have friends who, over time, deteriorate prior to death, most teen deaths are sudden and dramatic. Teens are generally ill-prepared for such losses, and adjustment is a complex

---

12. Perschy, *Helping Teens Work Through Grief*, 5.

process. Wofelt states, "Traumatic deaths make the *grief work* for teenagers complicated. They sometimes find it difficult to accept the intensity of the painful feelings of grief that they're experiencing. And, as a result of growing feelings of independence, teenagers don't want to accept adult help in coping with these feelings."[13]

Natural Disaster

Natural disasters produce an extensive impact on families, neighborhoods, communities, or, in cases like Hurricane Katrina, even regions of the country. Teenagers find their lives disrupted, sometimes in ways that impact the processes so important to overall development. Even the mildest of disasters disrupts the daily routines of teenagers and their families. If the disaster is extensive—a tornado that destroys a family's home, for instance—the teenager may have to deal with loss of privacy if the family has to relocate to temporary housing. Disasters can impact a teen's academic performance. A teenager may have trouble focusing on algebra if wildfires are raging in the canyon near where the teen's family resides. In the city where I live, a fire produced extensive damage to a middle school, and the seventh and eighth graders began the school year in portable trailers without a gym or cafeteria, making the focus on schoolwork more challenging. Other natural disasters may cost an adolescent his or her job or automobile, hindering progression toward independence. If a teenager must move following a disaster, he or she will have to leave friends, sports teams, church youth groups, and other sources of support and peer relationships. Natural disasters have the potential not only to disrupt daily functioning of teens, but to impact their overall developmental process.

Parental Divorce

Beginning in the 1960s, the divorce rate in the U.S. began to increase rapidly and continued to do so until about 1980. Since 1980, the divorce rate has held at a fairly constant rate. Alongside the climbing divorce rate, a type of conventional wisdom seemed to develop regarding the impact of divorce on children. This included the belief that children were better off living with one divorced parent than with two conflicted parents, and that teens could more easily adapt to divorce than could younger children. In more recent days, numerous marriage and family experts have questioned some of these early con-

---

13. Wofelt, *A Child's View of Grief,* 24.

clusions about divorce, including how and to what extent teenagers are affected when parents divorce.

According to Brooks and Seigel, "Adolescence appears to be the worst time in a child's life for parents to divorce. Such a decision at that time forces the child to handle two very difficult changes in life: (1) all of the physical and emotional transformations that arise during the teen years and (2) the emotional distress of divorce."[14]

While divorce can be difficult for both younger children and for teens, divorce affects teenagers quite differently than it affects children. Because children are limited in their ability to think well into the future, their sense of divorce is tied more to the immediate trauma of the event—not seeing one parent except on weekends, for example. Teens, on the other hand, are able to understand much more of what is taking place. Elkind states, "Teenagers, thanks to their ability to think in a new key, can appreciate the full impact of divorce—its emotional, personal, social, and financial repercussions."[15] For teens, especially younger adolescents, the divorce is also much more intertwined with identity formation. Seeing oneself as a child of divorced parents is more likely to produce feelings of shame and embarrassment in the teen than in a younger child.

The divorce of parents is, thus, a blow to teenagers. Bradley notes three key ways teens are shaped by the trauma of divorce. First, teens tend to withdraw and act uncaring in an effort to cope with the overwhelming emotional devastation produced by a parental breakup. Second, teens become cynical about important life values such as commitment and responsibility. Third, teens are robbed of parenting at a juncture when it's most crucial.[16] Bradley states, "Between the neurological instability of the adolescent brain and the moral instability of the adolescent world, teenage years are the last ones you want your kid to be navigating with newly divorced parents."[17] Following divorce, parents are often depleted and distracted and have reduced ability to provide the teenager with what he or she needs.

Divorce often forces teens to choose sides, to decide to stay with one parent and be separated from the other. At times, no matter who the teen chooses, the other parent is hurt and angry. To complicate matters, parents can use a child

---

14. Brooks and Siegel, *The Scared Child*, 99.
15. Elkind, *All Grown Up and No Place to Go*, 137–38.
16. Bradley, *Yes, Your Teen Is Crazy*, 144–45.
17. Ibid., 145.

as an informant or spy, asking the teen to report on the other parent. Some teens get caught in a tremendous tug-of-war between parents, while other teens learn to manipulate both parents, who often function out of a sense of guilt and not from the perspective of what is best for the child. Teens often become parentified, pulled into positions of confidant, friend, and advisor to parents, roles that are most appropriate for other adults to fill. When a parent starts dating, the teen commonly struggles with feelings of further rejection and a sense of being replaced. If a parent marries again, the teen must navigate the complex world of blended families and stepsiblings, an incredibly difficult task when combined with all the struggles of growing up.[18]

Further, the impact of divorce on teenagers continues well into the teen's future. When the teen becomes a young adult, commitment to a long-term relationship, especially to marriage, may be a challenge. "Why should I go through what my parents went through?" is a common question of young adult children of divorce. Similarly, the young adult may struggle with how anyone can have a successful marriage, and he or she may have doubts that anyone can have a good marriage. I've met many individuals in premarital counseling who start marriage, fearing that they won't be able to make it work. Such a belief can be dangerous to the prospect of having a satisfying marriage relationship.

Divorce also seems to leave a permanent imprint on the identity of the teen well into young adulthood. My wife has taught speech in college for many years, and the first speech her students give is a speech of introduction. When these adults introduce themselves to classmates, they frequently identify themselves as coming from a divorced family. My wife expresses amazement at the number of students who introduce themselves in this way; their parents' divorce has been integrated into the identity of these young adults, becoming part of how they see themselves.

A few decades ago, the conventional wisdom about divorce was that it was a difficult experience, but one that resilient children and teens would overcome. It's become much clearer in the past few years that divorce has an extensive impact on teenagers, disorienting them in the most difficult of developmental stages and becoming a weight they carry for years to come.

---

18. For an excellent and thorough discussion of how divorce and parental remarriage impacts teenagers, see Bradley's, "The Family Matters," in *Yes, Your Teen Is Crazy*. Bradley's extensive counseling work with teenagers allows him a rare glimpse into the teenager's world in the days following the divorce of parents.

HELPING TEENS COPE WITH TRAUMATIC EVENTS

Trying to provide help to teenagers following trauma or crisis events can be challenging. Knowing how to best help can be as confusing to the helper as the traumatic experience is to the teenager. This young person is, after all, at a time in life when he or she is naturally differentiating from parents, seeing the world in a more adult manner, and experiencing changing moods. There are several ways, however, in which a counselor, minister, or parent can help teens who have experienced a crisis or trauma event.

Be Patient as Teens Struggle

Most teenagers face numerous challenges even in ideal circumstances, but even more so if they've undergone a trauma event or a significant loss. Adult helpers must be patient when teens struggle. Because their moods can be more exaggerated than those of adults, teens may experience rage, sadness, hurt, fear, anxiety, or any number of other emotions. Adults must avoid correcting a teen for an emotion and should not try to talk the teen out of an emotion. Acknowledging the emotion, helping the teen label the emotion, and even normalizing the emotion are part of diffusing what the teen is experiencing, helping the teen make sense of, and cope with, what is taking place.

While helping a teen deal with emotions and accept them as natural responses to difficult circumstances, it's important to convey that the teen is still responsible for choices he or she makes. It's okay, for instance, for the teen to be angry, but it's not okay for him or her to punch a hole in the wall or vent anger on younger siblings. When teens are struggling with emotions, allowing outlets for them to vent in nondestructive ways can sometimes help.

Adults should also be patient with what teens interpret as crises. Some teens are so frequently involved in various crises, many of their own making, that it's hard for parents, teachers, or other adults to take these seriously or to be sympathetic. While it is helpful for adults to be low-key and calm when a child labors with a perceived crisis, adults should avoid being condescending or patronizing when a child is struggling. Adults do well to recall that, with all the changes going on, life for teens generally feels rather tumultuous, and any crisis only adds to these feelings. Adult patience and support help the teen read situations, make decisions, and cope with what has occurred.

Maintain Lines of Communication

Another aspect of helping teens cope is maintaining channels of communication between the teenager and adult helpers. A teenager may have trouble organizing and verbalizing thoughts and feelings, and may be prone to withdraw, act like everything is okay, or act out. Any of these three can be confusing to those trying to provide help. Encouraging an adolescent to talk, being patient if the teen does not talk, and listening nonjudgmentally when the teen does talk are all essential to maintaining communication.

In some instances, a teenager has an adult outside of the family with whom the teen feels safe. In such instances, this adult may be instrumental in helping the teen discuss difficult events. A trusted teacher, youth minister, or relative may be able to help the teen begin the process of talking about what has happened.

While teens often avoid talking to adults, they commonly feel comfortable talking with peers about crisis or trauma events. Following a traumatic event, debriefing groups of teens who were involved in the trauma provides an avenue for teens to verbalize thoughts and feelings in a setting where they feel safe and understood.

At times, a teen may find great benefit in talking with a counselor about a crisis or trauma event. Those working with teens should help the teen to find, if at all possible, a counselor with training and experience in working with adolescents. A counselor can help a teen decipher moods and beliefs, adjust to what has taken place, and make decisions about moving into the future. An effective counselor who specializes in adolescence can be a valuable, even crucial, component of the teenager's recovery process.

Allow the Teenager to Be a Teenager

As mentioned, in crisis or trauma circumstances, a teen may tend to move toward parentification or hypermaturity. A parent or family system, too, may covertly encourage the teenager to assume responsibilities beyond his or her stage of development, maturity level, and cognitive abilities. For several years I worked with teenagers in psychiatric hospitals. In these settings, I saw teens who had become family cooks and housecleaners following some family catastrophe. Other teens had become the primary caregivers for younger siblings. On a couple of occasions, I encountered teens performing large portions of homeschooling of younger siblings. Other teens had become the friend and confidant of a parent who lost a partner. One young teenager even was responsible for paying all the family bills. In each of these cases, teenagers were pulled into roles of being responsible for adult tasks or duties as parents struggled with depression, exhaustion, or both.

When a teenager has experienced a traumatic event or a significant loss, adults in the teen's world should avoid pulling the teen into an adult role for which the youngster is not prepared emotionally or physically. This doesn't mean that, in difficult circumstances, teenage family members should not assume more responsibility for helping the family. In many cases, responsibility of this nature is a healthy part of growing up. The problem occurs if a teenager is placed in a role beyond his or her level of maturity, carrying out duties that adults should be doing.

Conversely, in some crisis or trauma circumstances, a teen will become hyperdependent on parents, relatives, or adults in general. In these instances, adults who are in contact with the dependent teen can help him or her work toward individuation and independence. Neither overdependence nor hypermaturity will ultimately serve the young person well in adult life.

Help Teens Grieve

When teenagers experience a loss—whether the death of a friend or family member, or some more abstract type of loss—adult helpers should aid the teen in the grieving process. As do adults, teens need to grieve in order to work through the course of separating from the object or person that has been lost. This grieving is a necessary part of moving past the loss.

Perschy notes four key tasks in adolescent grieving.[19] First, teens must accept the reality of the loss. Second, they must experience the pain of the grief resulting from the loss. Third, teens must adjust to the environment without the missing person or lost object. Helping teens make such adjustments is crucial to the overall coping process. Last, teens should emotionally readjust to life without the lost person or object. Helping teens commemorate the loss aids in general adjustment and helps the teen move ahead with life.

Rituals can be an important part of teen adjustment. Adult helpers should work with teens to identify rituals that might be a helpful part of effectively coping with grief. In recent years, when a peer has been killed, teens have contributed to makeshift memorials, leaving notes, teddy bears, and other objects at a specific site in memory of the deceased friend. In a similar vein, some families who have lost a teenage child have allowed peers to write notes to the child

---

19. Perschy, *Helping Teens Work Through Grief,* 3–5.

Lamenting in community

on the casket. Rituals such as these become avenues for expressing grief and allow the teen a very concrete way of facing and responding to the death.

Eriksson and Griffin identify another method of aiding teens in the grief process, that of helping teens cope with loss through the use of lament psalms.[20] They advocate guiding teens to psalms of lament, such as Psalms 10; 61; 80; or 88. An adult can ask a teen if it's okay for a person to be disoriented, as the psalmists seem to be, and if it's acceptable to question God, as these individuals do. A teen can be encouraged to discuss or journal his or her own honest thoughts about what has taken place, expressing to God feelings of confusion, frustration, or even anger. This activity is especially helpful if done in a community of faith, where the community provides support and encouragement to adolescents struggling with a traumatic event. Eriksson and Griffin note, "In response to traumatic experiences, it is critically important for a community of faith to offer space for this kind of response to God. As youth workers, we may fear taking students to those places of doubt, anger, and disappointment with God. However, failing to create an environment for authentic lament can result in spiritually and psychologically short-circuiting the necessary healing process. This is a communal spiritual discipline we must not avoid. Authentic trust in God may take a long time, and kids need faithful adults to walk that difficult road with them."[21]

Walking alongside teens who are grieving can be challenging but rewarding. When adults assist teenagers in healthy grieving, the teen not only benefits in the present, but the helper also enables the teen to move toward the future without the baggage of unresolved grief.

CONCLUSION

Normal adolescence produces both exhilaration and trepidation, that sensation of walking along a precarious mountain path. When teens experience crises or trauma, they may feel like they're walking that path while dodging boulders falling from above. Caregivers who work with teens may also experience similar combinations of exhilaration and trepidation. Sometimes a caregiver may feel like he or she is standing between the teen and the drop-off. On other occasions, caregivers might feel like they're hanging onto a teen's sleeve

---

20. Eriksson and Griffin, "In the Aftermath."
21. Ibid.

while the teen leans over the edge. There are times, however, when the caregiver and the teen are able to slow down, breathe deeply, and look at the view. The caregiver may have the chance to help the teen make a safe journey along the path, avoiding some of the dangers. When that happens, the experience is of great value to both the teenager and the caregiver.

CHAPTER 12

CRISES AND DISASTERS IN THE CHURCH AND COMMUNITY

U
p to now, this book has addressed crises from the standpoint of the individual counselor or minister. Indeed, in many instances, a single caregiver provides comfort, assistance, and support when an individual or family experiences a crisis or trauma event. At times, however, a large-scale disaster may strike a church or community. In such circumstances, what is the role of the church in ministering to those who are affected? Do churches have a responsibility for preparing for larger crises and for effectively ministering when a more extensive crisis or disaster occurs?

According to Everly, churches have the opportunity to play a central role when crises transpire. He states, "It has been commonly observed that in times of crisis and disaster, many individuals seek out religious or spiritual leaders. Individuals in times of crisis will sometimes gather at houses of worship, or locations of religious or spiritual significance."[1] When a church is prepared for crisis events, reacts appropriately, and effectively ministers to those hurting, it becomes an incredible witness, not only to those directly involved in a crisis or disaster, but to the entire community. The church has the opportunity to be relevant, to express Christ's love in a very tangible manner, and to communicate to the watching world that it is not inert, uncaring, nor irrelevant.

DISASTERS DEFINED

A disaster is a large-scale crisis that generally occurs with little or no warning and impacts a specific segment of a community, an entire community, or even a region of a country. Halpern and Tramontin note that disasters tend to qualify

---

1. Everly, "Role of Pastoral Crisis Intervention," 139.

as crises, but not all crises are disasters, the difference being the scope of the event. They state, "A disaster implies sudden misfortune that results in the loss of life or property or in other forms of great harm or damage. Disaster's impact extends beyond just one person affecting, devastating, and sometimes eradicating an entire community."[2] Natural disasters include hurricanes, floods, tornadoes, drought, blizzards, prolonged heat or cold, fires, or mudslides. Other disasters are caused by humans and involve accidents, war, terrorism, or even biological or chemical contamination.

Three crucial elements of disasters are the scope, intensity, and duration of the event.[3] The scope of a disaster involves the breadth of how many individuals, families, businesses, and community institutions are affected. When the scope is broad, not only are individuals and families disrupted, but they may not have access to community services. Intensity gauges the strength of the direct impact of the disaster, ranging from low intensity to high intensity. High-intensity disasters usually involve death and destruction and take a greater physical and emotional toll on individuals and communities. A disaster's duration may be brief or extended. The longer a disaster persists, the more likely individuals will experience diminished physical and emotional resources. Disasters with uncertain duration may rapidly produce emotional strain when individuals become overly vigilant in their attempt to interpret the disaster situation. Disasters that are large in scope, intense, and of uncertain or extended duration tend to have the most devastating impact on a community and its residents.

HOW DISASTERS IMPACT A COMMUNITY

Researchers are just beginning to understand not only how trauma impacts individuals, but how groups of individuals such as families, churches, and communities are affected. Charles Figley, noted author and traumatology expert, identifies the term *systemic traumatology* as an area of trauma studies "concerned with the systemic (e.g., interpersonal and intra-relational) causes and consequences of traumatic events. This is one of the least studied, yet most important, areas within the field of traumatology."[4]

Figley notes that communities, when hit with a disaster, tend to follow a pattern in how they respond to such events, or a recognizable set of phases through

---

2. Halpern and Tramontin, *Disaster Mental Health*, 3.
3. Ibid., 20–22.
4. Figley, "AAMFT Clinical Update."

which they progress.[5] Understanding these phases provides direction to those seeking to offer aid in community disasters.

Predisaster Phase

Prior to a disaster, communities tend to function with a general lack of awareness, even a denial that anything catastrophic could happen. Disasters are events that occur elsewhere, in other communities or on the evening news. This lack of awareness fosters a reluctance to prepare for crisis events, and as a result, communities are commonly caught off guard, increasing the devastation to those involved. Most often, disasters strike with little or no warning, leaving communities ill prepared for the effects of widespread devastation.

In some instances, there may be warnings of an impending disaster, such as an approaching hurricane, wildfires sweeping through the countryside, or floodwaters rising. When warnings are given, individuals and families must assess the threat and decide how to respond, including whether to evacuate and, if so, what possessions to take. False alarms, as when a hurricane changes course just prior to landfall, may produce in individuals a hesitancy to take appropriate action during future disaster threats.

Impact Phase

When a large-scale disaster strikes, the impact on the community closely resembles the impact on individuals. Common responses are numbness, fear, and disbelief. Halpern and Tramontin observe that in the impact phase, "Fear and tension are extremely high at this time, but because the focus is in survival and on enduring an event intact, panic is often held at bay. People are mostly concerned for their own welfare and for their loved ones."[6] In most instances, individuals handle extreme events in the best way they can. During the impact phase, when a television news station interviews a disaster victim, it's not unusual for the person to appear numb or in shock. On other occasions, a person may comment about their losses: "They were just material possessions; we're strong—we'll rebuild."

Heroic Response Phase

In the immediate aftermath of a disaster, certain individuals display heroic responses. These heroic acts are often performed by first responders, as we all

---

5. Figley, "Disaster and Violence."
6. Halpern and Tramontin, *Disaster Mental Health*, 20.

witnessed in the days following the World Trade Center attacks. But ordinary citizens may also be involved in heroic rescue efforts, expending incredible amounts of energy to help family, friends, and even strangers. Heroic responses can be overt, noticed by the whole community, or may go unnoticed.

Inventory Phase

Following a disaster, individuals and families tend to first cope with the immediate concerns about safety and well-being. Soon, however, they turn their attention to inventorying losses around them. The greatest need in this phase is information about homes, property, pets, and about the community in general. Because communication channels are often disrupted in a disaster, information is difficult to obtain. In some instances, information is inaccurate or distorted, complicating the inventory process. Individuals may be blocked from obtaining information, as is the case when they are not immediately allowed to return to their neighborhoods or homes following certain disasters. Aid is most effective at this stage when it facilitates transmission of accurate information that allows individuals and families to inventory losses and damage.

Honeymoon Phase

In large disasters, the affected area often receives a great deal of attention. A variety of VIPs visit the community to offer condolences. Politicians survey the damage and pledge support. Media outlets shine their spotlights on the community and on those involved. Celebrities may arrive in a disaster-riddled city or region bringing their own publicity machines. Messages of care and comfort come from a wide array of outside sources.

This particular phase can be especially complicated. The caring interest from others feels good to survivors and the attention seems genuine. At this stage, however, survivors tend not to comprehend the full ramifications of what has occurred. While pledges of support provide hope and a sense that others are concerned, in most instances, politicians, the media, and VIPs leave, ending the honeymoon. Community members are left to pick up the pieces of their lives outside the spotlight that temporarily illuminated the community.

Disillusionment Phase

As things begin to settle down, individuals, families, and entire communities come more fully to understand the extent of the disaster's impact. In the disillusionment phase people become tired and irritable. Promises of aid and support may have been offered but often don't materialize, or might become entangled in government red tape and bureaucracy. In this phase, delayed trauma symptoms often emerge for the first time, making general coping more challenging. Those displaced from homes, jobs, friends, and life routines usually struggle. Some individuals experience hopelessness and helplessness. Thus, this particular phase can be quite difficult to navigate.

Reconstruction Phase

The process of rebuilding often takes months, or even years. Some individuals may not be able to rebuild and may be forced to relocate, attempting to start over in a new setting. During the rebuilding phase, individuals and families begin returning to normal, or at least to new patterns and routines of functioning. Many stricken communities plan for future disasters, using what they've learned from what worked and what went wrong, making adjustments for facing future difficulties. In ideal circumstances, a community may be stronger and closer for having experienced a disaster, and members of the community are often willing to provide support and assistance when other communities encounter similar situations.

Knowledge about the phases of community response to disaster can guide churches in planning for, and attempting to minister to, those suffering the impact. When a person is being brave immediately following a disaster, it doesn't mean that the person is immune from difficult times in the days ahead. A church, knowing the vital nature of accurate information surrounding a disaster, may help individuals obtain information during the phases when it is most necessary. Churches must avoid being like those who pledge their support and care, but disappear when the honeymoon phase ends. Churches must be available to minister throughout these phases, showing their care in the months and even the years that follow a large-scale disaster.

THE CHURCH'S INVOLVEMENT IN COMMUNITY DISASTER ASSISTANCE

When a church chooses to invest in its community through developing a strategy for responding to disasters, preparation is paramount. In addition to preparation, though, three other areas afford numerous opportunities for disaster relief ministry. The Lutheran Disaster Response Manual identifies them as rescue, relief, and recovery.[7]

Preparation

To be effective in ministering following a community disaster, churches must make plans for how they will respond. The North American Mission Board of the Southern Baptist Convention stresses the importance of preparation in disaster relief: "Churches must plan how they will respond to disasters, large and small, in their communities. These plans need to be well thought out and discussed by church leaders. . . . The unprepared church will miss valuable opportunities to minister while attempting to react to a disaster in their community."[8]

Many denominations have disaster relief organizations and support for individual churches who desire to carry out a disaster relief ministry. It appears that most local churches, however, are not aware of or fail to take advantage of the resources available. Southern Baptist, Evangelical Lutheran Church of America, Assemblies of God, Catholic, Episcopal, United Methodist, Evangelical Free, and Presbyterian denominations all have some form of support for local churches who wish to develop disaster response plans. (Appendix D gives a complete list of contact information for disaster relief ministries for each of these denominations.) Despite having this support available, most churches, rather than being proactive, seem to be reactive when disasters occur, doing the best they can to minister to those affected. Careful planning and preparation, though, greatly increase the effectiveness of churches in times of crisis.

Rescue

When a church is prepared, it's in a better position to act during the impact phase of a disaster. In this phase of a critical event, rescue efforts are the most crucial task—making sure people and property are safe. Generally, the rescue phase of disaster response is short-lived and conducted by professionals, including police and fire personnel. In some instances, such as witnessed following Hurricane Katrina, the rescue effort can be much more prolonged and may necessitate involvement of private citizens, organizations, and churches. While churches may not be involved in many aspects of rescue, they can provide

---

7. Lutheran Disaster Response, "Preparing for Disaster."
8. North American Mission Board, http://www.namb.net/site/c.9qKILUOzEpH/b .224451/ k.A400/Disaster_Relief.htm.

support for this part of the disaster process by supplying food and shelter to rescue personnel or to those immediately displaced by the crisis event.

Relief

Whereas rescue tends to take place during the disaster, the relief process generally begins when the situation stabilizes, and it can occur over an extended period of time. Relief work involves assessing needs of those most directly affected and making an effort to alleviate those needs. Again, this may necessitate providing food, shelter, and care to those who have been affected or displaced.

Recovery

Help with recovery entails aiding those affected as they move toward a pre-disaster level of functioning. Whereas relief focuses on immediate needs, recovery is geared toward the future. Recovery includes assistance with new housing, jobs, and transportation for those affected. It may mean relocating or rebuilding. Offering access to counseling services helps individuals and families mend and heal from the emotional trauma produced by extreme events. The recovery process generally takes months, even years, and is an opportunity for fruitful ministry to those who have experienced the disaster.

If a church decides to develop a disaster relief ministry, the church may choose to focus its attention on all of these avenues of help, or they may focus on a specific area such as relief or recovery. To be most effective, all churches desiring to assist in community crises must prepare and develop plans for how they will react. One component of planning and preparation is to identify specific ways a church will offer help when a disaster occurs.

WAYS A CHURCH CAN BE INVOLVED IN DISASTER RELIEF MINISTRY

A church can be involved in disaster ministry in a number of ways. These include making use of the church's facilities, utilizing the human resources available in the church, and providing an array of types of care to hurting individuals.

Use of the Church's Facilities in Times of Disaster

The church building itself may serve many different functions during a disaster. The church can be used to shelter and feed those who have been displaced. Following Hurricane Katrina, a number of churches in Louisiana, Mississippi, Alabama, and Texas housed hurricane evacuees. Many churches choose to function as collection or distribution points for food, clothing, or even furniture. Following the 2004 Florida hurricanes, numerous churches made their parking lots available for operations of food kitchens and food distribution to needy families. During a disaster, a church may offer to serve as a communications or staging center for rescue efforts. A church that makes use of its facilities for rescue, relief, or recovery creates unlimited ministry opportunities to those affected.

Using Human Resources in the Church

The body of Christ is made up of individuals representing a broad spectrum of talents and gifts. Many of these may be especially useful during times of community crisis. Some individuals are adept at providing comfort and encouragement. Others have a specific skill, such as carpentry. Another individual may have a truck, trailer, or van helpful for transporting supplies or people. Another person may have knowledge of, and access to, various community resources that can aid in relief or recovery. Still another person may possess financial resources that can be used for the needs of victims or for equipment for workers.

One essential component of effective disaster relief is knowing the human resources accessible in the church body. Prior to a community disaster, a church may choose to conduct a survey to determine what resources are available. Many individuals are willing to contribute their time, effort, or expertise as a part of a church's disaster relief ministry. Other individuals may not be able to participate directly, but are equipped to donate financial resources for disaster relief. Identifying all interested individuals, knowing what each can do, and having access to phone numbers and e-mail addresses will facilitate a church in organizing disaster preparedness.

Types of Care the Church Can Provide

When a disaster occurs, a church can minister in a number of ways. Some of what a church does depends on the personnel available as well as on the type of disaster.

1. *Meeting basic needs.* Perhaps the most fundamental type of care a church may provide is meeting the basic survival needs of those involved. This

generally includes helping individuals and families gain access to food, clothing, and shelter. Throughout the Gospels, we see Jesus concerned with meeting the basic needs of those He encounters. On two occasions (Mark 6:30–44; 8:1–13), He provides food to those who are following Him. Jesus says in Matthew 10:42, "And if anyone gives even a cup of cold water to one of these little ones because he is my disciple, I tell you the truth, he will certainly not lose his reward" (NIV). Both during and following disasters, people are often deprived of the most basic life needs, such as food, water, clothing, and shelter. Providing these can be one of the most direct and productive ways to minister.

2. *Cleanup and repair work.* Many types of disasters, especially natural disasters, leave a wake of destruction in the community, necessitating cleanup and repair work. Following a storm, a family may be without a roof on their house. Floods leave behind wet carpet, damaged furniture, and mud. A tornado or hurricane often causes trees or large branches to block driveways, yards, or roads. Providing assistance to families as they attempt to clear debris is a meaningful type of ministry. Following Hurricane Katrina, a group of men from my church rounded up a number of chainsaws, and at the request of a church in Mississippi, spent several days clearing fallen trees and large branches from the yards and roads of those in one small community. This specific ministry act was helpful to storm victims, but it also had a profound impact on the helpers.

3. *Transportation.* Disaster victims often temporarily or permanently lose transportation. Family vehicles may be damaged or destroyed, and in some instances, even public transportation is disrupted. Some churches are able to use church vehicles, including vans or busses, or individual church members may be available to transport individuals or families when needed.

4. *Counseling.* In some disaster events, individuals and families sustain numerous losses and could benefit from counseling. Some churches have the means to offer counseling services to those in need. Counseling may also be available through more informal channels, such as support groups. A church may choose to train laypersons to meet with individuals or families, listen to their concerns, pray with them, and offer general support and encouragement. Counseling may be more formal, with licensed and trained counselors utilized

to meet specific counseling-related needs. Churches might also offer crisis intervention counseling, during which individuals with specific training in crisis intervention work with survivors immediately following a severe trauma situation. If a church does not have access to counselors, developing a list of counselors to whom disaster victims can be referred is also beneficial.

5. *Financial support and advice.* Some churches may choose to provide financial support to those in need. In 2 Corinthians 8:1–15, Paul urges the church at Corinth to complete an offering they were collecting, which would be given to fellow believers in need. Paul refers to this offering as an "act of grace" (2 Cor. 8:6 NIV). In like manner, churches may choose to participate in an act of grace by providing for those in financial need following personal or community disaster.

Many churches have a benevolence or crisis fund to aid those in need. A church could also take up a collection following a disaster, which is then used to address specific needs produced by the crisis event. A financial contribution in the aftermath of a large-scale disaster is often even more useful than providing food or clothing, which has to be collected, stored, transported, and distributed. In some instances, churches have members with expertise in financial or business matters who agree to volunteer their time in order to provide financial advice to individuals regarding loans, insurance, financial aid, or other affairs necessitated by the disaster.

6. *Medical or dental care.* After certain disasters, teams of medical personnel may provide care to those most in need. Some individuals in the medical professions desire to use their skills to alleviate suffering following disasters. Medical teams may even be able to take short-term mission trips to other countries when disaster strikes abroad.

7. *Legal advice.* Some people find themselves in need of legal counsel after a disaster event. Churches may have lawyers willing to offer free legal advice to aid individuals in dealing with legal matters brought about by a catastrophic event.

A broad range of ministry opportunities is available following a disaster. Most churches, however, need to start small and develop a disaster relief plan that they're capable of carrying out in an effective manner. Some types of ministry depend on the personnel available. One church may have a number of carpenters, handymen, and others capable of constructing buildings or of doing repair work. Another congregation may have several members involved in medical professions. Still another church may have counselors and social workers as part of its congregation. A church must be attuned to its ministry strengths, personnel, and resources in developing its specific ministry focus for addressing needs when a disaster occurs.

DEVELOPING A DISASTER RESPONSE TEAM

A church that is interested in providing effective disaster relief should consider developing a disaster response team. A team of this nature is made up of church members who have the desire, ability, time, and gifts to help others following a tragedy. The purpose of a disaster response team is to be prepared to address emergency needs of individuals both in the church and in the community who experience a crisis or disaster. Development of a disaster response team requires planning, gaining church approval, and implementation of disaster relief efforts.

Planning

Those interested in beginning a disaster response team should prayerfully and thoroughly assess their church's potential and ability to carry out such a ministry. The planning process involves several components.

1. *Appointing leadership.* The disaster response team usually needs a person to head up the operation, and a team to carry out the tasks of the ministry. The Southern Baptist North American Mission Board recommends that the leadership of a team include a director, a resource coordinator, and a volunteer coordinator.[9] The director is responsible for the overall planning and functioning of the team. The resource coordinator assesses and obtains physical resources to be used by the team. The volunteer coordinator locates, enlists, and organizes volunteers to help with the relief ministry. Whether a church decides to develop a disaster relief committee, a task force, or a team, the church should identify a core group of leaders who will be responsible for carrying out the disaster relief ministry. Drawing individuals from a wide variety

---

9. Ibid.

of backgrounds should aid the team in carrying out a broad array of tasks.

2. *Develop financial plans for the ministry.* While a disaster response team may have good ideas and intentions, there must also be financial backing in order to perform the ministry. Thus, developing a budget for the ministry is a necessary element of the planning phase. A church may choose to support a disaster relief team as a part of its overall budget. In other instances, a team may be responsible for obtaining funding apart from the church budget. Planning includes discovering what resources are available and what resources would need to be purchased for the team.

3. *Survey members to determine human resources.* Planning includes knowing which individuals are willing to donate time and talents to help with disaster response. A disaster response team should develop detailed lists of individuals who are available for specific types of disasters, including how to contact these individuals on short notice.

4. *Identify potential disaster response activities and scope.* Prior to the occurrence of a crisis event, a team must identify the types of disasters to which the team is capable of responding. Not all teams will have the human, material, and financial resources to respond to every type of disaster. A team should, in most instances, start small, identifying what it can realistically and successfully accomplish. Also, a team must determine the scope of its response. Will it respond to disasters that occur nearby? Will it travel to disasters in surrounding communities or around the state? If a team intends to travel, it must be mobile on short notice, generally requiring some type of mobile response unit. In some cases, a team may plan to send members to overseas disasters as part of its mission effort. Identifying the type of activities and the distance the team will travel is a necessary part of the planning process.

Gaining Approval of the Church

After carefully planning disaster response, the team must make sure it has the approval and support of the church and church leadership. The church or church leaders must understand any financial commitment and must give approval for use of facilities, equipment, employed personnel, and for anything else that directly involves the church. When the church gives its blessing, there is greater likelihood that it will support the team financially and through prayer.

Implementing Disaster Relief Efforts

After planning and obtaining church support, the team is ready to respond when disasters occur. Team members must be trained and know what to do in specific types of crises. Leaders of the disaster response team must be able to communicate with other disaster relief entities and organizations about the role of the church's team. When a team responds to a crisis event, leaders must be aware of the physical and emotional well-being of team members. Following disaster relief efforts, the team should be willing to evaluate the overall relief effort, what was effective, what needs to change, and what further training is necessary. Regular evaluation leads to more effective future responses.

WORKING WITH OTHER CHURCHES AND AGENCIES

An important component of developing and carrying out a disaster response ministry is working with other entities, such as churches and community agencies. Churches must be sure they are cooperating with, rather than competing with, other relief entities, and that they not duplicate ministries and relief efforts already being carried out by other churches and agencies.

Churches should be aware, too, of what is being done within its own denomination. Often, disaster relief efforts at the denominational level are thoroughly developed, and denominational leaders have experience in helping individual churches prepare for and carry out effective relief efforts.

Churches should also be in contact with national entities regarding disaster relief. Organizations such as the Red Cross are often in charge of disaster relief efforts in a community and are gatekeepers for the participation of other groups who wish to help. Thus, in many instances, churches must work with such organizations in order to be directly involved in the overall relief efforts.

In its preparation phase, a church's communicating with local Red Cross officials helps them become aware of a church's disaster response team and may open doors for the team to be used in certain emergencies or disasters. Many city, county, and state governments, too, have disaster response teams or individuals. Identifying these individuals, connecting with them, and communicating what a particular church can provide increases the likelihood that a church will be involved in disaster relief.

PUBLIC RELATIONS

In some instances, a disaster happens within the church itself or to a group of church members participating in a church function. Thus, a church needs to have plans for assisting in disasters that occur in that church. Being clear about channels of communication, who is to be contacted, and steps to take when a disaster strikes are essential aspects of helping to mitigate problems.

One area that receives little attention is that of public relations. How does the church communicate to the community or to the media during or following a crisis event? If a disaster occurs in a church, the church may not be prepared for the onslaught of media representatives who arrive, wanting information from church leaders or members.

According to Morey, there are several things a church can do to effectively work with the media during disaster situations.[10]

- The minister should communicate with other church leaders prior to making public statements or speaking to the media.
- The church should designate a spokesperson; other church leaders or representatives should refrain from communicating with the media. The spokesperson may be the minister or another church leader who can accurately represent the message the church desires to convey. The church's representative should dress as professionally as possible as this lends credibility to the message.
- Before speaking to the media, the spokesperson must be clear about what he or she desires to communicate and should only speak to the media when prepared. When speaking, the representative needs to avoid speculating and should focus on giving factual information. Attempts at humor are never appropriate during a crisis event.
- Church leaders should be aware that any information given to reporters can end up on the news. Being judicious in releasing information is always wise when communicating with the media.

A church's approach to dealing with the media will also depend to some extent on the nature of the crisis. If the church or church members are victims of a disaster, the content of a media release will vary from that of an event

---

10. Morey, "Crisis Communication for Ministers Conference," 36–41.

for which the church may be to blame, as in the case of ministerial abuse or misconduct.

Forming relationships with media personnel prior to being involved in a crisis could benefit the church when a crisis occurs.[11] Again, preparation and foresight may pay off in the long run.

CONCLUSION

If not in a church, disasters will happen in the proximity of a church or in the community where the church resides. A church can choose to be a passive observer, feeling helpless to assist in such matters. A church may choose to react, to do the best it can with limited knowledge, resources, and effectiveness. Or a church can make the choice to develop plans and strategies to implement when such instances do take place. The church that plans and carries out a disaster response ministry has the greatest likelihood of not only ministering most effectively to hurting people in Christ's name, but ultimately of generating appreciation for the church and for its part in the community. A successful partnership between church and community, in which the community recognizes the valuable role the church plays, opens many different doors to convey the good news of Christ.

---

11. Ibid., 41.

CHAPTER 13

CARING FOR THE CAREGIVERS

A THERAPIST'S STORY

JENNIFER WAS A SUCCESSFUL THERAPIST. She was well-liked by her clients and respected by her professional peers. One morning, Jennifer received a call from a local pastor, asking her to help with a crisis situation. A young single woman who was a member of the pastor's church had been murdered in her home. Those at the crime scene notified the woman's mother, who came to her daughter's house, arriving before rescue and police personnel. The pastor asked Jennifer to assist in ministering to the family of the deceased woman and especially to the mother who had witnessed the crime scene.

Jennifer accompanied church staff members to the mother's apartment, where police were interviewing friends and family members. At the apartment, Jennifer not only heard details of the murder, but caught a glimpse of a crime scene photograph held by one of the detectives.

Having trouble concentrating, eating, and sleeping, Jennifer contacted me a few days later. She was distraught, not only over the horrible incident that had happened to the family, but over her own response to the events. As we talked further, Jennifer told me that, prior to her training to become a therapist, she lived in a war ravaged region of the world. While in this part of the world, she had many traumatic experiences, including being in a marketplace with her child when a man was shot nearby. It became obvious to both Jennifer and me that her being exposed to the murder of the single woman was not only stressful for Jennifer to hear, but it reminded her of traumatic situations she had experienced in her own life, the combination of which seemed to be producing the effects of trauma in Jennifer.

INTRODUCTION

Ministry and, more specifically, ministry to those who are in crisis situations can be demanding and even grueling. There seems to be a certain wear and tear on caregivers, and this stress is multiplied if the person, whether a minister or counselor, works with those who've undergone extreme or traumatic situations.

The Bible appears to recognize the strain on those who seek to help others. In 2 Thessalonians 3:13, Paul encourages believers, saying, "But as for you, brethren, do not grow weary of doing good." He makes a similar statement in Galatians 6:9, where he says, "Let us not lose heart in doing good, for in due time we will reap if we do not grow weary." Paul acknowledges that it's possible for any believer to run low on energy, to become fatigued, or even exhausted. Elijah, the great Old Testament prophet, is an excellent example of exhaustion in ministry.

ELIJAH: AN EXHAUSTED PROPHET

First Kings provides an account of a man of God experiencing discouragement and fatigue. Israel has been experiencing a drought for an extended period of time due to the wickedness of Ahab, King of Israel. Elijah, one of the great prophets of the Old Testament, not only tells Ahab there will be no rain (1 Kings 17:1), but God sends Elijah to the king to challenge him and his wife, Jezebel, to a contest between their gods and the true God. Ahab gathers 850 of his prophets and meets Elijah on top of Mount Carmel. In the contest arranged by Elijah, the prophets of Baal and Asherah assemble a sacrifice on their altar, then call on the name of their gods to provide fire for the sacrifice. Despite numerous pleas to their gods, their incessant dancing and praying, nothing happens.

Elijah rebuilds the altar to the Lord, lays his sacrifice on it, then douses the sacrifice with water. Elijah prays to God, asking Him to answer and to reveal Himself to those observing this strange contest. First Kings 18:38 recounts what happens: "Then the fire of the LORD fell and consumed the burnt offering and the wood and the stones and the dust, and licked up the water that was in the trench." When the observers witness this, they fall to the ground to worship the true God. Elijah orders the false prophets killed, then tells Ahab that the people of Israel are about to experience their first rain in years.

Elijah accomplished a great victory in the name of the Lord. He had a front row seat to an incredible display of God's holiness, His power, and His provision. A single prophet wins the contest against hundreds of others. We'd assume that Elijah would be ecstatic after this victory and that he would long bask in the afterglow of this amazing experience.

After Ahab reports all the events to Jezebel, she threatens to kill Elijah. Elijah, fearing Jezebel, flees to the wilderness, where he hides. First Kings 19:4–5 tells what happens to Elijah following his victory: "But he himself went a day's journey into the wilderness, and came and sat down under a juniper tree; and he requested for himself that he might die, and said, 'It is enough; now, O LORD, take my life, for I am not better than my fathers.' He lay down and slept under a juniper tree."

After the great religious triumph, Elijah experienced an emotional and physical crash. He was afraid, discouraged, exhausted, and even suicidal. This great man of God underwent a period of extreme difficulty in the midst of following and serving God.

Later, we'll consider how God responded to Elijah in the wilderness, how God provided for Elijah, and how He addressed the needs of His prophet. The passage above, though, clearly demonstrates that those who minister can experience times of personal struggle, doubt, and exhaustion.

Living the Christian life requires a certain amount of energy expenditure, and even more so if ministering to others who are facing some type of crisis. Beyond fatigue, however, a caregiver who works with those in crisis may wrestle with burnout or may even develop symptoms of traumatized individuals.

An essential component of effective crisis ministry, then, is providing help to other caregivers, and for those caregivers to recognize their own stress and be aware of strategies for self-care. Caregivers should be cognizant of what makes them vulnerable, of how a person might be affected, and of strategies for effectively coping with the stress that results from providing crisis care.

THE REWARDS AND CHALLENGES OF HELPING

Assisting hurting individuals produces both immense rewards and numerous challenges. Caregivers experience a great deal of satisfaction when they see a hurting person overcome obstacles and grow. Providing crisis ministry gives the helper the feeling of being used by God and of functioning as a contributing part of the body of Christ. Often, a helper senses being a conduit of God's grace or mercy to a struggling person or family. Helping a person walk through the valley and emerge on the other side produces a thrill. The helper often is able to see a hurting person's resilience, courage, and strength in the face of difficulties. Laurie Anne Perlman, a trauma therapist and expert on counselor self-care, believes that helping others brings about a transformation in the helper. She says, "This transformation includes personal growth, a deeper connection with both individuals and the human experience, and a greater awareness of all aspects of life."[1]

While it's true that there are many benefits of helping, there are also difficulties. Figure 13.1 identifies some of the unique challenges related to helping others following a crisis or trauma event.

Figure 13.1. Challenges of Crisis Ministry

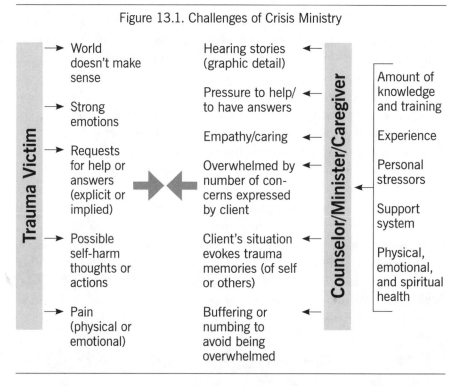

Caregivers frequently work with victims when the hurting person is at his or her worst. The trauma victim often experiences confusion, and the world doesn't make sense. In many instances, the person's pain is palpable and can be

---

1. Perlman, "Self-Care for Trauma Therapists," 51.

accompanied by feelings of helplessness, hopelessness, and various other strong emotions. The hurting person often wants help and answers, whether or not he or she verbalize these requests. Some trauma survivors may have thoughts of self-harm or suicide, which places further demands on caregivers for appropriate care.

The caregiver seldom has easy pathways of alleviating the person's pain and must walk with the person through difficult times. If the helper works with individuals who've experienced extreme trauma, the caregiver is commonly exposed to some of the worst aspects of what one human being can do to another, often hearing repeated, graphic accounts of what occurred to the victim. Rarely are there easy solutions or resolutions to the struggles faced by trauma or crisis victims, but the helper commonly feels pressure to provide answers and to proceed with wisdom. Caregivers usually function by empathetically engaging with hurting individuals, but this can be overwhelming when the victim has experienced extreme trauma. If, though, the helper numbs or buffers to avoid being overpowered by the situation, the helper's effectiveness is often diminished. In crisis ministry, the helper can be overwhelmed by the sheer number of problems a trauma victim is facing, and it's challenging to know where to begin and how to proceed. In some instances, the trauma event conveyed by the client can remind the caregiver of personal trauma experiences or of trauma events of past clients.

The helper not only feels the impact of what occurs in the interchange between helper and client, but the caregiver's own experience plays a part in aiding the hurting person. The caregiver's amount of knowledge and training about crisis counseling contributes to his or her effectiveness, as does the helper's experience in this type of ministry. If the helper is coping with a number of personal stressors extraneous to counseling, his or her ability to provide quality care may be compromised. Caregiver effectiveness is also influenced by the helper's support system, and by the helper's own spiritual, physical, and emotional health—or lack thereof.

The crisis ministry journey is long and arduous. In some instances, glimmers of hope are dim and rare. Like the victim, the helper may find him- or herself becoming disoriented, discouraged, and, in some cases, experiencing symptoms that may parallel symptoms of the trauma or crisis survivor.

It would be impossible for the helper to avoid all of the challenges inherent in helping. Can a care provider take steps, though, to minimize or mitigate some of the more extreme hazards that result from helping? To answer this question, it is first necessary to identify and define some of the difficulties caregivers may experience.

CRISIS MINISTRY: IMPACT ON CAREGIVERS

Even when producing the best of outcomes, crisis ministry is inherently challenging. In some instances, these challenges may cause the counselor or minister to experience increased amounts of stress, accompanied by weariness, fatigue, and exhaustion. Should these continue over a period of time, the caregiver is in danger of developing burnout. In more serious circumstances, caregivers may experience secondary traumatic stress (STS), resulting in symptoms similar to PTSD. Below, each of these possible outcomes is given closer attention.

Weariness or Exhaustion

Helping others requires the caregiver to utilize both emotional and physical energy. The more extensive the situation requiring crisis care, the more energy caregivers tend to expend. It's not unusual for caregivers to find themselves tired, drained, even exhausted. Counselors often have a large caseload, seeing many individuals in difficult circumstances. When a greater percentage of clients are undergoing crises, the counselor is more likely to become weary from helping. Ministers, too, commonly find themselves dealing with multiple crises, some of them quite extensive. A minister often addresses crises in addition to an already full slate of responsibilities and duties. The wearing nature of helping others frequently results in the caregiver feeling depleted or exhausted.

By itself, exhaustion or weariness is usually a temporary state. If the crisis ministry situation comes to an end, if the caregiver gets adequate rest and relaxation, or if the caregiver finds relief from other life stressors, the fatigue may subside. Caregiver exhaustion becomes more critical, however, if the helping situation is ongoing, or if other ministry crises arise. If exhaustion is prolonged, the minister or counselor may be in danger of developing burnout.

Burnout

Corey, Corey, and Callanan define burnout as "a state of physical, emotional, intellectual, and spiritual exhaustion characterized by feelings of helplessness and hopelessness."[2] James and Gilliland similarly note, "[Burnout] is

---

2. Corey, Corey, and Callanan, *Issues and Ethics in the Helping Professions*, 60.

experienced as a state of physical, mental and emotional exhaustion caused by long-term involvement in emotionally demanding situations. It is accompanied by an array of symptoms including physical depletion, feelings of helplessness and hopelessness, disillusionment, negative self-concept, and negative attitudes toward work, people, and life itself."[3] Burnout, then, is both an emotional and biological process. Demands and stressors produce physiological changes such as headaches, backaches, ulcers, high blood pressure, ongoing fatigue, lowered resistance, and increased susceptibility to illness.

Burnout occurs over time and can be a slow, gradual process. An individual experiencing burnout tends to notice a steady decline in felt effectiveness, sense of purpose, and the belief that what the person is doing makes a difference. Because burnout occurs over a period of time, individuals may have some difficulty recognizing whether or not they're in a state of burnout.

A number of work-related conditions contribute to the likelihood of a person's experiencing burnout. Extreme or unrealistic job demands, especially when combined with unclear job expectations, produce stress, which contributes to burnout. Ongoing conflict with supervisors, coworkers, or clients, or jobs dealing with individuals in distress adds to the strain a worker experiences. A worker who has tasks that are never completed, where there is always more to do, tends not to achieve the satisfaction of ending the task. Add to these a worker's lack of recognition or support for his or her contribution—especially if the worker regularly receives criticism despite the his or her efforts—the likelihood of burnout then increases.

Ministers and counselors are individuals whose professions render them susceptible to burnout. Job demands are high and often unrealistic, accompanied by constant overt and implicit demands. Those encountered by ministers and counselors are often in states of physical, emotional, or spiritual crises. The work of ministers and counselors is never fully complete, there's always more to do, and it's not uncommon for them to wonder if they should have done more in helping others. Those in caregiving professions must be aware of the potential for burnout, especially surrounding crisis events and subsequent ministry.

Secondary Traumatic Stress

In the last fifteen years, several terms have been used to identify what happens to caregivers who are negatively impacted by working with those who've experienced traumatic events. The three most common terms are *secondary*

---

3. James and Gilliland, *Crisis Intervention Strategies*, 480.

traumatic stress, *vicarious traumatization*, and *compassion fatigue*. These terms are generally used interchangeably and tend to refer to identical processes. Figley identifies secondary traumatic stress as "the natural, consequent behaviors and emotions resulting from *knowledge about* a traumatizing event experienced by a significant other. It is the stress resulting from *helping or wanting to help* a traumatized or suffering person."[4] Chrestman refers to the terms vicarious traumatization, contact victimization, and secondary post-traumatic stress reaction, defining these terms as "disruptive and painful psychological effects which may develop in mental health professionals who work with survivors of traumatic events."[5]

Secondary traumatic stress can be all-encompassing in the life of a caregiver. According to Perlman, STS often affects the caregiver at a number of different levels. "It can have an impact on the helper's sense of self, worldview, spirituality, affect tolerance, interpersonal relationships, and imagery system of memory."[6]

Secondary traumatic stress is not the same as general occupational stress experienced by therapists or ministers, nor is it equivalent to burnout. All helping professions produce stress on the helper, and in some instances, the amount and extent of stress leads to burnout. But STS is not the same as burnout. Perry notes that the distinguishing difference between STS and burnout is that the latter tends to emerge gradually and becomes progressively worse, whereas STS emerges suddenly, sometimes with little warning.[7] Conversely, whereas STS can, in some instances, subside rapidly, recovery from burnout is generally a slower process. Stamm also distinguishes between STS and burnout, stating that for burnout "examination of etiology generally shows increased work load and institutional stress are the precipitating factors, not trauma."[8]

Secondary traumatic stress is generally a short-term reaction to working with a trauma victim. The symptoms may emerge, be somewhat mild, and may disappear in a brief period of time. For some helpers, however, the symptoms are more extensive and longer lasting, even to the point of becoming chronic. Figley distinguishes between STS and secondary traumatic stress disorder (STSD). In the latter, the symptoms experienced by the helper are almost

---

4. Figley, "Compassion Fatigue," 10 (italics in the original).
5. Chrestman, "Secondary Exposure to Trauma," 29–30.
6. Perlman, "Self-Care for Trauma Therapists," 52.
7. Perry, "The Cost of Caring."
8. Stamm, "Work-Related Secondary Traumatic Stress," 1.

identical to PTSD. He states, "Therefore, STSD is a syndrome of symptoms nearly identical to PTSD except that exposure to a traumatizing event experienced by one person becomes a traumatizing event for the second person. Thus, the STSD symptoms are directly connected to the person experiencing primary traumatic stress."[9]

In the best of circumstances, caregiving is obviously not easy. In some instances, caregivers are, in fact, negatively affected by the helping process. This negative impact can be mild, including discouragement or weariness, but it may also be quite extensive, including a sense of emotional paralysis, intrusive thoughts about traumatic events experienced by clients or by the caregiver, or even relationship disruption. Knowing all this leads to other concerns, including who is vulnerable, and why certain caregivers seem to be at risk.

WHO IS VULNERABLE TO SECONDARY TRAUMATIC STRESS?

Are there specific caregivers who are more likely to experience STS? Are those who function in certain types of caregiving professions at higher risk? There appear to be certain aspects of helping others that increase the likelihood a caregiver will experience secondary trauma.

First Responders and Healthcare Workers

In the early 1990s, as researchers began better to understand the nature of secondary stress and trauma, two groups of people were identified as especially vulnerable to STS. The initial group identified is first responders, including police, fire, and emergency medical personnel, in other words, those who are consistently exposed to extreme trauma as a part of their profession. Perhaps this has never been more evident than in the days following the attacks on the World Trade Center towers. At a conference sponsored by Columbia University and New York Presbyterian Hospital in collaboration with the New York Police Department, Kevin Barry noted that one year after the bombings, first responders were struggling with many of the symptoms of STS. These symptoms included anger, depression, hypervigilence, family discord, unwanted images of the event, sleep disruption, and concentration difficulties.[10] For some of the

---

9. Figley, "Compassion Fatigue," 11.
10. Barry, "September 11, A Year Later," 3.

9/11 first responders, these symptoms were mild and transient. For others, the symptoms were more persistent, closely resembling PTSD.

The second group at risk is health-care providers, including counselors, social workers, or anyone else who has direct contact with trauma survivors, attempting to assist them following a trauma event. As the understanding of STS has continued to develop, researchers notice still other groups at risk, including ministers. Perlman notes that clergy are among the groups who can undergo secondary trauma.[11] Stamm agrees that clergy are vulnerable, stating that in the research, "Clergy receive little attention but may be exposed to a great deal of traumatic material as a result of their work."[12] In brief, helpers who attempt to provide care to those who have been traumatized are at risk themselves, including ministers, Christian counselors, and anyone who offers aid to trauma victims.

Those with Strong Empathy Skills

Empathy is basic to any kind of counseling, crisis or otherwise. The ability of the caregiver to empathize with the trauma survivor helps reduce the victim's sense of isolation, knowing that another person cares. Figley observes that while empathy is an essential ingredient of crisis or trauma counseling, it may negatively impact the helper. He states, "Empathy is a key factor in the *induction* of traumatic material from the primary to the secondary 'victim.' Thus, the process of empathizing with a traumatized person helps us understand that person's experience of being traumatized, but in the process, we may be traumatized, as well."[13] Thus, one of the characteristics that makes a caregiver effective may also contribute to that helper's being affected by the other person's trauma. Here, the helper is in somewhat of a dilemma. If he or she continues to be empathetic, the act of empathy may contribute further to the secondary trauma of the caregiver. On the other hand, if the caregiver becomes hardened or numb toward trauma victims' experiences, the caregiver is ultimately less effective.

Those Who Work with Children

Another group of helpers who are especially at risk for STS are people who work with children who've been traumatized or have experienced some type of

---

11. Perlman, "Self-Care for Trauma Therapists," 52.
12. Stamm, "Work-Related Secondary Traumatic Stress," 1.
13. Figley, "Compassion Fatigue," 20.

extreme crisis event. Perry notes that children are the most vulnerable members of our society, and when a child has been harmed, it tends to provoke a strong reaction in adult helpers. He states, "At times, the senseless and almost evil nature of some of the trauma inflicted on children shakes one's sense of humanity."[14] When a caregiver works with children and must listen to repeated stories of trauma, the result can be an increased likelihood of developing secondary trauma.

Those with Personal History of Trauma

A caregiver who him- or herself has undergone a traumatic event is more likely to experience STS. The story of Jennifer at the beginning of the chapter is an example of a client's trauma that activates memories of the therapist's own trauma. Perry notes that many therapists have experienced some notable loss or personal tragedy. He observes, "To some extent, the pain of experiences can be 're-activated.' Therefore, when professionals work with an individual who has suffered a similar trauma the experience often triggers painful reminders of their own trauma."[15] Kassam-Adams believes that any caregiver who has a personal history of sexual trauma is more likely to succumb to secondary trauma when working with sexual trauma victims.[16]

Other Contributing Factors

Researchers have identified other characteristics of individuals who are most vulnerable to STS. Chrestman notes that inexperienced therapists or those who carry a large caseload of trauma clients are more likely to experience secondary trauma.[17] Figley sees a connection between a caregiver's motivation and secondary trauma, stating that those who see themselves as rescuers or saviors are more likely to suffer the effects of secondary trauma.[18]

COPING STRATEGIES FOR THE EFFECTIVE CAREGIVER

What can a caregiver do to reduce the likelihood of experiencing unproductive fatigue or exhaustion, and what can be done to avoid burnout? If a helper

---

14. Perry, "The Cost of Caring," 8.
15. Ibid.
16. Kassam-Adams, "Risks of Treating Sexual Trauma," 45.
17. Chrestman, "Secondary Exposure to Trauma," 31.
18. Figley, "Compassion Fatigue," 9.

does experience exhaustion, burnout, or STS, what should he or she do to cope most effectively? To answer these questions, we'll first consider God's care for Elijah when he hid in the wilderness, exhausted and alone. Next, we'll examine spiritual, emotional, physical, professional, and relational strategies the caregiver can employ in an effort to stay vital and healthy in providing crisis care to those who are hurting.

God's Care for Elijah

Following his triumphant encounter with the priests of Baal, Elijah flees to the wilderness, sits down under a tree, and asks God to end his life. God's response provides insight into His concern for and care of those who minister to others in His name. First, God allows Elijah to rest (1 Kings 19:5). Whether from the overall strain of ministry, the pressure of the contest between prophets, or the energy expended in fleeing from Jezebel, Elijah was exhausted. Next, God feeds His prophet. An angel awakens Elijah and instructs him to eat: "Then he looked and behold, there was at his head a bread cake baked on hot stones, and a jar of water. So he ate and drank and lay down again" (1 Kings 19:6). God provided nourishment and rest for Elijah, not just once, but twice. After Elijah rests again, God tells him to eat yet one more time (vv. 7–8).

After Elijah is rested and fed, God takes him on a journey, far away from others, where the prophet meets alone with God. In addition to providing for Elijah's physical needs, God then addressed his spiritual concerns. Elijah voices his frustration to God, including how the wicked people are behaving, and his sense of futility in ministry. On two occasions (vv. 10, 14), Elijah complains that he's the only one fighting God's battles. In this, we see the prophet's sense of isolation.

God's response to Elijah is noteworthy. He reveals Himself to Elijah through the quietness of a gentle breeze. It appears that God pulls Elijah away from the active noise of ministry to enable the prophet to hear God's voice. God then reassures Elijah that he is not alone; seven thousand others exist who have not prostituted themselves to foreign gods (1 Kings 19:18). God gives Elijah instructions for returning to ministry, where once again we see this strong man of God fighting God's battles.

In this encounter between God and Elijah, God did not scold, punish, or reject Elijah for his discouragement and exhaustion. He provided for Elijah, physically, emotionally, and spiritually. He allowed Elijah to retreat from ministry and then prepared him to reenter the fray. God helped Elijah rejuvenate in order to continue doing the work to which God called him.

God's care of and provision for Elijah is instructive regarding the needs of caregivers and how they can maintain vitality as well as healthy functioning in crisis ministry. Caregivers can employ a number of coping strategies in order to lessen the likelihood of succumbing to fatigue, exhaustion, burnout, or STS.

Spiritual Coping Strategies

Above all else, the Christian caregiver must strive to maintain spiritual vitality. Such vitality is necessary not only in a general, day-to-day ministry, but especially as the caregiver is involved in ministering to those in crisis. Spiritual self-care entails several components.

Remember Who You Are

The caregiver is human and not divine. As a human being, the helper is subject to all the experiences that happen to humans: weariness, fatigue, joy, sadness, pain, discouragement, and so on. As a human, the caregiver cannot fix or remove a person's suffering, but is able to provide support and care. While the caregiver can be used by God to help hurting people, the caregiver is neither superman nor savior. Rather, helpers should most accurately see themselves as part of God's plan, as part of His care for others. But caregivers should remember that they are *part* of God's care, not all of it.

Maintain Spiritual Disciplines

Even in the midst of stressful ministry, helpers should strive to maintain spiritual well-being through regular spiritual disciplines. Activities like prayer, Bible study, and worship should never be neglected for any length of time in the helping process. Time away from ministry not only rejuvenates the helper, but reflects Jesus' practice of regularly pulling away from the crowds of followers and from His disciples in order to pray and meditate.[19]

Seek Balance in Ministry

Caregivers should strive for vitality by seeking a balance in ministry. Those who provide a great deal of crisis ministry especially need to be alert to

---

19. Luke 4:42; 5:16; and 6:12 all give instances of Jesus leaving His followers behind and taking time for prayer and meditation.

opportunities for other kinds of ministry. For years I worked with teenagers who were hospitalized due to psychiatric problems or chemical abuse. During these years, I also chose to teach a teenage Sunday school class. This allowed me to balance troubled teens with those who were more typical. In the last several years, a large portion of my counseling has been with couples in marital distress. Throughout this period, my wife and I have also taught a newlywed Sunday school class, working with young couples who are in love and excited about marriage. Those who do crisis ministry can attempt to balance this difficult work with something that is more consistently refreshing.

Avoid Functioning in Your Own Strength

As most ministers know, it's tempting to try helping others in one's own strength. If crisis ministry occurs over a period of time, a caregiver may lose focus on the source of power he or she has for providing care. A minister ends up working diligently, but in his or her own strength. Effective caregiving requires staying connected to God and functioning through the strength He provides. Isaiah 40:31 is an excellent verse for those involved in the sometimes arduous task of helping others: "Yet those who wait for the LORD will gain new strength; they will mount up with wings like eagles, they will run and not get tired, they will walk and not become weary." When the caregiver allows God to be the source of renewed energy, that caregiver is much better prepared for the demands of crisis ministry.

Physical Coping Strategies

In addition to the caregiver's addressing spiritual components of healthy functioning, he or she must also focus on physical aspects of self-care. When God deals with Elijah in the wilderness, He first attends to the physical needs of the prophet. Taking care of physical needs allows the helper to have the stamina necessary for ministering to others.

Recognize and Address Stress

The helper must be alert to personal stressors long before being involved in crisis ministry. Being aware of these sources of stress enables the caregiver to deal with the stressors in an appropriate and healthy manner. Having too many unresolved stressors prior to engaging in crisis ministry greatly reduces the likelihood of effective helping.

Pace Yourself in the Midst of Crisis Ministry

Earlier in my career, I faced crisis ministry by throwing myself into the crisis situation and, on some occasions, functioning at maximum speed while helping those in need. Following those first attempts at extensive crisis ministry, I was mentally and physically exhausted. Crisis ministry demands a great deal from the caregiver. From those early ministry attempts, I learned to pace myself through later crises. By the night of the Wedgwood church shootings, I had learned to tell myself to conserve my expenditure of energy. In the days that followed, one of my colleagues and I would remind each other of the necessity of this pacing, saying, "This is a marathon, not a sprint." This saying helped us remember to conserve energy where possible in order to be available throughout the entire crisis. The minister who paces him- or herself is more likely to provide consistent, sustained care.

Remember to Rest

While the Bible possesses numerous references to work, it also has a great deal to say about rest. God created for six days, then rested on the sabbath. God commanded the Israelites to follow this same pattern, saying, "Six days you shall labor and do all your work, but the seventh day is a sabbath of the LORD your God; in it you shall not do any work" (Exod. 20:9–10). The Israelites were to plow their ground and prune their vineyards for six years, but leave these alone on the seventh (Lev. 25:3–4). In all of these examples, there is a work-rest rhythm. God's people were to work diligently, but they were also to rest. Conversely, those involved in crisis ministry are often tempted to skip periods of rest, believing that they're needed in the midst of the crisis. Lack of adequate rest, however, leaves one vulnerable to fatigue, exhaustion, and burnout.

Take Care of Your Body

When caregivers are involved in crisis ministry, they have a tendency to eat in unhealthy ways and neglect exercise routines in order to keep up with the demands of the situation. First Corinthians 6:19 makes clear that our bodies are the temple of the Holy Spirit. As such, the caregiver's body needs care, including the avoidance of junk food, which is so easy to grab when things are stressful, and the maintenance of an exercise schedule. Regular times of recreation also help the caregiver move in the direction of maintaining balance in life.

Emotional Coping Strategies

Crisis ministry involves strong emotions, both from the crisis survivor and from the caregiver. Healthy coping includes being aware of the emotional processes that are a part of crisis ministry and striving to function in an emotionally healthy manner.

Avoid Becoming Numb to Emotions

In an effort to avoid being overwhelmed by the emotions evoked in crisis ministry, it's possible for the caregiver to become numb to emotions such as sadness, anger, frustration, anxiety, or despair. Whether intentionally or unintentionally, the caregiver can narrow his or her range of emotions to avoid the pain or anxiety that is often a part of crisis ministry. If a caregiver becomes numb to emotions, whether his or her own or those of the crisis victim, the helper's effectiveness is likely to be diminished.

Utilize Appropriate Channels to Express Emotions

Like the trauma victim, the caregiver can be tempted to modulate strong emotions through nonproductive and unhealthy avenues. Using alcohol or drugs to numb emotions, using sex or pornography to distract oneself from what is painful, or spending money to divert one's attention from the struggles of crisis ministry—all are destructive avenues of attempting to cope. Caregivers may also find themselves watching excessive amounts of television, spending money compulsively, spending hour after hour at the computer, or overeating. When a helper feels strong emotions related to crisis ministry, appropriate channels of coping might include talking with a colleague or supervisor, exercising, strategizing, or praying. Acknowledging strong emotions and the toll they take assists the caregiver in making wise choices about addressing such emotions. Some caregivers choose to journal thoughts and feelings. Others may talk to friends, colleagues, or loved ones about what they're experiencing. Recognizing the emotional component of crisis ministry allows helpers to avoid becoming impaired in their ability help.

Seek Your Own Counseling, if Necessary

In some instances, the counselor or minister may seek his or her own counseling for struggles related to crisis ministry. Admitting the need may be difficult for the helper, but at times it's also a wise course of action and a means of maintaining vitality. If a caregiver struggles with burnout, he or she might benefit from counseling. If a caregiver experiences STS, especially that which is ongoing, seeking guidance from an experienced trauma counselor may help the caregiver deal with his or her own struggles, thereby allowing the caregiver to continue ministering to those who are hurting.

Relational Coping Strategies

Being connected to others in healthy relationships is one of the most powerful forms of dealing with helper-related stress. Caregivers should seek to develop, maintain, and nurture relationships with other individuals and with family members. But while healthy relationships provide an incredible source of support for the helper, relationships can also be the basis of additional stress and strain, especially if these associations are emotionally taxing. Caregivers must take care of their own relationships.

Avoid Isolating   *Important*

Like the trauma victim, the helper may at times feel lonely or disconnected from significant relationships. This sense of isolation can be especially acute when the caregiver is maintaining confidentiality and, therefore, cannot talk about his or her cases with others in the caregiver's general support network. When Elijah was in the wilderness, one of his complaints to God was his being the only one still trying to serve God. Elijah felt isolated and believed he was alone in his quest. Staying connected to others who are able to provide support helps the caregiver maintain emotional balance.

Nurture Relationships

The caregiver should not only maintain relationships, but must work to cultivate these relationships, even during the most stressful times of helping others. If a caregiver fails to nurture family relationships and friendships, these can easily become additional sources of stress and strain. On several occasions, in the middle of extremely stressful crisis ministry situations, I made a point of spending time talking to and playing with each of my children. Sometimes my best stress reliever was to roll on the floor and chase my two-year-old twins around the house, and hear them giggle at the games we'd make up. Similarly, talking with my wife, listening to her talk about her world, and spending time caring for our marriage helps me maintain my emotional balance. Taking time to stay invested in my family reminds me of the positive things in my life and keeps me anchored in the real world, increasing my effectiveness as I work with those in troubled circumstances. Nurturing relationships, then, is an essential component of effective coping.

Professional Coping Strategies

On a professional level, too, a caregiver can take steps to reduce and adjust to stress. A caregiver should attempt many of these prior to entering a crisis ministry situation; others are necessary during the time one is providing crisis care.

Keep Current in the Crisis Ministry Field

Crisis ministers need to be involved in ongoing training in regard to crisis ministry. Because the field is growing, new information and approaches aid the caregiver in being most effective when helping others. Reading books and journal articles, talking to experienced crisis ministers or counselors, and attending training seminars are all methods of updating skills and expanding knowledge about helping others. When a crisis minister has a growing base of information about the field, it reduces the likelihood of being ignorant to the stressors inherent in the field.

Connect with Peers Who Provide Crisis Ministry

One of the best ways to keep fresh in crisis ministry is to find others who function in a similar capacity. Trading stories, discussing approaches, and even laughing together allow the caregiver to find relief amid the strain of ministering to others.

Ask for Help

In crisis ministry, a caregiver will sometimes need help, advice, encouragement, or support. The crisis minister needs to identify other experienced crisis ministers who may be able to provide support, consultation, or encouragement. If the crisis minister functions isolated from professional peers, there is a higher likelihood of stress, exhaustion, and burnout. Asking for help is not a sign of weakness, but rather an indicator of humility and wisdom.

CONCLUSION

"Should the air pressure change in the cabin, a mask will drop from the overhead compartment." The flight attendant's voice crackled over the plane's loudspeaker system. "First, attach your own mask securely," she continued, "pulling on the tabs to keep it in place. Next, help those around you to make sure their masks are secure."

I'd never thought much about this last part of the safety instructions, which I'd heard many times before, until my first flight with my children. The instruction seemed backward and went against my parental instincts. Shouldn't I attach my children's masks first, making sure they're okay, before securing mine? Well, no. If a parent becomes disoriented due to oxygen deprivation, he or she will be of little help to a child. In this scenario, both might suffer. Rather, the parent must assure that he or she will be able to breathe, and then assist the child.

In the same manner, caregivers must see that their oxygen masks have dropped down, that the lines are clear, and that the masks are correctly in place. When properly caring for oneself, the caregiver is better positioned to then help others. The caregiver who becomes depleted, overexerted, exhausted, or who suffers from burnout or secondary traumatic stress will likely be of diminished value both as a counselor or minister, and as a person. The crisis minister cares for him- or herself by attending to his or her spiritual, emotional, and physical needs. The caregiver utilizes professional support, training, and resources, and strives to maintain healthy relationships with others. When the crisis minister remains vital and healthy, he or she is far more likely to be effective in helping others face, and cope with, life's difficulties.

A FINAL WORD

After Saul dies, David becomes king of Israel. First Chronicles 12 gives the account of David's supporters gathering at Hebron to help David consolidate his hold on the kingdom. Many of the tribes of Israel send David their best men, trained for war. Judah contributes men who are experts with shields and swords (1 Chron. 12:24). Simeon sends "mighty men of valor" (1 Chron. 12:25). Other tribes supply David with brave men, military leaders, fierce soldiers, and those who have earned fame in their own tribes. All these men come to Hebron, prepared to help David fight God's battles.

One tribe's offering to David seems out of place. According to 1 Chronicles 12:32, Issachar sends David, "men who understood the times, with knowledge of what Israel should do." Unlike the other tribes who provide their best warriors to support David, Issachar supplies men who are able to see the bigger picture, who have the ability to comprehend the larger political and military landscapes. Thompson observes that the men of Issachar are able to shrewdly observe what is transpiring in and around Israel and have the skill of discerning what is taking place socially and politically.[1] Keil and Delitzsch note that the men of Issachar have insight, experience, and understand what is unfolding around them.[2] The tribe of Issachar seems to recognize that battles are not always fought with military strength alone; some battles require wisdom, planning, and an ability to appreciate what is occurring from the vantage of a larger perspective.

I find myself wondering if counselors are like the men of Issachar. The battles that crisis caregivers fight are not military ones, involving armies and weapons of war. These battles are fought in the counseling office, at the disaster sight, sometimes in the homes of those who are experiencing a crisis or loss, and often on one's knees in prayer.

---

1. Thompson, *1, 2 Chronicles*, 9:126–27.
2. Keil and Delitzsch, *The Book of Chronicles*, 193.

I believe the counseling field needs individuals like the men of Issachar, people who understand the times and who possess knowledge of what to do when crises occur. We live in times during which people will experience difficult events like many of those described in this book. Those in crisis ministry understand that crises and traumatic experiences inevitably take place and that, for many, the impact will be devastating. This book was written to provide caregivers with knowledge of what to do when people experience difficult circumstances, when individuals go through crises, trauma, grief, or loss, and of how to effectively minister to those who are hurting.

The men of Issachar arrived to help David fight God's battles and to advance God's kingdom by lending their knowledge, expertise, and wisdom. Counselors and ministers trained in crisis ministry serve as parts of the body of Christ who help those in the most difficult, painful, and trying of circumstances. In doing so, crisis caregivers are helping to fight God's battles, to make His name known, and to advance His kingdom, all for the glory of God.

SYMPTOMS OF TRAUMA

All individuals who go through a traumatic event will likely experience symptoms. These may occur immediately after the traumatic event or in the days following. Look over the list below and place a check by symptoms you have noticed.

	Immediately After the Event	Between the Event and Now	Currently
Cognitive Symptoms			
Difficulty concentrating	_____	_____	_____
Flashbacks	_____	_____	_____
Reacting to similar circumstances	_____	_____	_____
Guilt	_____	_____	_____
Futurelessness	_____	_____	_____
Blank times or "blank outs"	_____	_____	_____
Altered worldview/belief system	_____	_____	_____
Other: _____	_____	_____	_____
Emotional Symptoms			
Numbness	_____	_____	_____
Anger	_____	_____	_____
Sadness	_____	_____	_____
Feeling helpless	_____	_____	_____
Feeling hopeless	_____	_____	_____
Mood swings	_____	_____	_____
Self-harm thoughts	_____	_____	_____
Hypervigilence			
Easily startled	_____	_____	_____
Overly aware of surroundings	_____	_____	_____
Other: _____	_____	_____	_____

Behavioral Symptoms

Sleep disturbance
    Sleeping more   _____   _____   _____
    Sleeping less   _____   _____   _____
Nightmares or disturbing dreams   _____   _____   _____
Sleeping, but not feeling rested   _____   _____   _____
Eating disturbance
    Eating more   _____   _____   _____
    Eating less   _____   _____   _____
    Upset stomach   _____   _____   _____
Trouble completing routine tasks
    At work   _____   _____   _____
    At home   _____   _____   _____
    At school   _____   _____   _____
Overcautious   _____   _____   _____
Taking risks   _____   _____   _____
Substance use/abuse   _____   _____   _____
Other: _____   _____   _____   _____

Spiritual Symptoms

Questions about God's existence   _____   _____   _____
Questions about God's character   _____   _____   _____
Anger at God   _____   _____   _____
Difficulty with religious practices
or expressions
    Church attendance   _____   _____   _____
    Bible reading   _____   _____   _____
    Prayer   _____   _____   _____
Other: _____   _____   _____   _____

Relationship Symptoms

Relationship withdrawal   _____   _____   _____
Relationship strain or conflict   _____   _____   _____
Difficulty being alone   _____   _____   _____
Other: _____   _____   _____   _____

GRIEF SYMPTOM SHEET

E veryone who experiences the death of a loved one goes through the grief in different ways. Please look over the areas below and identify how you are being affected by the loss of your loved one.

1. Place a check beside the emotions you tend to notice most.

_____ Sadness	_____ Hurt	_____ Anguish
_____ Fear	_____ Loneliness	_____ Helplessness
_____ Longing	_____ Lethargy	_____ Guilt
_____ Emptiness	_____ Weariness	_____ Confusion
_____ Anger	_____ Frustration	_____ Irritation
_____ Rage	_____ Numbness	_____ Discouragement
_____ Relief	_____ Isolation	_____ Regret
_____ Despair	_____ Abandonment	_____ Vulnerability
_____ Other: _____		
_____ Other: _____		

2. Are any of these emotions a concern for you?

3. Place a check beside any of the following that are difficult for you.

   _____ Being alone

   _____ Being around others

   _____ Getting out of bed

   _____ Seeing my loved one's belongings

   _____ Concentrating on routine tasks

     _____ Eating regularly
     _____ Maintaining regular sleep patterns
     _____ Talking to others about the death of my loved one
     _____ Attending activities
     _____ Controlling my emotions
     _____ Recalling information

4. Place a check beside any of the following that are true for you.
   _____ Sometimes, I forget what I'm doing or find my mind wandering.
   _____ I feel better when I can talk about my loved one.
   _____ I feel anxious if I can't recall what my loved one looked like or the sound of his or her voice.
   _____ Occasionally, I expect to see my loved one walk around a corner or come through the door.
   _____ Sometimes I think I hear my loved one's voice.
   _____ Sometimes I think I see my loved one.
   _____ I often dream of my loved one.
   _____ I find myself drained of energy.
   _____ Occasionally, my chest feels tight and I have trouble breathing.
   _____ I cry at unexpected times.
   _____ I have trouble finding words to express how I feel.
   _____ I sometimes worry that if I start to feel better, I'm being disloyal to my loved one.

5. What part of the grief process concerns you most?

6. How has grief affected your spiritual life? Place a check by the statements that are true for you.
   _____ My spiritual life is a source of comfort to me.
   _____ My spiritual life has been more difficult recently.
   _____ I take comfort in reading my Bible.

_____ I attend church/participate in religious activities as much as I did prior to the death of my loved one.

_____ I have questions about God that were not present prior to the death of my loved one.

7. Are there any other aspects of your grief that would help your counselor most accurately understand what is taking place for you?

HOLIDAY/ANNIVERSARY CHECKLIST

A fter the death of a loved one, certain times of the day, week, or year may seem more complicated, painful, or challenging. Look over the lists below and identify any times that seem especially difficult for you.

Daily

_____ Mornings   _____ Nighttime

_____ Mealtimes   _____ Other: _____

_____ Coming home   _____ Other: _____
      from work

_____ Evenings

Weekly

_____ Mondays   _____ Fridays

_____ Tuesdays   _____ Saturdays

_____ Wednesdays   _____ Sundays

_____ Thursdays   _____ Other: _____

Anniversaries

_____ My birthday

_____ Deceased loved one's birthday

_____ Child/children's birthday/s

_____ The anniversary of the death

_____ Wedding anniversary

_____ Other: _____

Holidays

_____	New Year's Eve/Day	_____	Annual family trips/activities
_____	Valentine's Day	_____	Fourth of July
_____	Easter	_____	Halloween
_____	Mother's Day	_____	Thanksgiving
_____	Memorial Day	_____	Christmas Eve/Day
_____	Father's Day	_____	Other: _____

Seasons

_____	Spring	_____	Fall
_____	Summer	_____	Winter

DENOMINATIONAL DISASTER RELIEF SERVICES

Assemblies of God

Benevolences Disaster Relief
1445 N. Boonville Ave.
Springfield, MO 65802-1894
417-862-2781
http://ag.org/disaster/

Catholic Church

Catholic Charities
P.O. Box 25168
Alexandria, VA 22313-9788
http://www.catholiccharitiesusa.org/

Episcopal Church

Episcopal Relief and Development
815 Second Avenue
New York, NY 10017
800-334-7626 ext. 5129
http://er-d.org/

Evangelical Free Church of America

ReachGlobal
(EFCA International Mission)
901 East 78th Street
Minneapolis, MN 55420
800-745-2202 or 952-854-1300
http://www.efca.org/international/compassion/

Evangelical Lutheran Church in America

8765 W. Higgins Road
Chicago, IL 60631
800-638-3522 or 773-380-2700
http://www.elca.org/disaster/

Presbyterian Church (USA)

Presbyterian Disaster Assistance
100 Witherspoon Street
Louisville, KY 40202
999-728-7228 ext. 5839
http://www.pcusa.org/pda/

Southern Baptist Convention

North American Mission Board
4200 North Point Parkway
Alpharetta, GA 30022-4176
770-410-6000
http://www.namb.net

United Methodist Church

United Methodist Committee on Relief
General Board of Global Ministries
Room 330
475 Riverside Drive
New York, NY 10115
212-870-3816
http://www.umc.org/

BIBLIOGRAPHY

Anderson, A. A. *The Book of Psalms, Volume 1 (Psalms 1–72)*. The New Century Bible Commentary. Edited by Ronald Clements. Grand Rapids: Eerdmans, 1983.

Barlow, David, and Mark Durand. *Abnormal Psychology: An Integrative Approach*. 4th ed. Belmont, CA: Wadsworth, 2005.

Barry, Kevin. "September 11, A Year Late." *Journal of Pastoral Counseling* 37 (2002): 3–9.

Berger, Kathleen. *The Developing Person Through the Life Span*. 6th ed. New York: Worth Publishers, 2005.

Bock, Darrell. *Baker Exegetical Commentary on the New Testament*. Edited by Moises Silva. Grand Rapids: Baker, 1996.

Boice, James Montgomery. *The Gospel of John: An Expositional Commentary*. Vol. 3. Grand Rapids: Zondervan, 1977.

Boss, Pauline. *Loss, Trauma, and Resilience: Therapeutic Work with Ambiguous Loss*. New York: W. W. Norton and Company, 2006.

Bradley, Michael J. *Yes, Your Teen Is Crazy*. Gig Harbor, WA: Harbor Press, 2003.

Brooks, Barbara, and Paula Siegel. *The Scared Child: Helping Kids Overcome Traumatic Events*. New York: John Wiley & Sons, 1996.

Chrestman, Kelly. "Secondary Exposure to Trauma and Self Reported Distress Among Therapists." In *Secondary Traumatic Stress*, edited by B. Hudnall Stamm, 29–36. 2d ed. Lutherville, MD: Sidran Press, 1999.

Clinton, Tim, and George Ohlschlager. "The Movements of Grief as a Healing Journey." *Christian Counseling Today* 11, no. 2 (2003): 16–22.

Cooper, Lamar Eugene, Sr. *Ezekiel*. The New American Commentary. Vol. 17. Edited by E. Ray Clendenen. Nashville: Broadman & Holman, 1994.

Corey, Gerald, Marianne Schneider Corey, and Patrick Callanan. *Issues and Ethics in the Helping Professions*. 7th ed. Belmont, CA: Brooks/Cole, 2007.

Elkind, David. *All Grown Up and No Place to Go*. Rev. ed. Reading, MA: Perseus Books, 1998.

Eriksson, Cynthia, and Brad Griffin, "In the Aftermath: Processing Trauma Through the Lens of Lament." Fuller Theological Seminary. http://www.cyfm.net/article.php?article=Lens_of_Lament.html.

Everly, George. "The Role of Pastoral Crisis Intervention in Disasters, Terrorism, Violence, and Other Community Crises." *International Journal of Emergency Mental Health* 2, no. 3 (2000): 139–42.

Everly, George, and Jeffrey Mitchell. *Critical Incident Stress Management.* 2d ed. Ellicott City, MD: Chevron Publishing Corporation, 1999.

Figley, Charles. "AAMFT Clinical Update: Post-Traumatic Stress Disorder." American Association for Marriage and Family Therapy. http://www.aamft.org/families/Consumer_Updates/PTSD_AAMFT_Clinical _Update.htm (accessed June 22, 2006).

———. "Compassion Fatigue: Toward a New Understanding of the Costs of Caring." In *Secondary Traumatic Stress,* edited by B. Hudnall Stamm, 3–28. 2d ed. Lutherville, MD: Sidran Press, 1999.

———. "Disaster and Violence: Picking Up the Family Pieces and Keeping Them Together." Keynote address, American Association of Marriage and Family Therapists Conference, Dallas, TX, October 1998.

Fitzgerald, Helen. *The Grieving Child.* New York: Simon & Schuster, 1992.

Foster, Lewis. *Zondervan NIV Study Bible.* Edited by Kenneth L. Barker. Grand Rapids: Zondervan, 2002.

Geldenhuys, Norval. *The New International Commentary on the Gospel of Luke.* Grand Rapids: Eerdmans, 1988.

Halpern, James, and Mary Tramontin. *Disaster Mental Health: Theory and Practice.* Belmont, CA: Thomson Brooks/Cole, 2007.

Holmes, David. *Abnormal Psychology.* 4th ed. Boston: Allyn and Bacon, 2001.

Hyer, Lee. *Trauma Victim: Theoretical Issues and Practical Issues.* Muncie, IN: Accelerated Development, 1994.

James, Richard, and Burl Gilliland. *Crisis Intervention Strategies.* 5th ed. Belmont, CA: Thomson Brooks/Cole, 2005.

Jones, Ian F. *The Counsel of Heaven on Earth.* Nashville: Broadman & Holman, 2006.

Kanel, Kristi. *A Guide to Crisis Intervention.* 3d ed. Belmont, CA: Thomson Brooks/Cole, 2007.

Kassam-Adams, Nancy. "The Risks of Treating Sexual Trauma: Stress and Secondary Trauma in Psychotherapists." In *Secondary Traumatic Stress,* edited by B. Hudnall Stamm, 37–48. 2d ed. Lutherville, MD: Sidran Press, 1999.

Keil, C. F., and F. Delitzsch. *The Book of Chronicles*. Commentaries on the Old Testament. Translated by Andrew Harper. Grand Rapids: Eerdmans, 1950.

Landreth, Garry L. *Play Therapy: The Art of the Relationship*. Muncie, IN: Accelerated Development, 1991.

Lewis, C. S. *A Grief Observed*. New York: Bantam Books, 1961.

Lukens, Horace C., Jr. "Essential Elements for Ethical Counsel." *Christian Counseling Ethics*, edited by Randolph K. Sander, 43–56. Downers Grove, IL: InterVarsity Press, 1997.

Lutheran Disaster Response. "Preparing for Disaster: A Guide for Lutheran Congregations." http://www.ldr.org/prepare/PrepDisaster.pdf (accessed 24 June 2006).

Lyles, Michael R. "Trauma and PTSD: A Clinical Overview" *Christian Counseling Today* 11, no. 2 (2003): 48–53.

Morey, Gary. "Crisis Communication for Ministers Conference." Master's thesis, Southwestern Baptist Theological Seminary, 2002.

North American Mission Board. http://www.namb.net/site/c.9qKILUOzEpH/b .224451/k.A400/Disaster_Relief.htm (accessed June 22, 2006).

Oden, Thomas. *Crisis Ministries*. Classical Pastoral Care Series. Vol. 4. Grand Rapids: Baker, 1994.

Perlman, Laurie Anne. "Self-Care for Trauma Therapists: Ameliorating Vicarious Traumatization." In *Secondary Traumatic Stress*, edited by B. Hudnall Stamm, 51–64. 2d ed. Lutherville, MD: Sidran Press, 1999.

Perry, Bruce D. "The Cost of Caring: Secondary Traumatic Stress and the Impact of Working with High-Risk Children and Families." Child Trauma Academy. http://www.childtrauma.org/ctamaterials/SecTrma2_03_v2.pdf (accessed June 14, 2006).

Perschy, Mary Kelly. *Helping Teens Work Through Grief*. Bristol, PA: Accelerated Development, 1999.

Rosen, Gerald M., ed. *Posttraumatic Stress Disorder: Issues and Controversies*. John West Sussex, England: John Wiley & Sons, 2004.

Rosenbloom, Dena, and Mary Beth Williams. *Life After Trauma: A Workbook for Healing*. New York: Guilford Press, 1999.

Salmond, S. D. F. *The Century Bible*. London: Blackwood, Le Bes, & Co, n.d.

Santrock, John. *Life-Span Development*. 3d ed. Dubuque, IA: Wm. C. Brown Publishers, 1989.

Stagg, Frank. *Matthew and Mark*. Broadman Bible Commentary. Vol. 8. Edited by Clifton J. Allen, Nashville: Broadman, 1969.

Stamm, B. Hudnall, ed. *Secondary Traumatic Stress.* 2d ed. Lutherville, MD: Sidran Press, 1999.

———. "Work-Related Secondary Traumatic Stress." *PTSD Research Quarterly* (Spring 1997): 1–8.

Sue, David, Derald Wing Sue, and Stanley Sue. *Understanding Abnormal Behavior.* 7th ed. Boston: Houghton Mifflin Company, 2003.

Terr, Lenore. *Too Scared to Cry.* New York: BasicBooks, 1990.

———. *Unchained Memories.* New York: BasicBooks, 1994.

Thompson, J. A. *1, 2 Chronicles.* New American Commentary. Vol. 9. Edited by E. Ray Clendenen. Nashville: Broadman & Holman, 1994.

Trenchard, Warren. *The Student's Complete Vocabulary Guide to the Greek New Testament.* Grand Rapids: Zondervan, 1992.

Wolfelt, Alan. *A Child's View of Grief.* Ft. Collins, CO: Service Corporation International, 1990.

Wright, H. Norman. "Crisis Intervention and Emergency Practice." In *Competent Christian Counseling*, edited by Timothy Clinton and George Ohlschlager, 1:600–614. Colorado Springs: Waterbrook Press, 2002.

———. *Experiencing Grief.* Nashville: Broadman & Holman, 2004.

———. *The New Guide to Crisis and Trauma Counseling.* Ventura, CA: Regal Books, 2003.

———. *Recovering from the Losses of Life.* Nashville: Lifeway Press, 1995.

Zonnebelt-Smeenge, Susan, and Robert Devries. "Establishing Core Positive Constructs in Grief Therapy." *Christian Counseling Today* 11, no. 2 (2003): 26–30.

Scripture Index